Exile and Return Among the East Timorese

Contemporary Ethnography

Kirin Narayan and Paul Stoller, Series Editors

A complete list of books in the series is available from the publisher.

Exile and Return Among the East Timorese

Amanda Wise

PENN

University of Pennsylvania Press

Philadelphia

10 9 8 7 6 5 4 3 2 1

Published by
University of Pennsylvania Press
Philadelphia, Pennsylvania 19104-4112

Library of Congress Cataloging-in-Publication Data

Wise, Amanda.
    Exile and return among the East Timorese / Amanda Wise.
        p.   cm. — (Contemporary ethnography)
    ISBN-13: 978-0-8122-3909-6
    ISBN-10: 0-8122-3909-1 (cloth : alk. paper)
    Includes bibliographical references and index.
    1. Political refugees—East Timor. 2. Political refugees—Australia—Sydney (N.S.W.)—
Social conditions. 3. Exiles—East Timor. 4. Exiles—Australia—Sydney (N.S.W.)—Social
conditions. 5. East Timorese—Australia—Sydney (N.S.W.). 6. Return migration—East
Timor. I. Title. II. Series

HV640.5.E19 W57   2006
959.87'032—dc22   2005042361

This book is dedicated to my parents, Frederick and Joan Wise, and to my loving, supportive, and ever patient partner Selvaraj Velayutham.

Contents

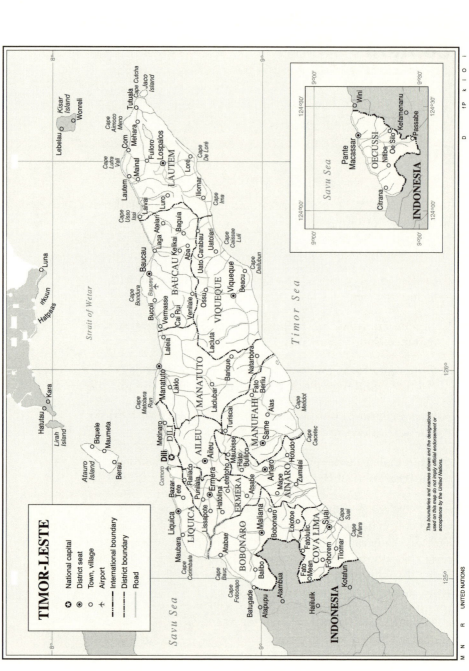

Map 1. Timor-Leste. Courtesy United Nations Publications Board.

Introduction: "We can't hang Xanana there!" On the Politics of Representing Community

It is often said that East Timor's President Xanana Gusmão, former guerrilla fighter and national hero, is the Nelson Mandela of Southeast Asia. A romantic, saint-like figure, he became an icon for East Timor's cause, appearing on posters and T-shirts in his beret, reminiscent of the famous image of Ché Guevara. Every solidarity supporter had his picture on their wall, and East Timorese children graffiti his likeness together with messages of resistance. Described as "poet, resistance fighter and peace maker," Xanana has become a hero for our times. What a surprise, then, to find myself in a local museum in Sydney's western suburbs, mediating a dispute between museum management and members of the East Timorese community, the latter demanding Xanana's image be moved to a less prominent location.

In 2001 I was asked to curate an exhibition in partnership with two East Timorese artists and a group of East Timorese youth. The exhibition, "Leaving the Crocodile,"[1] was held at the Liverpool Regional Museum to celebrate the history of the East Timorese community in Sydney and to reflect on their present situation following the 1999 referendum that led to East Timor's independence. I worked with them for more than a year to collect items for the exhibition. The youth group also took charge of a video camera for twelve months, during which time they persuaded friends, family, and community members, in living rooms and at East Timorese community events, to be interviewed on a range of issues having to do with living in Australia and their thoughts about the future. After much thought and discussion about how the exhibition should be presented, we settled on a format for the display, centered on two separate rooms. Artworks produced by the youth group, visually articulating their identity issues as young East Timorese in Australia, would be on display in the first room visitors encountered on entering the exhibition space. The room would also include photographs documenting the non-political aspects of the community from 1975 to 2001. These included photographs of community groups over the years, cultural items from family collections, and photo-portraits and accompanying interviews with six selected community members. Those featured a community leader, a kung fu teacher, a fashion designer, a gay man, a young woman involved in the resistance, and José Ramos-Horta's mother. The group wanted this room to feel welcoming, to emanate a sense of warmth, hope, and joy. It featured a giant version of East Timor's crocodile icon fashioned from bright yellow paper napkins (made by a member of the community with assistance from the youth group) and a wall-sized mural of a sacred tree in magenta and sky-blue. The centerpiece was formed by six-and-a-half-foot wooden totem poles, with visual stories painted on them by members of the youth group (Figure 1).

The process of painting these poles is a story in itself. Most of the poles featured a hybrid combination of imagery from East Timor and life in Australia. However, one young man was somewhat embarrassed because his pole didn't have anything "East Timorese" on it; it featured

Figure 1. One of the poles for the exhibition. Photo by Manuel Branco.

some images from the Sydney Olympics and a dragonlike figure. Some of the girls thought that was all right; perhaps the dragon represented the Chinese influence in East Timor. But, in fact, he sheepishly admitted, the dragon was the symbol of his favorite rugby team. So even at the young age of seventeen, this young man was feeling pressure to identify with an ethnicity he didn't feel particularly attached to. We included the pole as it was, once I'd convinced them that they didn't have to show "ethnic" symbols if they did not wish to.

The second room contained historical photographs, artifacts, and documents pertaining to the Sydney East Timorese community's contribution to the independence struggle. The two rooms were split because there was a consensus among the group that they were tired of seeing the sad pictures from the struggle over and over again. They felt that now that East Timor was independent, perhaps it was the time to show a more hopeful side of the community.

The whole process of planning this very community-driven exhibition was amazingly enlightening. While we were working in the museum in the two weeks leading up to the opening, members of the East Timorese community would wander in and look around, offering suggestions on what was missing or what should be hung where, or giggle over old photos in which they recognized themselves or someone they knew. Many would bring in new photographs or items (although the cut-off date had long since passed), imploring me to include them, as they believed the objects or photographs were absolutely essential to the story. I'd either have refuse diplomatically or find an extra corner to squeeze the item in. In the end, the exhibition was crammed with all sorts of items, some of which held meaning only for the East Timorese community. The chaotic nature of the collection we ended up with drove the museum's exhibition designer crazy. As he was responsible for the overall aesthetic look of the exhibition, we had many arguments over the community's right to include what they wanted as against his desire to make it a visually clean and appealing space that foregrounded images that would appeal to the general public.

Which brings me back to the wonderful poster of Xanana Gusmão. Perhaps four feet high—in striking colors of red, yellow, and black—it featured Xanana in military garb and beret, looking like a brave resistance fighter (Figure 2). Behind its new glass frame it looked even more exquisite, so much so that the designer chose it to hang in the middle of a blank wall, the first to meet the eye on entering the exhibition space, flanked on either side by East Timorese traditional weavings. It was certainly visually striking, and the museum staff gathered around to admire the designer's skill at positioning it thus. And then, in wandered a group of East Timorese, who collectively exclaimed, "You can't hang Xanana

Figure 2. Poster of Xanana used in the exhibition.

there!!!" They were horrified. Because the image was in the middle between the two weavings, they thought the display looked somewhat like
a shrine. In such a prominent position, they were very worried that
it would look like "we were all FRETILIN supporters"[2] and that half
the community would boycott the exhibition. The by now ashen-faced
designer tried fruitlessly to convince them it was all in the name of aes-
thetics, and besides, didn't everyone love Xanana?

There are all kinds of disputes, dislikes, and complex political alle-
giances in the community, all beyond the usual view of the public, who
are unaware that not all East Timorese love Xanana or have a homogeneous picture of themselves. However, the group was also worried that
the poster would turn the exhibition into another political display, mim-
icking those put on by the solidarity and independence campaign over
the years. This was *their* exhibition. Eventually they came to a compromise.
An alternative poster was found, not as striking as the first, but promoting
the first democratic elections in East Timor. Xanana was shuffled off to
the second room to appear on a wall alongside a range of other pictures,
positioned so that it wouldn't look like we were supporting him over other
people.

The opening day eventually arrived, but it too highlighted some complex politics of representation. We had invited a group of East Timorese
youth to perform traditional East Timorese dances and had also asked
the dance group from the East Timorese-Chinese community to perform. They were very hesitant when I invited them. One prominent
member of their association said to me, "You don't want our dancers, do
you? People will want to see real East Timorese dancing, not us." The
Timorese-Chinese repertoire included a hybrid mix of Chinese and Portuguese folk dances, performed in gold and maroon Indonesian *kabaya*.
I thought they were lovely, but the dancers were convinced they didn't
belong at our exhibition. Eventually though, they acquiesced, and were
so well received by the audience that they had to perform an encore.
But one audience member was surprised. She came to me and said, "I
thought East Timorese were dark with curly hair!"

In the end, the exhibition was generally very well received. But
inevitably there were discussions and debates among members of the
community who weren't involved in helping to put it together. The ubiquitous "grandmothers" wandered through, closely inspecting each and
every item. Some of the old ladies complained because we had asked the
young people to put the exhibition together. They felt that the young
people hadn't "learned the culture yet," and therefore, how on earth
could they possibly do a good job at representing the community? For
them, culture very much equaled the high culture of traditional East
Timor, not the quotidian, hybrid cultures on display. Similarly, some

older members of the community thought there should be more artifacts that expressed "real culture": baskets, carvings, and weavings, that
sort of thing. They were concerned that their culture was not being presented "at its best." Perhaps they felt that it was a bit like bringing out
the best china when guests come over, rather than using the chipped
and mismatched pieces used every day. In one section, we had set up a
display in a suitcase featuring a child's dress, which was worn by one
woman during her escape in 1975. We presented it in the suitcase surrounded by embroidered pieces, carvings, and other cultural items families had brought with them to Australia. Some East Timorese visitors
to the exhibition said that we should have gone to East Timor to get
"proper" cultural items, rather than the ones we found in the community. There was a sense of loss among them, as though the items available in Australia didn't quite measure up to the "true" culture of East
Timor. There were also some objections from those politically involved,
annoyed at not having received a more prominent position, or that the
version of history portrayed did not fit with their view, or upset that certain individuals were not included. Others felt the struggle should have
occupied a more prominent place, because it was "real" history.

The exhibition process reminded me in important ways that "community" is never seamless. Identities are often under debate; they are
ever in process. There are always struggles around official representations
of the "culture," arguments over who should have the power to determine those representations, and struggles over who gets to be included
in its official definition. But perhaps most important, the exhibition process reminded me that, contrary to the way East Timorese have often been
represented—as mute victims, simply there to personify East Timor's suffering—there is in fact a whole everyday world in suburban Sydney where
East Timorese live, love, work, form friendships, relationships, alliances
and sometimes disputes, where debates over identity and politics actually
happen. There is a whole social world, which lies beyond the struggle
and beyond the sad pictures of East Timorese as victims. At the same
time, there is also a great deal invested by members of that community
in holding dear their identities as refugees and their role in East Timor's
fight for independence.[3] East Timor's historic vote for independence in
August 1999,[4] following more than four hundred years of European and
then Indonesian colonization, created enormous upheaval and confusion among the East Timorese refugee diaspora living in Australia. With
so much invested in the "return" of East Timor, and many identifying so
strongly as "exiles," the "return of the homeland" challenges the very
basis on which many have imagined themselves since fleeing to Australia.

*   *   *

This book is about the small East Timorese community in Sydney, Australia, focusing on the period immediately following East Timor's independence. I draw on key debates on diasporic and transnational identities in fields such as cultural studies, contemporary anthropology, and cultural geography to address the two key aims of the book. The first is to explore the various dynamics that have shaped the cultural identities, both personal and collective, of members of the East Timorese diaspora in Australia. The second is to understand the challenges posed to these people by a newly independent East Timor. As refugees and forced migrants, who for the most part left East Timor fifteen to twenty years earlier, the East Timorese in Australia have an ambivalent relationship to their homeland. For this reason, issues to do with identity, home, and belonging have always been complex and often traumatic. Rather than having moved gradually from displacement to settlement, refugee communities such as the East Timorese might more accurately be defined as exiles. However, as the literature on exile has shown, the exile experience is no straightforward one. It is not a question of remaining an intact community in exile, awaiting the opportunity of safe return. The exile experience itself affects community and individual identities. Individuals, communities, homelands, and countries of refuge are always situated within and in relation to a changing grid of circumstances and power relationships. The question of "return," then, becomes fraught with ambivalence and contradiction. It is this ambivalence that forms the undercurrent of this book.

The research was undertaken in Sydney between 1999 and 2002, and in East Timor in early 2001. Much of my ethnographic study was conducted during the period I spent working as a volunteer for two East Timorese community organizations in Sydney's western suburbs. From this involvement, friendships inevitably developed, and I was privileged to be welcomed into many East Timorese homes and families and invited to many community events. The twelve months I spent curating the exhibition with the youth group made perhaps the greatest contribution to my understanding of the community. I learned a great deal during the process of meeting with and interviewing community members and collecting photographs, letters, cultural items, newspaper clippings, and documents from their homes. Inevitably, I spent many hours in living rooms hearing their owners reflect on the memories these objects evoked for them. The exhibition reminded me that, although I employ the term "community" as shorthand to refer to my research subjects, there is little basis to infer that "community" in this case is in any way homogeneous or all-encompassing. It is, unsurprisingly, made up of different subgroups, factions, and individuals who move between them, or don't identify with the "community" at all.

One of the more important choices I made when embarking on this research was to try to avoid as much as possible interviewing members of the community in the context of formal East Timorese political groups. There were a number of important politically oriented organizations in Sydney whose primary function was to advance the East Timorese independence struggle and to provide aid to those suffering in East Timor under the Indonesian regime. They have subsequently focused their efforts on the reconstruction of East Timor. Although I respect their work, I felt that they were not the place to "get to know the community," as it were, in part because only a small percentage of East Timorese were actively involved with them. While I spent time with and interviewed some community members who were active in politics, I tried to keep this relationship separate from the formal political realm. Similarly, I tried to avoid too much contact with the various Australia-East Timor solidarity groups. This may seem an odd decision, given my wholehearted support for the East Timorese cause. However, I sensed early on that individuals in the community moved between "official" versions of themselves in dealing with "outsiders," usually in the political realm, and a more quotidian Timoreseness that operates on the ground in the everyday spaces of suburban Sydney. Staying away from official groups also meant I was able to avoid getting caught up in factional disputes and avoid the trap of being perceived as in alliance with one side or the other. I was able, therefore, to have access to many different parts of the community.

The timing of this research is an important factor. The referendum that made East Timor's independence possible was held at the end of August 1999, followed by violence and devastation wreaked on the tiny territory for the whole month of September, until the arrival of the Australian-led multinational peacekeeping force. From November 1999, the East Timorese in Australia began returning home to visit, and large numbers of the key leaders in the community left to take positions in the new government. East Timor was formally granted independence on 20 May 2002, after two-and-a-half years of United Nations administration. For East Timorese in Australia, the referendum came as a great surprise. The period during which I undertook my research was therefore one of immense transition for the community, both physical and psychological. This book, then, must be seen in this light. It documents this important transition period, the twilight phase, if you like, between exile and whatever lies after. At the time of writing, the East Timorese in Australia were only just beginning to settle into post-exile patterns. It will be some time yet before this process has played itself out. Toward the end of the book, I look at how members of the community have responded to some of the difficult challenges they face in renegotiating a space for themselves in this new geopolitical landscape. Throughout, my primary aim has been to give a grounded ethnographic base to refugee studies and to contemporary debates on diaspora, ethnicity, belonging, home, and identity. Most important, I wanted to understand what happens when exiles, diasporas and refugees are able to go home. That is, what happens when imagined and real homes collide?

To answer this question, I traveled to East Timor in early 2001. Initially, I was reluctant to go, for several reasons. At that time, East Timor had been descended upon by thousands of academics, NGOs, UN civilian staff, and all manner of concerned individuals and organizations wanting to see first hand and participate in the creation of a new nation. I felt very strongly at the time that the last thing East Timor needed was another "concerned" researcher poking around the ruins of Dili. However, throughout my research, just about every one of my research participants urged me to go, and they were all eager to hear about my findings upon my return. Every person, academic and otherwise, would ask, "so . . . have you been to East Timor?" My original position was that my study was on the East Timorese diaspora in Australia, and that therefore there was no need to travel to East Timor. But as time went on I began to see an increasingly transnational (or translocal, as I term it in later chapters) character to the community, with much coming and going between the two places. I therefore felt justified in taking a field trip to Dili, where most Sydney returnees are living. I rented a room next to the central marketplace and linked up with a range of returnees, mostly interviewing them in their homes. Those I interviewed seemed very pleased to have the opportunity to pour their hearts out to someone neutral about the good and bad aspects of their return. Their stories appear in the final chapter, "From Exile to Diaspora."

The words of my Timorese interviewees are a central feature of the book. I quote individuals at length and structure some chapters around them, in order to emphasize the centrality of their stories. Although I theorize fairly extensively about what I have seen and heard, in the end, the point is not to be "about theory" for theory's sake, but to set it in dialogue with ethnographic material to find new ways to understand the experiences of those in my research. I have also used photographs quite liberally throughout to try to "bring to life" my research subjects. The photographs I have included are not there to provide material for a textual reading; rather, their presence is intended to give a sense of color, shape, form, life, and bodily character to the community this book represents.

Naturally, as the researcher, I am as much present in this book as my participants. There was often a blurring of boundaries between friend, researcher, volunteer, activist, and adviser. I felt strongly that the relationship should be based on reciprocity. Many in the community gave generously of their time; in return, I offered my skills and volunteered with East Timorese community organizations. I acted as mentor, tutored East Timorese students, helped in fundraising, and helped organize community events. For example, the young woman who helped me recruit a number of my interviewees was tireless in her assistance. In return, I was glad to be able to help her develop a women's health information kit, which she was able to translate for use in East Timor, and to provide her a reference when she was seeking employment. A few times East Timorese parents approached me for advice on how their children might get into a university, and I was pleased to be able to offer them practical assistance. All these situations helped alleviate the enduring sense I had of intruding into their lives for selfish academic purposes. Such feelings were present throughout much of my research. I was very aware that this was a community that had experienced a great deal of trauma, and that I would need to employ a great deal of sensitivity in interrogating "official versions" of East Timoreseness.

The issue of trauma was an important one. Because so much had been said about that aspect of the East Timorese, I felt that it wasn't my role to force my participants to relive their sad past. I therefore tried to tread very lightly in interviews so as not to bring up painful memories, unless of course the interviewees made it very clear that they wished to share them. Understandably, some people did not wish to be interviewed at all, fearing that (as in their past experiences with interviewers) they would be expected to repeat horrible stories. My hesitation also stemmed from my own discomfort with such stories. I found it very difficult to hear of the terrible experiences of those people I had come to know and like. A few times interviewees broke down after reflecting on painful memories of their own accord. I found this extremely difficult. I knew from my debriefing with a trauma counselor that I should try not to show my distress because the person might feel guilty for upsetting me. But those times when it actually happened, I found it hard to resist crying myself, and felt that I needed to hug the person, but was never quite sure (given the counselor's advice) if that was the right thing to do. Several times I cut short interviews and "changed hats," turning off the tape, reverting to the role of friend. Other times I would hide my distress, only to find myself in the car on the way home crying my eyes out. At one stage I was doing several interviews over an intensive period, constantly hearing sad stories, a period I found enormously distressing and stressful. For these reasons, I learned to avoid certain topics.

Except for a short section in Chapter 4, I chose in the end to avoid repeating these stories in this book, as similar accounts are well-documented elsewhere (see Turner 1992, 45; Winters 1999). I felt that it would simply be gratuitous to include them, but their pain and sadness permeate every aspect of the book. However, I also wanted to show how East

Timorese lives are much more than the sum of their trauma. As a friend and researcher, I have also left out certain parts of interviews that might cause arguments or other problems in the community, because I judged that it was not my role to contribute unnecessarily to their difficulties.

Points of Departure:
Refugees, Diasporas, and the Politics of Home

My research began its life as a study of a diaspora community who happened to be refugees. Coming from a cultural studies background and having wandered into cultural anthropology and, to some extent, cultural geography over the years, I came to the study of refugees in a very roundabout manner. However, I quickly discovered that it is a field dominated by sociology and policy studies. I believe my background outside the specialist field of refugee studies has allowed me to take a perspective that is different from the usual work in this area; for this reason, I feel I have developed some insights that may make a worthwhile contribution to the study of refugee communities and settlement.

I found the literature on refugees, return, and repatriation to be surprisingly scarce. That which does exist often focuses on mass repatriations of refugees from camps *in* the third world, *to* the third world, such as repatriation projects from neighboring countries to Rwanda, Cambodia, or Eritrea. There is little material available on the specific experiences of refugees living in Western "host" countries, nor on the question of return and repatriation of long-term refugee communities in the West such as the East Timorese, who have for the most part settled and integrated into their new country of residence, yet who still attach great value to their identities as exiles. Moreover, this body of literature on return and repatriation is, for the most part, devoid of the voices of the refugees written about, preferring macro-level analysis based on primarily quantitative data.[5] A perusal through such material (see Bariangaber 2001; Black and Koser 1999; Inui 1998; McDowell and Eastmond 2002) reveals that with few exceptions authors do not feature the actual words of refugees interviewed (if they have been interviewed at all). Assefaw Bariangaber's work (2001) is a good example. A case study of repatriation patterns of Ethiopian refugees in Sudan, it is a quantitative analysis of how a range of variables (age, gender, ethnicity, reason and context of original flight) map onto the decision to voluntarily repatriate.

Certainly, this kind of macrosocial analysis is important for policy purposes. Work that explores how many and who will return home, and statistical sociological measures such as numbers in housing, employment and so on, are useful general indicators of repatriation issues, and are helpful in the allocation of resources. However, while offering a broad set of patterns, the lack of qualitative voice leaves unexplored the messy reality of life for many refugees. Such work is not able to offer insight into the kinds of dialogic processes that shape how individuals and communities make meaning of their situation, and it denies any intimate understanding of an individual's relationship to either the host or the original home. Such approaches cannot offer any nuance in understanding the *experience* and meanings attached not only to repatriation, but also to the *possibility* of return. I hope that my work complements this earlier body of literature by offering an exploration of some of the social, cultural and subjective processes at work and the complex and intersecting processes that affect a person's experience of exile and return.

The tendency toward voiceless macro-analyses of mass movements of people functions, Liisa Malkki argues, to render refugees as "speechless emissaries" (Malkki 1997b). Malkki's pioneering work offers a challenge to the discursive and methodological language of much work on refugee issues. The language of humanitarian discourse (such as the literature reflected on above) has a tendency to treat refugees as its object. In Malkki's view, this discourse functions to dehistoricize and universalize refugees. Refugees are not seen as individual, specific persons who act in the world, who have families, friends, personalities, goals, narratives and so forth, but are framed as "pure universal victims." In this way, argues Malkki (224), such discourses deny those in the refugee category the opportunity to be seen as historical actors rather than simply mute victims. As a result, such studies have the effect of silencing the individuals they want to understand. The most far-reaching effect of such representational regimes

is the systematic, if unintended, silencing of persons who find themselves in the classificatory space, "refugee." That is, refugees suffer from a peculiar kind of speechlessness in the face of the national and international organisations whose object of care and control they are. Their accounts are disqualified almost a priori, while the languages of refugee relief, policy science, and "development" claim the production of authoritative narratives about the refugees. (234)

Instead, work in this area must insist on acknowledging the human suffering, narrative authority, historical agency, and political memory of the subjects (rather than objects) of research and assistance (234). Following Malkki's formulation, I attempt to present East Timorese experiences in this way, by making use of lengthy narratives drawn from interviews, and focusing on the intricacies and shifting patterns of meaning-making with respect to identity and belonging, exile and return.

Despite the reservations highlighted by Malkki, there are insights from the literature on returning that are useful in framing some key issues of relevance to this book. Allen and Morsink's important collection, *When*

Refugees Go Home (1994), argues that it is imperative to treat the category "returnee" with caution. Rather than an undifferentiated mass, returnees are in reality as diverse as any other group. They caution that research into repatriation must recognize the particularities of each group and those within it. In the same volume, Stein (1994) warns that many "returnees" who voluntarily repatriate do so not because of some long-held yearning to return to the homeland but in response to a deterioration in conditions in the country of asylum. Conversely, a growing literature on return indicates that for many groups an end to conflict does not necessarily precipitate a desire to return. For example, research on Eritrean and Bosnian refugees by Al-Ali, Black, and Koser (2001) indicates that Eritrean refugees who have citizenship rights in their European host countries are overwhelmingly reluctant to return to Eritrea. However, the continued maintenance of ties to their homeland challenges the notion that their wish not to return home indicates a desire to cut off from it.

These findings are equally important in the East Timorese case. They remind us that one must focus both on conditions in the homeland and on a refugee's experience in the host country. This is especially imperative in the case of refugee communities such as the East Timorese who have been living for a protracted period in a wealthy country such as Australia. Moreover, as McDowell and Eastmond note, recent critical ethnographic work on refugee return questions the dominant discourse among relief agencies and policymakers, which posits that repatriation is the most favorable and natural solution to exile. This newer work questions the basic assumption of this discourse on the grounds that it draws on increasingly discredited essentialist notions of a natural link between community, culture, and place (2002, 1).

Similarly, Malkki (1997b, 65) points out that naturalizing the link between people, identity, and place leads to a perception of migrants and refugees as "displaced" and therefore pathological subjects. Objectifying refugees in this way leads to the perception of them as an undifferentiated mass, requiring intervention to "put down new roots." While keeping in mind the centrality of different kinds of power and capital to the achievement of home, I want to avoid the trap of equating the East Timorese experience with powerlessness. Refugees are too frequently represented as helpless subjects requiring expert intervention. In contrast, I wish to explore some of the processes by which East Timorese are managing, in very active ways, their own sense of belonging. Although at the time of writing it was too early to ascertain how the transition from exile will play out, there are some emerging trends that I believe are signs of some of the ways East Timorese people are attempting to reconfigure a sense of home now that the category of exile is no longer available.

In the course of my research I realized too that I was not just studying a refugee community. The East Timorese are refugees living in a wealthy Western country and, most important, are refugees who now have the opportunity to return. This reinforced the worth of enlisting perspectives from my "home territory," the study of diasporic and transnational identities. However, with a few exceptions (see Al-Ali, Black, and Koser 2001; Fuglerud 1999; Kaminsky 1999; Wahlbeck 1998; Zetter 1994), diaspora studies emanating from anthropology, cultural studies, and so on have not so far taken into account experiences that are specific to diasporic communities made up of refugees. With the exception of work in Jewish studies, the field of diaspora and transnational studies has not yet fully explored the interconnections between issues of trauma, the symbolic centrality of exile, questions of long-distance nationalism, and the implications with respect to the reality of return. Moreover, although the "homing desire" is often read as central to the diasporic experience, only rarely do we see a case where the return home becomes a real possibility. I believe this is the most important element of this book. For all the symbolic rhetoric of exile and return, what happens when it shifts from the realm of the symbolic to the practical, messy and contradictory ground of reality?

With respect to terminology, there are a number of terms I use throughout the book. Echoing Robin Cohen's notion of the "victim diaspora" (Cohen 1997), I use the term "refugee diaspora" to describe the East Timorese in Australia. Cohen has developed a typology of diaspora that includes victim, labor, trade, imperial, homeland-oriented, and cultural diasporas. He suggests that the African, Armenian, Palestinian, Jewish, and Irish diasporas most closely match the profile of a classic victim diaspora. Victim diasporas are characterized by a decisive "break event" in their histories, such as slavery, forced exile, or massacre. They usually cling to a collective memory and myth about the homeland and seek to ensure its safety and prosperity when it is in danger (54).

Based on Safran's classic model (1991), the East Timorese case conforms to those more general features of diaspora described by Cohen, which include a strong ethnic group consciousness; a sense of empathy with other co-ethnic members; an idealization of the homeland and a collective commitment to its maintenance, restoration, safety and prosperity, or creation; and the development of a return movement (Cohen 1997, 26).

I use the term "refugee diaspora" for several reasons. First, I employ it to flag a connection to both refugee and diaspora studies. I also use "refugee diaspora" rather than "victim diaspora" to reflect the fact that the East Timorese in Australia themselves generally prefer the term "refugee" as a self-descriptor, and because I believe this term highlights the fact that East Timorese are "recent victims." The fact that East Timorese have only recently fled their homeland suggests firsthand experiences of trauma rather than the more mythologized version in some of the other groups, such as the African or Jewish diasporas, that Cohen includes in his "victim" category. I also support Werbner's more anthropological view that diasporas are "communities of co-responsibility," expressed through material gestures such as charitable giving and political mobilization (Werbner 1998, 12). With Werbner's concept in mind, I take up Tölölyan's manifesto on diaspora, published in the preface to the first issue of the *Diaspora* journal. Following Tölölyan, I invoke the notion of diaspora to explore the "traces of struggles over and contradictions within ideas and practices of identity, homeland and nation" (Tölölyan 1991, 3) in the East Timorese refugee diaspora.

I also use the terms "exile" and "community of suffering" throughout the book. I employ the term "exile" principally because it has functioned as an important identity marker for members of the East Timorese community. I use it to signify what Rushdie has called the "dream of glorious return" (quoted in Naficy 1991, 287), a dream, Naficy argues, that remains alluring only as long as it remains unrealized. What is interesting about the East Timorese case is that, due to real political events (gaining national independence), the East Timorese in Australia and elsewhere have had to make a shift from "exile" to "diaspora." The first is an identity forced upon a group, the second has an element, I argue, of voluntariness.

I argue throughout the book that the dream of return has been maintained and reproduced through what I term the East Timorese "community of suffering." Following Werbner, I deploy this concept to describe the particular kind of community formed in the face of physical or symbolic violence toward a group (Werbner 1997a, 235). Werbner argues that the important aspect of ethnic violence is that it targets "the body, the body politic, the material bases of physical and socio-political reproduction, and the emblematic representations of subjectivity, personhood and society" (237). In the East Timorese case, violence against the body and body politic occurred through ritualized torture and violence perpetrated by the Indonesian military against the populace, subsequently revealed in smuggled photographs shown to members of the diaspora. Such practices symbolically and affectively bind the pain of the individual victim to the fate of the ethnic collectivity. Violence against one is violence against all. Similarly, the military tactics of dispossessing East Timorese of land and banning the use of local languages in schools represented orchestrated means of violating communal symbols and property. Such violations, Werbner argues following Bhabha, result in a sedimented memory of common suffering which becomes the shared affective-symbolic resource for future solidarities founded in "victimization and suffering" (238).

Outline of the Book

As Foucault (1974) and others after him remind us, all histories leave sediment that influence the present in complex ways. There are three key historical layers of relevance to the East Timorese community. The first of these is the historical context of East Timor's four hundred years of colonization by the Portuguese, followed by invasion and occupation by the Indonesians in 1975. The second is the period of living in Portugal and then Australia; the final layer is East Timor's "return." Each layer has left traces that affect how East Timorese in Australia experience their present identities. I track these layers in the opening chapters to set the scene for the more theoretical exploration of the complex and shifting patterns of East Timorese identities in the diaspora. In Chapter 1, "East Timor: A History of the Present," I provide a background—from Portuguese colonization to Indonesian occupation and finally independence—and give an overview of some of the social and cultural categories formed in Portuguese Timor prior to 1975. Although the chapter is primarily descriptive, I insert, where I can, narratives from East Timorese that offer personal recollections of these histories. It is especially imperative to recount this history in the East Timorese case because the complex patterns of colonization, occupation, and migration have left shifting and sometimes contradictory marks on the way East Timorese understand and make meaning of themselves and their situation today.

Chapter 2, "Leaving the Crocodile," presents a series of accounts from East Timorese refugees in Australia about their flight from East Timor and their early experiences in Australia. I sketch some important community background, including numbers and settlement patterns, and an overview of the key issues in the community, such as East Timorese politics in Sydney, the differences between the Timorese-Chinese and the wider East Timorese community, and information on important settlement issues.

In Chapter 3, "Nation, Transnation, Diaspora," I begin the theoretical analysis. My aim is to map some of the "imaginative resources" that have contributed to the collective imagination of the East Timorese community in Sydney. That is, I explore some of the primary content of what Appadurai (1996) and Werbner (1997a) have called the "diasporic public sphere." In addition to mapping the "cultural products" and symbolic production of the East Timorese diasporic public sphere, I take up the important work of Gupta and Ferguson (1997) to explore the intercommunal and transnational links entailed therein, and the implications of these on the shape of East Timorese diasporic identity.

Although I keep the body present throughout the book, I make central questions of embodiment and affect and explore their role in East

Timorese identities in exile in Chapter 4, "Embodying Exile." Here I consider the performative dimensions (protests, church rituals, singing and dancing) of the political campaign for East Timor's independence. The chapter looks at how these have created a context for "retraumatizing" bodies and memories, channeling them into a political "community of suffering" and contributing to a heightened sense of the morality of exile identity among many in the community.

Chapter 5, "Locating East Timoreseness in Australia," shifts the focus from the political to the everyday. Following Nederveen Pieterse (2001), I introduce the concept of "disappearing boundaries" and explore the interaction between what Gerd Baumann (1997) calls "dominant" and "demotic" discourses. I take up these concepts to explore narratives from five East Timorese of various backgrounds, drawing heavily on in-depth interviews to look at their complex patterns of belonging and identity. I consider how these identity patterns form at the intersection of a range of relationships such as class, place, Portugueseness, Chineseness, or Australianness.

Finally, Chapter 6, "From Exile to Diaspora?" draws together conclusions in previous chapters to reflect on questions of home and return now that East Timor has gained independence. I introduce a number of characters whose stories articulate different experiences of the *possibility* and *actuality* of return and explore how these might connect with some of the issues to do with questions of exile, hybridity, and transnational and translocal sensibilities. Who is returning and why? How have they experienced return? How do those still in the diaspora experience the possibility of return, and how does this sit with former exile identities? How does the post-exile situation mesh with questions of home and belonging? How do the *reality* and *possibility* of return challenge meanings attached to East Timoreseness among the diaspora and returnees? I consider these questions to reflect on how the possibility or reality of the "return home" has impacted on senses of self, identity, home, exile and belonging experienced by members of the East Timorese community. Following Appadurai (1995), I introduce the concept of translocality as a way of articulating what I see to be an important trend emerging in the East Timorese community. Rather than any mass repatriation, there appears to be an increasingly translocal involvement in both East Timor and Australia. I argue that translocality can be read as one mode through which East Timorese who are still in Australia and those who have returned are actively renegotiating a new sense of "home" as a means of dealing with some of the difficult issues of partial belonging that former exiles inevitably face.

Chapter 1
East Timor: A History of the Present

> The nation fills the void left in the uprooting of communities and kin, and turns that loss into the language of metaphor. Metaphor, as the etymology of the word suggests, transfers the meaning of home and belonging, across the "middle passage" . . . across those distances, and cultural differences, that span the imagined community of the nation-people.
>
> —Homi Bhabha

On 30 August 1999, the people of East Timor voted overwhelmingly in favor of independence from Indonesia. This at once joyful and tragic founding moment marked the return of the long awaited homeland for thousands of East Timorese exiles abroad.

For the East Timorese refugee diaspora, the imagining of East Timor as a nation is central to their imagining of self in exile. The weight of this tiny new nation's violent past is so great, and inscribes such pain, that for many East Timorese in exile, maintaining a sense of national identity has become an act of personal and collective survival. It is important to emphasize the very real ways in which resistance and national identities hold deeply affective meaning and importance for the East Timorese in East Timor and abroad. To begin to understand the meaning of "home" and "identity" for the East Timorese refugee diaspora, it is essential to understand the particular historical genealogies,[1] the *conditions of possibility*, for an East Timorese imagined community.

Avtar Brah implores us to ask not simply who travels but when, how and under what circumstances, and moreover, to ask what socioeconomic, political, and cultural conditions mark the trajectories of these journeys, and what regimes of power inscribe the formation of the diaspora? (1996, 114). Implied in her manifesto is a call to reflect not just on the present, but on the historical "identity trajectories," the forces that bring a group into being and shape its sense of collective identity. Taking this as my starting point, the aim of this chapter is to articulate the significant parts of East Timor's recent and older history that have provided the raw material for imagining East Timor as a nation. I explore the social, historical, cultural and discursive limits and possibilities for imagining East Timor and "East Timoreseness" in exile. What is this "East Timor" nation for which so many have fought? How has it been imagined? And what has allowed it to "be"? Have all East Timorese been fighting for the same "East Timor"? What are the patterns of history and meaning that frame this "imagined community"?

As East Timor began the difficult transition from nation in resistance to newly imagined nation and those in exile began to return, the differing histories of East Timor's national identity became painfully manifest. To use the term "imagined community" does not denote falseness or artificiality. All communities, as Anderson's (1991) work attests, are "imagined." The imagination, as liberation movements have long been aware, is constitutive of institutions, practices and processes of inclusion and exclusion that have very real "in the world" meanings and effects. Indeed, colonial liberation movements recognize that psychological liberation is a precondition for decolonization. And so, in the same way that it is important to see the constructedness of the colonizer's imagination and its effects, it is also salient to take the same reflexive view of any imagined community of resistance. As the recent history of many new postcolonial nations has demonstrated, there is always the danger of falling back into the dangerous space of overt essentialism, thus perpetuating the cycle of colonization in new ways.

Part One: Histories

The Creation of Portuguese East Timor

The narrow, mountainous island of Timor lies about 350 miles northeast of Darwin, the northernmost city in Australia, in the southeastern end of the Indonesian archipelago. "East Timor" did not exist as an entity prior to Portuguese colonization in the sixteenth century. Today's East Timor encompasses half the island of Timor, the small enclave of Oecussi located within West Timor on the north coast near the border, and the small island of Atauro, located off the coast of Dili (see map, p. vii).[2]

Early Portuguese contact with East Timor came via a 1566 settlement of Dominican Friars. They built a fortress on the island of Solor, just northwest of Timor, for converts from Solor and Flores. An early mestiço population developed during this period. Known as "black Portuguese" or *topasses*—a term thought to be derived from either the Gujerati word *tupasse,* meaning translator, or the term *topee walas,* meaning "hat men"—they formed a distinct and powerful ethnic community, controlling trading networks between Solor, Larantuka, and Timor (Taylor 1999).[3]

Timor's abundant sandalwood was a valuable commodity that attracted Catholicized topasses and Portuguese. The Portuguese "officially" invaded around 1642—moving from the coast to control internal trade. During this time, the Dutch were working their way into Timor from the west, finally defeating the western capital Kupang in 1653. Kupang, nevertheless, remained firmly under the power of the local topasses until the 1730s, when the Dutch incited local tribes to rise up against them. The topasses for the first time turned to the Portuguese for support in their defense, but were defeated overwhelmingly in 1749, thus ensuring a Dutch presence in the west and creating a clear territorial division between East and West Timor (Taylor 1999).

Taylor (1999, 3) argues that, by accident of history, the "healthy respect" that ensued between *topasses* and Portuguese meant that neither sought to spread their influence beyond the local kingdom level, thus leaving East Timorese cultural life and social structures, at a general level, relatively untouched. Gradually East Timor became less and less important to the Portuguese colonial empire.

Portugal's colonial rule in East Timor is often seen as a rather benign form of rule, particularly as compared to Portugal's other colonies such as Mozambique and Angola and the Dutch rule in West Timor. However, the comparatively favorable conditions in East Timor should be seen as resulting mostly from distance, isolation from other colonies, and neglect as Portugal directed attention and resources elsewhere in its empire. The Portuguese were not kind-hearted rulers in East Timor, as is sometimes argued. There was a healthy slave trade in the nineteenth century,[4] and until Portugal's Caetano regime fell in 1974, the use of forced labor to build roads, cultivate cash crops, and the like was common (Taylor 1999, 11, 22).

Indeed, contrary to the popular view that East Timor had no independence movement when decolonization began in 1974, there was, in fact, always resistance among the people of East Timor to foreign invaders.[5] There were many resistance battles in the eighteenth century, and Portugal, for this reason, gave up attempts to administer the territory as a whole in 1769. However, control was reasserted at the end of the nineteenth century, and the use of forced labor produced widespread anger and led to a major uprising from 1910 to 1912, which was eventually crushed by the Portuguese (Taylor 1999, 11). In 1959 there were again riots and uprisings, and fifty-eight East Timorese were exiled to Angola and Mozambique for their role (Taylor 1999, 21). This event and its subsequent retelling became a formative moment for those who became important in the East Timorese independence movement. It is interesting to note, in light of more recent silence on West Timor and "Timorese-ness," that after the 1959 uprising one of the group's leaders stated that "We are not interested in the government of Indonesia, but in the inte-gration of East and West Timor. We have ancient links—we never had a border before Portugal colonised Timor" (Taylor 1999, 21). In recent years, however, West Timor has been mentioned rarely, and I have heard no reference among East Timorese to ideas about integration with it. East Timorese in Timor and Australia generally speak of West Timorese as a different people, more Indonesianized and lacking the benefits of Portuguese influence.

It is interesting that this connection with West Timor has been com-pletely silenced. Since East Timor was rebelling against Portuguese colo-nization, the anticolonial movement at the time of those earlier uprisings had to make links to some "cultural common past" with the indigenous West Timorese. This was the only available means of rebellion, relying on encompassing West Timor in the precolonial vision for which they were fighting. But when they began to fight against Indonesian colo-nization this became harder, because West Timor had no independence movement that could bond East and West together in "pain." Therefore, claims to independence have relied on their *difference* from West Timor, premised on the Portugueseness of the East to justify claims for inde-pendence from Indonesia.

World War II and the Japanese Invasion

East Timor became a pawn in World War II when Australia, despite Por-tugal's neutral status, moved into East Timor to defend itself from Jap-anese encroachment from the north. Approximately 400 Australian troops were sent to Timor in 1941. They moved into East Timor from the West, seeking "friendlier natives." The Dutch had far less positive relations with the Timorese in West Timor than the Portuguese did with the East Timorese. The Timorese in the West were inclined to associate "whiteness" with "badness" and hence, for the Australian soldiers, there was a risk of the locals betraying them to the Japanese (Kenneally 2001). The soldiers were reportedly well received in East Timor, and there are many accounts of East Timorese sacrifice and bravery to protect the sol-diers, who by that time had been virtually abandoned by the Australian military. The Australians fought, according to many accounts, for two years as a kind of guerrilla army with little ammunition or other supplies such as food. This meant that they relied heavily on the protection and support of the East Timorese. With the help of the East Timorese, the Australian troops inflicted some 1,500 casualties on the 20,000-strong Japanese force. The Australians were eventually forced to retreat in 1943.

These troops felt an enormous debt to the East Timorese. Many soldiers were looked after by villagers, who provided protection, medical aid, and food, acted as guides through the mountains, and relayed clandestine messages. Many soldiers left IOU notes with families they became close to, notes promising that one day the debt would be repaid. Needless to say, many of these troops felt enormous guilt at being forced to abandon their East Timorese helpers to the Japanese upon their retreat. Indeed several of the Australian veterans were very active in the East Timor solidarity movements as a means of repaying that debt. Here is an example from Paddy Kenneally, a Timor veteran and independence supporter:

I remember, the Japanese captured, shot, and bayoneted fifteen Australian soldiers. . . . One of the fifteen was still alive and a Timorese woman got some men to take him to her village. His wounds were dressed and he was hidden from Japanese patrols searching for him. The Timorese fed, sheltered and supported us the whole time we were there. And look how we repaid them! (Paddy Kenneally, in Wise 2001, 20)

After the Australians were evacuated, the East Timorese carried on fighting the Japanese, and their eventual defeat brought bitter retribution from the Japanese occupying forces for the remainder of the war. Few Australian lives were lost. Although around 500 East Timorese were evacuated to Darwin with the Australians, the Australian government deliberately excluded native East Timorese, confining the eligible evacuees to Portuguese and mestiços. It is estimated that some 40,000 East Timorese died as a direct result of the war between 1941 and 1946. These deaths resulted from bombing raids of both allied and Japanese forces, from retaliation against East Timorese for assisting the Australian soldiers, and many also resulted from forced labor by the Japanese, as well as starvation and disease (Taylor 1999).

During the Japanese occupation, my mother, sister and myself took refuge in the mountains with my uncle. Because my father and some of his colleagues aligned themselves with the Australians, he went with the Australian Commandos to Remexio. My father told my uncle to take me and my sister with his family if my mother didn't want to run any more. So my sister and I followed my uncle to Uatulari/Alimbata. We stayed there for a few months until the Japanese forces arrived and we caught an Australian ship and came to Australia. I arrived in Australia with my uncle, aunt and my cousins. Since my father was following the Australian Army, my mother stayed alone and was caught by the Japanese and killed and burned. (Natalina Ramos-Horta, mother of José)[6]

Following the devastation of the war and the Japanese occupation, Portugal resumed its rule of the territory. However, the sandalwood trade, East Timor's main commodity, had declined, and the colony's only revenue came from small-scale production of coffee. Portugal remained a poor nation and spent little on developing the tiny colony. Portugal's economic situation worsened as time went on: beginning in 1961 with the wars fought in its African colonies, Mozambique and Angola, it gradually became depleted and exhausted. The winds of change finally blew in East Timor's direction (Taylor 1999).

Decolonization

Two dictators ruled Portugal for fifty years, Antonio Salazar from 1932 to 1968, and Marcello Caetano in 1968–1974. In April 1974, the Portuguese army staged what became popularly known as the "Carnation Revolution" in Lisbon, leading to the collapse of Europe's last colonial empire. Almost immediately a policy of decolonization was implemented.

Decolonization took place in the face of massive illiteracy in East Timor, which in turn had a strong bearing on who would become prominent in East Timor's political landscape. Primary school enrollment increased from 8,000 in 1954 to approximately 57,000 in 1974, but 93 percent of the population remained illiterate in 1973. There was a small increase in participation at the secondary level, creating a small, educated urban elite. Few East Timorese proceeded to higher education, only two students per year before 1970 but by 1974 there were 39 university students, most moving into areas such as government administration, health, and education. This group formed the core of those who later became involved in East Timor's first political parties (Taylor 1999; Morlanes 1991).

From as early as the 1960s and well established by 1973, the year before the Carnation Revolution, there were loose gatherings of politically minded, educated East Timorese elites, discussing their dissatisfaction with colonial rule. These clandestine meetings often took place in the Daré Seminary near Dili, where many had been educated. They published articles in local Catholic newspapers such as *A Provincia de Timor* and *Suara*, and later in *A Voz de Timor* (where a young J. A. Gusmão published political pieces in 1975 and José Ramos-Horta worked as a journalist) (Nicol 1978).

Following the Lisbon coup on 5 May 1974, the governor of East Timor issued a proclamation allowing the establishment of political associations, not political parties. These associations subsequently became East Timor's first political parties. The first to be established, on 11 May, was the Timorese Democratic Union (UDT). UDT's leadership consisted primarily of three main groups: administrative elites, plantation owners, and some *liurai* (East Timorese royalty). Its charter promised development in a Portuguese cultural framework, espoused democratic principles, and rejected integration with any foreign country.

The second association to appear was the Association for a Democratic East Timor (ASDT). Its power base was made up of young urban elites (its leadership had an average age of just thirty), many retaining strong ties to their rural areas of origin. It espoused democratic-socialist principles and the need for literacy and health programs, agricultural development, and pride in East Timorese culture. It also advocated full participation of all sections of East Timorese society. In September 1974, ASDT became FRETILIN—the Frente Revolucionario do Timor Leste Independente, or Revolutionary Front for an Independent East Timor (Nicol 1978; Taylor 1999; Morlanes 1991). Key founding members were Xavier do Amaral, Nicolau Lobato, and José Ramos-Horta. Luís Cardoso (Cardoso 2000) describes the leading characters in East Timor's resistance as all "in love with poetry and the latest ideas from Europe." Lobato (son of the catechism teacher from Soibada, and later tortured and murdered by the Indonesians) would in the early days be seen walking through Dili always with a book under his arm, deep in thought. Xanana (José Alexandre) Gusmão, the young and charismatic leader who would succeed Lobato as leader of FRETILIN (and its military wing, FALINTIL Forcas Armadas de Libertacão Nacional de Timor-Leste), was also somewhat of a poet. Xanana was remembered fondly by Cardoso (2000) as a goalkeeper during peacetime soccer matches, "spread-eagled on the ground, too busy making up sonnets to actually stop any goals."

The third key group to form, on 25 May 1974, was the Association for the Integration of Timor into Indonesia, later to change its name to the more palatable Timorese Popular Democratic Association, APODETI. It advocated autonomous integration into Indonesia, compulsory teaching of the Indonesian language, free education, medical assistance, and the right to strike. It is now widely known that this party was clandestinely supported and funded by the Indonesian government (see Taylor 1999; Dunn 1996; Jolliffe 1978; Nicol 1978). APODETI's most prominent support came from Dili's small Muslim community and from a key liurai from near the border with West Timor.

UDT and FRETILIN both gained popular support. Local elections were conducted in February and March 1975. There was much enthusiasm for political expression, with large rallies throughout the county. FRETILIN, which had gained much popularity in rural areas by implementing democratic and grassroots rural development and literacy programs, won more than 55 percent of the vote, with UDT close behind. Between the two parties, they had the support of up to 90 percent of the population. APODETI had negligible support, with only 300 members, in spite of generous financial support from Jakarta (Nicol 1978; Taylor 1999; Morlanes 1991).

Little did these young political actors know that their tiny nation was of such interest to its neighbor, Indonesia, and to Malaysia and Australia, with their eye on oil reserves in the Timor Strait (Dunn 1996; Taylor 1999). The United States, too, had economic and military strategic interests in the region, what with the war in Vietnam, its concerns with cold war politics, and its history of support for the Sukarno regime in overthrowing communism. At the same time, elements in Lisbon were contemplating an easy integration of East Timor with Indonesia, in the same way that Goa had become part of India. All provided a frightening backdrop to the process of decolonization in East Timor.

Coup

In 1974, the Indonesians implemented an operation to destabilize East Timor. The operation was code-named Operasi Komodo. A range of tactics was used, including propaganda broadcasts, providing financial support to those with leanings toward Jakarta, and attempts to exploit bad feelings among UDT leaders about their election loss by creating suspicion in their minds. UDT split into two camps: pro-independence and those more sympathetic to the possibilities of integration with Indonesia. On the night of 10 August 1975, UDT forces loyal to the latter position mounted a coup against FRETILIN. On 20 August, FRETILIN launched a counter-attack. Three weeks of fighting ensued; up to 2,000 were killed. In the midst of the chaos, the Portuguese fled on 27 August to Atauro Island, abandoning control completely. The Portuguese army was unwilling and unable to intervene.

I was five years old, in a village near Remexio. My family was UDT and the majority of the people in the area were FRETILIN. There was open hostility toward us, so my family decided to move to Dili where they thought it would be safer. A truck was hired and my uncle's family, my own family, my grandfather, an unmarried aunty and another aunty with her two children set off for Dili. On the way there was a road block. Our truck was ordered back to Remexio. We were all jailed in the local primary school to await "justice" the next day. Our captors were awaiting the ringleaders to organise what one would call popular justice. To the adults, death was certain, while the children were oblivious to the terror around them. I remember laughing a lot because all my cousins were there. The next day, as the ringleaders were due to arrive, the East Timorese national army beat them to it and liberated us. Someone had mercifully informed Dili of what was happening. We were taken to Dili, and placed in the UDT compound. The place was teeming with UDT families who had fled their homes in fear of their safety. From the compound we could hear the endless sounds of gunfire throughout the nights. (Julieta, 27, in Wise 2001, 15)

By mid-September, UDT forces had retreated into West Timor. FRETILIN effectively regained control, immediately forming an administration, and began to develop health, social and education programs.

Invasion and the Indonesian Occupation

FRETILIN's rule and East Timor's independence lasted just three short months. Taking advantage of East Timor's political instability, Indonesia invaded for the purpose of "restoring order." Five Australian journalists, there to report on rumors of the impending invasion, were killed in the village of Balibo by Indonesian troops on 16 October 1975. The Australian and Indonesian governments went to great lengths to cover up these murders, reporting that the victims had been accidentally caught in crossfire from FRETILIN troops (see Taudevin 1999; Jolliffe 1978; Nicol 1978). Full-scale invasion began in the early hours of 8 December, with attacks by troops on land and from the sea and by aerial bombing raids. The initial attack, by all accounts, was vicious and made no attempt to avoid civilian casualties. Days of murder, rape, and looting followed. In the early days, the Chinese in Dili were singled out for selective killings. Around 500 Chinese were killed the first day. Entire families of East Timorese were shot for displaying FRETILIN flags. So began almost twenty-five years of horror for the people of East Timor. Bodies would be piled up and thrown out to sea (Taylor 1999).

On the day of the invasion, I remember sitting at home with my grandfather and brother, sisters and cousins when members of the Indonesian military parachuted over our neighbourhood, one landing literally in our yard. "Sit still and be quiet," warned our grandfather. Whilst gathering his chute, the Indonesian paused, looked at us, just as we were looking at him, and then he left. This strange event heralded the beginning of the confusion, fear and suffering that was to follow. I remember fleeing with some of my family to head toward the seeming safety of the hospital, only to be turned back by men with guns. I remember a gun being held to my head by a man full of bravado who was then verbally abused by my brave cousin: "He's just a boy you idiot! What can he know!" . . . I remember working for the Red Cross a year later, distributing necessities to people who had fled to the mountains and then surrendered, unsure of the future, running into the bushes, hearing whispers of atrocities committed against those we knew and those we loved. (Paulo, 36, in Wise 2001, 14)

Full-scale attacks lasted for four years. Despite the size of the invading force, which by April 1976 numbered 35,000, compared to approximately 20,000 FALINTIL troops (FRETILIN's military wing), the Indonesians controlled only coastal regions, due to the difficult and mountainous terrain in the middle of the island, where most East Timorese lived.

We were hiding in a building, and they told us all to lie down in front of that building, and we couldn't move, you know. And then, after we went inside, and one of the FALINTIL troops who was there with us, he tried to, you know, tried to take off the FALINTIL uniform, but unfortunately he was killed by an Indonesian just beside me, and it was terrible. (Fabiola, 35)

Most accounts estimate the number killed in East Timor during the early years of the occupation as at least 200,000. And many more have died since, a devastating figure, considering that the total population in 1975 had been 680,000. This period has been compared with the Pol Pot "final solution" in Cambodia; in per capita numerical comparison, it far exceeds it. Genocide was carried out through wholesale bombing with napalm, starvation, and mass murder. Adam Malik, Indonesia's foreign minister at the time, told reporters: "50,000, or perhaps even 80,000 people may have been killed during the war in East Timor. So what? It was a war. . . . Why all the fuss?" (*Sydney Morning Herald*, 5 April 1977). Such comments reflect the Indonesian military's perceptions of East Timorese as for the most part "backwards, undeveloped and basically sub-human" (Anderson 2001, 235).

In the years following there was a series of campaigns, including the now infamous "encirclement and annihilation" campaign, posited as the "final solution." The military rounded up thousands of East Timorese "walkers" and forced them to form a human chain to encircle the island from the East and from the West to "flush out" guerrilla resistance fighters from the mountains. Many thousands died from starvation or murder during this campaign.

They killed people, took more away, committed rape, took people's sons and husbands without any of us knowing where, even to this day! They oppressed people. People could not speak up, we lived in fear. The years that they occupied East Timor, they did nothing right, just commit crimes. [I lost three of my own children . . .] Fernandazinha was killed by a bomb explosion dropped from an American plane that was sold to the Indonesians. The youngest one was captured and killed in Ainaro. . . . He was so innocent, never held a gun in his life. His name is Guilherme. . . . Nuno was also killed. . . . In 1978 there were severe attacks by Indonesian forces, so a lot of people died during this time and the Timorese guerrillas moved around a lot and my son, Nuno, got sick and was caught by Indonesian forces and tortured to death. (Natalina Ramos-Horta)

A strategy of cultural and social genocide, or "Indonesianization" ensued. As many as 80 percent of villagers were resettled in town, where they had no means of support, or put into concentration camps, or "model villages," as they were euphemistically known. Forced labor was rife. These camps destroyed local social systems, were psychologically devastating, and caused an enormous increase in diseases such as malaria and tuberculosis. Furthermore, those sent to them lost ownership of their traditional lands (Taylor 1999, 105–6).

There was a great deal of investment in infrastructure, including schools, hospitals, and government offices, in an attempt to show the impressive benefits of integration with Indonesia compared to the underdeveloped state in which the Portuguese left East Timor. Schools became a prime site of "Indonesian indoctrination." Teaching Portuguese was banned, and schooling in Indonesian became compulsory. Children had to learn the Indonesian "Pancasila," the national ideology of Indonesia, word for word, and to sing the Indonesian national anthem each morning. They also had to attend special classes to learn about Indonesian nationhood.

There was an ongoing and systematic program of forced birth control by injecting the contraceptive Depo-Provera into women in clinics, women who were unconscious after operations, and young girls in high schools (Taylor 1999, 158–60). From 1989 a program of resettlement commenced, bringing migrants from other parts of Indonesia to "Indonesianize" the population. Dili's streets and markets soon began to resemble a Javanese town. By the late 1990s, Indonesians were estimated to be 20 percent of the population (Taylor 1999, 124). This followed thirteen years of East Timor being a closed territory. Opening to Indonesian settlers also opened the territory to other outsiders, which helped to get news out of the territory.

A culture of suspicion and mistrust was deliberately cultivated as a tactic of fragmentation and control. East Timorese were conscripted into the military, and "informers" were employed. It is estimated that there was one informer for every ten to fifteen people. The military aimed to have at least one informer attached to every four family groups. This policy created a frightening environment of suspicion, division, and mistrust among many East Timorese, which carries through to this day.

It would be impossible to account for all the atrocities, all the "disappearances," tortures, rapes, forced prostitution, and murders since the invasion. However, perhaps the most important event, in terms of acting as a kind of "turning point" in East Timor history by catching the world's attention, was the 1991 Santa Cruz (or Dili) Massacre. On 12 November, a Catholic mass was held in Dili at the Motael Church to commemorate the death of a young student, Sebastiao Gomes, who had been shot dead by troops at the church two weeks earlier. The mourners walked to the cemetery to place flowers on his grave and were fired on by the Indonesian military at random, and without provocation. It is estimated that between 250 and 400 people were killed. Although not an uncommon event in East Timor, this was different. A British cameraman in the crowd filmed the event. The film was subsequently smuggled out of the country and broadcast around the world.

Resistance

From the very beginning, the FALINTIL resistance had popular support. For the first three years FRETILIN fought in a more traditional mode under a central command. In FRETILIN-controlled areas during this time, they ran classes on food production, housing, education, and health care. However, after massive bombing their forces were depleted by almost 80 percent and were virtually at the point of extinction. In 1981, under the new commander Xanana Gusmão, FALINTIL broke up into mobile guerrilla units and, backed by a very successful clandestine support network, moved into the mountains. The activities of the underground network included supplying intelligence, food, and medicine to the FALINTIL fighters and organizing demonstrations in Dili and elsewhere. The resistance, including both soldiers and the clandestine network, was renowned for its amazing tactical skills, as was the will of the people in general to resist, despite widespread intimidation and torture. The clandestine network was aware of the importance of international media attention. However for thirteen years East Timor was closed to foreign media. The network would secretly plan media "incidents," such as organizing a demonstration during the pope's visit in 1989, to attract international attention and support. Fabiola, a former member of the clandestine resistance in East Timor and Indonesia describes the sophisticated methods their network employed:

To get information, I would have to approach the Intelligence Officers and . . . I didn't like, but you have to act like a prostitute or something like that, to get information without the Indonesians suspecting. So sometimes it's a lot of sacrifice. But one thing in my mind, because my principle, that I decide to get involved in the struggle, I have to continue until the end. . . . That's why I continued to work clandestinely in that area. And then, also, because—because it's very easy for me, because I was working for the only East Timorese NGO there. . . . Because that organisation also had a lot of support from different countries, like United States, like US Aid, or from Canada. And . . . it had a lot of facilities there that I could use, like photocopy machines, and everything. Faxes, and that. But with the clandestine network it works like each category kept separate. So, some, like, if you are responsible to organise the protest, just the protest. You don't involve in other things. Those that involve in collecting facts have to take their information to the bush, it's like: A, B, C, D. But D only knows C. But they don't know B and A. That way, if one is caught and tells, it can't get back down the chain. (Fabiola, 35)

In 1994 Gusmão was successful at organizing a coalition of the disparate parties to form a single resistance movement, bringing together UDT and FRETILIN. It was called the Conselho Naçional da Resistençia Maubere or National Council of Maubere Resistance (CNRM), later the National Council of Timorese Resistance (CNRT). Maubere is an interesting term in itself. José Ramos-Horta coined the term at the beginning of the development of FRETILIN to characterize FRETILIN's version of social democracy. Originally a Mumbai (an East Timor language) word meaning "man," "dweller of the mountains," it became used in a derogatory expression meaning "poor" and "ignorant." It was appropriated by

FRETILIN to designate "the People," to identify East Timorese as different from Portuguese, Chinese, and others, and particularly referenced the nonassimilated East Timorese. According to Ramos-Horta, it proved to be the single most successful political emblem of FRETILIN's campaign, a symbol of cultural identity, pride, and belonging (Ramos-Horta 1987, 37).

Gusmão himself was captured by the Indonesians in 1992, sentenced to life imprisonment in Jakarta, and released after the fall of the Suharto regime in 1998. East Timor's diplomat José Ramos-Horta left East Timor before the 1974 invasion and remained in exile until independence in 1999. During those years, Ramos-Horta traveled the world seeking support and awareness for East Timor's cause, working with the UN and the various international East Timor Solidarity movements. Ramos-Horta and East Timor's Bishop Carlos Belo were joint winners of the Nobel Peace Prize in 1996 for their role in East Timor's quest for independence. This event, coupled with the news of the Dili massacre in 1991, finally brought international attention to their cause.

Political Exiles and Students in Early East Timorese Nationalist Politics

Ramos-Horta was born in East Timor in 1949 to an East Timorese mother and a Portuguese father. His father was what was known as a *deportado*. The deportados were exiled from Portugal to East Timor for their leftist politics by the fascist Salazar regime. They brought political ideas from Europe with them and frequently remained in East Timor and married local women. José Ramos-Horta went to school at Soibada and the Liceau in East Timor, both of which produced a number of leading figures in East Timorese politics. Following his early involvement in politics, Ramos-Horta was himself exiled, in 1970–71, to Mozambique. Here he was exposed to a range of ideas circulating within the anticolonial politics of southern Africa at the time. Back in East Timor, the political leaders such as Ramos-Horta, Lobato, and Gusmão were reading people such as Frantz Fanon, Albert Memmi, W. E. B. Du Bois, Aimé Césaire, and Amilcar Cabral, all significant influences on the shape of FRETILIN's political discourse.

Many of these key political figures studied at the famous Daré Seminary, in the hills behind Dili. Run by politically progressive Jesuit priests, the Daré Seminary school was renowned for its robust political culture and progressive ideas. It produced many of the most important leaders in East Timorese politics. In addition, many East Timorese from assimilado families went on to study at universities in Portugal, returning with a healthy stock of 1960s European political ideas.

Of course, "assimilado" was a mechanism of colonial divide and rule tactics. Although many represented the elite's interests which were the core of the more pro-Portuguese UDT party, many from mestiço and other assimilado families went on ironically to be key players in creating an East Timorese national identity based on the romantic notion of the Maubere peasant peoples as a core political strategy. These historical trajectories are important to this discussion because Portugal's colonial/class structures in East Timor created a political class, many of whose members now occupy the diaspora.

The Church and Religion

The Catholic Church has had as long and significant an influence in East Timor as has Portuguese colonization. The Catholic Church's earlier "civilizing mission" eventually meant that many of the East Timorese elite were educated at the only higher education institution in East Timor, the Daré Seminary. Run by fairly radical Jesuit priests, it was a breeding ground for the early East Timorese independence leaders. The Catholic Church still runs a large network of schools and orphanages in East Timor. Support for the Catholic Church has increased phenomenally since the Indonesian invasion. Before 1975, most East Timorese were animists, and despite the Church's best efforts, fewer than 30 percent had converted by the end of Portuguese rule. This changed dramatically in the ensuing years. Indonesia requires all its citizens to identify with one of the five "official" religions. Unsurprisingly, East Timorese people chose Catholicism as a form of resistance against the predominantly Muslim invaders. Today somewhere around 90 percent of East Timorese claim to be Catholic. East Timorese knew that becoming a member of the Catholic Church would afford some measure of protection, and it also offered a ritual outlet to express their collective suffering. Catholic clergy often put their own lives at risk to protect East Timorese who were harassed by the military, and churches became places of refuge to hide from danger (Taylor 1999).

Anderson argues that the Catholic Church in East Timor substituted for the print media in forming a sense of collective national identity. The Church made the strategic decision to give services only in Tetum, raising it from a lingua franca to the language of East Timorese national identity (Anderson 2001, 238). The Catholic Church resisted attempts to incorporate the East Timor church into the wider Indonesian church, instead administering East Timor as a separate entity. The pope appointed East Timor's Bishop Belo an apostolic administrator of a Italian diocese that had been dormant for centuries, through which he was responsible for East Timor and answered directly to the pope. When John Paul II visited the territory in 1989, rather than kissing the ground when he stepped off the plane in East Timor, as was customary for him on arriving in a new country, he put a crucifix on a pillow on the ground and kissed it instead. This was seen by some commentators to be a symbolic statement in support of Indonesia's sovereignty over East Timor. However, Catholic commentators and East Timorese argue the opposite. Had he kissed the ground upon arriving he would have infuriated his Indonesian hosts, since it is a gesture reserved for visits to independent states. There was much expectation among Catholic East Timorese that he would kiss the ground as a gesture to the illegality of Indonesia's occupation. Instead, he knelt and kissed the crucifix on the pillow. This was perceived by East Timorese as a sign that he did not accept Indonesia's sovereignty over the territory. The pope's visit provided a major rallying point for the independence campaigners, especially the fact that it brought a great deal of international attention to the territory.

Transnational Connections Between Portugal and Its Colonies

East Timor was just one small outpost of the Portuguese empire, but the relationships cemented by this period of colonization are of ongoing importance for contemporary East Timorese. Portugal remained an unfailing advocate in international forums for an independent East Timor, and now that independence has been won, Portugal is playing an important part in the reconstruction process.

Political actors in the East Timorese diaspora also cultivated links with other ex-Portuguese colonies such as Brazil and Mozambique. Drawing on the shared experience of decolonization, relationships were established with the Community of Portuguese Speaking Countries (CPSP). Similar relationships were developed with many non-Western nations. During his twenty-four years as East Timor's exiled diplomat, Ramos-Horta traveled widely in Latin America, drawing large crowds and significant support.

An example of such support is the São Paulo Manifesto. In 1997, the São Paulo Parliamentary Front for East Timorese Independence, a group composed of representatives from all twelve parties in Brazil's São Paulo parliament, published a manifesto outlining its support for the liberation struggle of East Timor's people (CDPM 1997). The manifesto reads in part:

We, Parliamentarians of São Paulo, have decided to actively oppose the unjust, violent and illegal domination of East Timor by Indonesian troops on 7 December 1975. We speak the same language as our Timorese brothers, and condemn the fact that the people of Timor are forbidden to use it because the occupier considers it subversive to do so. . . . We intend, therefore, to start using our influence with the Brazilian Foreign Office, to defend our East Timorese brothers' freedom and independence; to promote solidarity with the Timorese people; to call for an immediate end to Indonesia's occupation of East Timor, and for the self-determination and independence of its people; to defend cultural diversity and religious freedom, and to press the Brazilian Government to recognise FRETILIN as the legitimate representative of East Timor.

The manifesto shows the success of the East Timorese independence movement's strategy to link into the rhetoric of brotherhood among the formerly colonized. Notice too the significant references to the banning of the Portuguese language in East Timor, and the issue of religious freedom.

Former Portuguese colonies in Africa have also supported East Timor's cause. Links have been cultivated from the Timorese diaspora in Portugal and Australia with countries such as Mozambique, Angola, Cap Verde, and São Tomé and Príncipe. These countries helped the East Timorese continue their struggle, demonstrating consistent and vocal support over the years in United Nations forums.

Independence

Following the Asian currency crisis in 1997, Indonesia was left devastated with many Indonesians experiencing food shortages and rapid inflation. The Suharto regime failed to regain control of the economy, and on 21 May 1998 he was forced to resign in the face of continual mass demonstrations, replaced by B. J. Habibie. The Indonesian public viewed Suharto's pervasive corruption, cronyism and nepotism as responsible for the crisis. Key generals also resigned, including the despised generals Probawo and Wiranto, both key figures in the military operations in East Timor.

In June, July, and September 1998 there were discussion forums in Dili calling for a referendum on the territory's future, and in Jakarta students began for the first time to be brave enough to protest outside the prison where Xanana Gusmão was being held, calling for his release. President Habibie, in the face of internal and international pressure, indicated he was prepared to offer a "special status" to East Timor. The independence movement roundly rejected this. On 27 January 1999, to the surprise of all, in a move widely interpreted as an attempt to distinguish himself from Suharto (with elections looming) and to gain international prestige, Habibie offered to hold a referendum in East Timor on its future. "I will prove to the world that I can make a major contribution to world peace as mandated by our Constitution," he stated in the *Jakarta Post* on 16 February 1999. On 30 August 1999, East Timor had the chance at last to vote on its future. East Timorese people voted overwhelmingly in favor of breaking with Indonesia. With a voter turnout of 98 percent, 78 percent of the population voted for independence. Like their counterparts at home, East Timorese in Australia were allowed to vote in the referendum at polling stations set up in the Liverpool area for Sydney East Timorese. Paolo reflects on his memories of the referendum day in Sydney:

it was a very uplifting day. It was a really beautiful day, a sunny day. And I got there early, actually. Because that sense of—I can't wait to vote. You know? And people were there early—there was a long queue and I think um . . . there was a lot of media there—and um . . . I think yes— well. It was a really, really happy day. People were just so, so happy. You can . . . (stops . . . closes eyes . . . Long pause . . . breaks down). (Paulo, 36)

The news was not all good, however. After twenty-five years the Indonesian military was less than thrilled at the prospect of letting East Timor go. Since the announcement of the referendum in January, the military had been busy organizing and arming local militia groups to threaten people leading up to the vote. The day following the referendum with its vote of 78 percent in favor of independence, Indonesian-armed and -trained East Timorese militia went on a violent rampage implementing their planned "scorched earth" policy.

The referendum day in Sydney. . . . It was like the first time in my entire life— oh! It's my right, you know? I'm not forced by anybody, and then I can become a part of this community, of the East Timorese community, to choose the nation's future. The people of East Timor's future. . . . And then I actually watched all that happened in East Timor on Australian media, . . . it was terrible. It was terrible, not just because of my family—I have family, I have friends, but especially the people of East Timor. The innocent people, you know. So, it was very sad, very frustrating, very stressed out. You know, for me, I even postponed uni and my studies. (Fabiola, 35)

At least 1,000 people were killed in the ensuing violence, which the Indonesian military did nothing to quell. Many East Timorese took refuge in the Dili UN compound. However, on 10 September, UNAMET, the UN body set up to conduct the referendum, evacuated all their staff, leaving the East Timorese without any foreign support. The UN also left many local staff behind, who faced reprisals from militias. Many East Timorese fled to the mountains. Militias forcibly herded some 200,000 East Timorese across the border into West Timor, to end up in squalid refugee camps.[7] Throughout September there were pleas for the international community, Australia in particular, to send troops to stop the violence, since the Indonesian military (who had been granted the right to oversee the elections and maintain order) refused to act. Until the UNAMET evacuation, there were some 400 journalists in Dili sending reports to the outside world. As a result, there was a huge public outcry from nations such as Australia, the U.S., and Portugal. In Australia there was a series of large street marches, with many tens of thousands calling for international intervention. It was claimed that these were the largest marches in Australia since Vietnam. Indonesia was against UN intervention and continually denied the violence. However, in the face of such overwhelming public pressure, and with the U.S. threatening to cut military ties, the UN finally sanctioned a peace "enforcing" force, known as INTER-FET. Indonesian troops looted property, and virtually burned Dili to the ground, as their parting gesture. On 21 September 1999, after three weeks of violence, the first troops of an Australian-led force landed in Dili. As Taylor (1999) points out, for many East Timorese it was too little too late.

they organised the protests here, I was in the protests for the intervention of peacekeeping force. I'm very—how do you say—very thankful for Australia to lead, to lead in the fight, to be the first in the decision to go to East Timor, with all the pressure from Indonesia. That's why, also, to the Australian community that support us a lot. Since 1975, you know, after the occupation. The government is totally different now, but the Australian people are very supportive. (Josefa, 36)

After the initial Australian troops secured the territory, in early 2000 the original INTERFET force handed responsibility to a multinational peacekeeping force, which included troops from Australia, New Zealand, Jordan, Brazil, and Portugal, among others. At the same time, the United Nations Transitional Administration in East Timor (UNTAET) was established in order to

provide security and maintain law and order throughout the territory of East Timor; to establish an effective administration; to assist in the development of civil and social services; to ensure the coordination and delivery of humanitarian assistance, rehabilitation and development assistance; to support capacity-building for self-government; and to assist in the establishment of conditions for sustainable development. (UN 2002)

Consequently, a large contingent of international UN and NGO civilian staff descended on East Timor, bringing with them inflated international salaries, which led to a bizarre dual economy in East Timor centered on the capital, Dili. The *Olympia*—a huge floating hotel, with a disco and flashing lights visible on its decks—anchored in Dili harbor (where just months before, dead bodies were floating) to house the influx of internationals. Hotels in converted shipping containers charging $U.S.80 a night sprang up all over the small city, as did expensive bars, discos, and cafes, all, of course, out of reach of all but the elite of East Timorese society.

In the two and a half years of UNTAET operations, there was a shadow administration, the East Timor Transitional Administration (ETTA), made up of East Timorese in training to take over when UNTAET left. On 30

August 2001 East Timorese went to the polls to elect an 88-member Con-
stituent Assembly to take office 22 March 2002; FRETILIN won resound-
ingly, and on 14 April Xanana Gusmão was elected president in East
Timor's first presidential election. On 20 May, East Timor was formally
granted independence. Large celebrations were held throughout the
country. In Dili, in front of an audience of international leaders, including Portugal's president Antonio Sampaio, Indonesia's president Mega-
wati Sukarnoputri, Australia's prime minister John Howard, and former
U.S. president Bill Clinton, the UN flag was finally lowered and the new
nation, Timor Leste, was declared. The UNTAET mission wound down
during 2002, with only a skeleton staff remaining. The economic bubble, which came with the international presence, has burst, and there is
still massive unemployment, a lack of basic infrastructure, and other development needs. There is, however, still a commitment by international
donors, the largest being Japan, Portugal, and Australia (in that order),
and it is hoped funds from the rich oil fields of the Timor Strait will
begin to flow soon, since in May 2005 Australia and East Timor signed an
agreement for joint development of the fields.

Sociocultural and Population Characteristics

Traditional Structures

Traditionally East Timor was made up of a series of kingdoms called *rai*,
their rulers known as *liurai*. These *rai* did not necessarily correspond to
East Timor's 31 languages. Each *rai* comprised several territorial divisions known as *suco*, which in turn comprised anywhere between three
and thirty *cnua*, or villages. Suco and cnua were ruled by chiefs. The liurai, chiefs of suco, and occasionally chiefs of cnua were known as *dato* or
dato fakun (important people). All dato received a tax called *rai-ten* in
exchange for granting gathering, planting, and hunting rights to their
land. Liurai were elected by other dato, based on an elected hereditary
system (Morlanes 1991; Thatcher 1991).

The next rung down on the traditional hierarchical ladder was occupied by *tumukum*, the ordinary chiefs of villages who attended to the daily
matters of their people. The next were *ema*, "the people" or "free men."
Finally, at the bottom, were slaves, who were either captives of war or "personal" slaves exchanged, bought, or acquired through the dowry system
barlaque (Morlanes 1991). It should be noted that personal slaves would
frequently be taken into the household and fed, educated, and treated as
one of the family. In fact, many refugees brought their slaves (although
they are never called this) with them to Australia as family members.
Frequently these people were orphans or children of very poor homes.

Colonial Structures

As was common practice among colonizers, the Portuguese made use of existing traditional cultural structures to control the colony. They used strategies such as enflaming ethnic rivalries and embracing the liurai class, giving them direct access to the governor. *Liurai* were encouraged to take on Portuguese culture as a marker of status, and the colonizers maintained structures whereby the liurai class would benefit from colonization.

Following the 1912 uprisings, however, the Portuguese introduced a system to undermine traditional kinship alliances, which had assisted the uprisings. The administration officially abolished "kingdoms," effectively undermining the power of liurai, and redivided the colony into administrative units based for the most part on the smaller *suco* subdivisions. Groups of *sucos* were administered as an administrative district called a *posto*. However, this had little effect; although the liurai kingdoms were formally abolished, *suco* heads always had to make sure "unofficially," that they were supported by the liurai in their actions. Thus, colonial and traditional systems coexisted.

With the advent of the Estado Novo of Antonio Salazar in Portugal, the "civilizing mission" in Portugal's colonies began to be formalized. The Portuguese administration broke the population into three racial categories and five subsequent categories describing Portuguese cultural and educational accomplishments. The racial categories were (1) Portuguese ("white"); (2) *mestiço* ("white"/indigenous mix or other racial mix); (3) indigene or native ("pure" native to the island) (Thatcher 1991; Morlanes 1991). The cultural and educational hierarchy was as follows:

1. Portuguese
2. Educated-acculturated *mestiço*
3. Educated-acculturated indigene
4. Noneducated, nonacculturated *mestiço*
5. Noneducated, nonacculturated indigene

Portuguese from Portugal were known as *metropolitano*, coming mainly from Lisbon. Both educated-acculturated mestiços and indigenes were identified as assimilado. These two groups were called *baino* (civilized indigene) by other noneducated, nonassimilated indigenes and mestiços. Noneducated and assimilated indigenes were known as *gentio* (meaning non-Christian or nonbaptized), *timor* (meaning son of Timor, ignorant), *O nativo dos pés descalços* (barefooted native), and *calade* (stupid or ignorant). By 1975, less than one-third of this group were Catholics, while most were animists (Morlanes 1991, 52–53). An individual had to achieve a series of educational and "cultural" requirements to attain assimilado status and Portuguese citizenship. A person had to speak Portuguese, earn sufficient income to maintain his family, and prove he was "of good character." For those in business and administration, these criteria were waived. Assimilados could also vote in elections, unlike the majority of the "unassimilated."

The liurai class generally had the advantage of Portuguese education. They often married Portuguese and were extremely wealthy and politically powerful. According to Thatcher, the assimilado class, those considered *civilizado*, were a small number of the population. In the 1950 Portuguese Timor Census, for example, 7,471 of 434,907 Timor-born people were counted as assimilados. Of these, 1,541 were indigenous Timorese, 48 Indian, 110 Arab, 568 white, 54 black, 3128 Chinese, and 2022 mestiço (Thatcher 1991, 32–37).

Education, Class, and Gender

Class in East Timor was very rigid, and therefore occupational structures were too. Portuguese occupied the top administrative positions, while the assimilated, educated mestiço were mostly employed in the middle and lower level positions in the civil service or worked as nurses; some owned coffee plantations. The Chinese dominated the commercial sector, and the indigenous population were primarily employed as laborers on coffee plantations or were fishermen or village-based subsistence farmers. In the cities, some found work as servants, cooks, cleaners, nannies, or gardeners (Morlanes 1991, 74–75). Women occupied (and in rural East Timor still do) a largely subordinate status. According to Ines de Almeida, a woman was expected to marry at the age of fifteen or sixteen in an arranged union, with a bride price of about three buffalo, a coral necklace, and $100 paid to her parents. She was expected to cut wood, wash clothes, work in the field, cook meals, and look after numerous babies. Often girls were not sent to school (ETRA 2000).

Population and Ethnic Groupings

East Timor is, contrary to popular perception, an ethnically diverse place. Henry Forbes, a British anthropologist and traveler writing in 1885, describes the scene of Dili thus:

The streets of Dili itself offer to the traveller a fine studio for ethnological investigation, for a curious mixture of nationalities other than European rub shoulders with each other. . . . Tall erect indigenes mingle with Negroes from the Portuguese possessions of Mozambique and the coasts of Africa, most of them here in the capacity of soldiers or condemned criminals; tall, lithe East Indians from Goa and its neighbourhood; Chinese and Bugis of Macassar with Arabs and

Malays and natives from Alior, Savu, Roti and Flores, besides a crowd in whose veins the degree of comminglement of blood of all these races would defy the acutest computation. (quoted in Thatcher 1991, 67)

This vignette illustrates well the very mixed nature of East Timor, and indeed, the somewhat misleading nature of the official categories outlined above. Here, Nicolau reflects on his memories of East Timor's cosmopolitan racial mix:

I remember, people used to say, the African ones, they put their life to the soccer. In Timor, any club you go, all people from Africa background. And then the Chinese are good in Kung Fu, Karate. In Timor, if we go any other house that is Chinese—there is always picture of Kung Fu—like Bruce Lee. And they tend to practice Kung Fu. If you go to the Indian they do what the Indians do. And there is also Timorese there too—mixed up. Yes. Lot of Timorese if they like Martial Arts—they hang around with the—in Timor—if you see a Timorese person hanging around with the Chinese—we say—this person—must like practice martial arts. We tend to see the African—Timorese-African—they will tend to like soccer. If you look at the Portuguese—then someone with them—you know that this person is intellectual. If a Timorese person hang around with a white person—that means that this person is an intellectual. Or he is one of an elite man. Oh yes. I'm old enough to remember this sort of stuff! (Nicolau, 33)

The approximate population of East Timor in 1975 is disputed, although generally estimated to be between 609,000 and 680,000. The population breakdown in Table 1, given by Luis Thomaz in 1974–75 (cited in Morlanes 1991, 48) is useful in that it shows ethnic groups other than Portuguese, mestiço and indigene. In addition, there was and still is a small Arab population in Dili, of approximately 340. This community reportedly descended from a group of traders from Yemen. For some reason they have been excluded from the above count. A second point is the small number counted in the mestiço category. It is widely understood to be a great underestimation. A large number of East Timorese at that time would have been from mixed backgrounds. Indeed, the majority of East Timorese could claim ancestry from more than one racial category.

TABLE 1. East Timor—number of people by ancestral category, 1974–75

Ancestry	Number	Percent of total population
European (Portuguese)	1463	0.24
Chinese	6120	1
mestiços (mix)	1939	0.32
Goanese	42	
Cap Verdians (Negroes)	22	
Timorese (indigenous)	599891	98.4
Total population	609477	

Most of the Chinese population resided in Dili and were engaged in the commercial sector. In fact it is estimated the Chinese community occupied 98 percent of East Timor's commercial sector, including virtually all importing and exporting. For the most part "middle class," having access to the benefits of schooling and the cultural prestige of honorary *assimilado*, the Chinese nevertheless had their own internal structures. A study by Rank (1977) shows that the community would refer to "rich" and "poor" Chinese. The wealthier class collaborated easily with the Portuguese, while cooks, waiters, bus drivers, and laborers were treated as poorly as the poorer urban East Timorese (Taylor 1999). In 1976–77, Dili's 6,000-strong Chinese population represented approximately 50.5 percent of the total active working, waged, and salaried population of the district (Morlanes 1991, 70). According to Taylor (1999, 16), because the Chinese were at the end of the trading chain, directly linked with consumers, they were often stereotyped by East Timorese as being wealthy opportunists out to exploit them, an image that bore little resemblance to the reality of many poorer Chinese in the villages. For these reasons many Chinese were prime targets of the Indonesians when they invaded, which is why such a large number of Timorese Chinese fled. In the following chapter I take up their story, as well as that of East Timorese who fled the civil war to Australia in 1975, and later those who fled the Indonesian occupiers, before moving on to introduce some of the important patterns and characteristics that exist in the East Timorese community in Sydney.

Chapter 2
Leaving the Crocodile: The East Timorese Community in Sydney

When Crocodile changed
To a piece of earth
From there I started to exist
From there I started to breathe
From there I started to move
      —Maria Immaculada dos Reis-Piedade (2001)

From 1975 to 1999, many East Timorese refugees came to Australia because of its proximity and the existence of a large East Timorese community who were able to offer a much needed support network. The first
East Timorese to arrive in Australia were fleeing the civil war between
UDT and FRETILIN. The invasion of East Timor by Indonesia on 7
December 1975 forced many more East Timorese to flee their homeland,
and they continued to come for the next twenty-four years. East Timorese refugees came to Australia in several waves, beginning with those who
fled the civil war and ending with the students and others who escaped
in the mid- to late 1990s. The process of flight was painful and traumatic
for all who had to leave East Timor, regardless of when, how, or from
whom they were fleeing.

The first East Timorese refugees arrived in Australia in Darwin on 15
August 1975 on board the Dutch vessel the M.V. *Macdili*. The *Macdili*, a
small cargo ship, left Dili on 12 August with 272 people on board, 249
of them Portuguese working for the administration and members of the
Portuguese army. The second group arrived on the Norwegian vessel the
S.S. *Lloyd Bakke*, which happened to be off the coast of East Timor when
it heard an SOS from the Portuguese governor. The ship collected 1,150
individuals and brought them to Darwin. The *Macdili* made a second trip
to Dili. Due to intensified fighting, it was forced to anchor offshore. On

the night of 27 August, around 700 people, including members of the Chinese community sheltering on the beach, amid bombing, boarded cattle barges that took them to the ship (see Figure 3).

There was a misunderstanding between the two parties—UDT and FRETILIN. They called it civil war, but now I think it is a misunderstanding, because we were not prepared to govern a country. The boat made two trips. I came with the second boat. The boat was called the *Macdili*. The second boat that I was on came on the 28th of August and arrived in Darwin on the 29th. It was a cargo boat that had been hired by Chinese businessmen, which used to come to East Timor every month to import and export goods. So, this boat was there when the civil war broke out in East Timor. So people went to the boat to come to Australia. They wanted to take the Chinese people first, but we were at the harbor and then we escaped at the same time with the governor when he went with his team. They went to Atauro, the island off Timor. And then that night we escaped with them—on small boats, cattle barges, to the bigger cargo boat, then we came to Australia. We left everything behind of course. I came with my mum, one brother, and two sisters, and plus others that my mum was looking after, adopted brother, and adopted sisters, we all came together. So we arrived in Australia in Darwin on the 29th of August 1975. We came with a group of about 500 people, mainly children, and their mothers, they had to leave their husbands behind. We never thought we'd stay here for good. We were just waiting for the situation to stabilize so that we could go back. (Nancy, early 50s)

Figure 3. A typical middle-class East Timorese family in Timor around 1970. Courtesy Brigida de Andrade.

In total, 2,581 refugees arrived on the three ships. All were escaping the violence of the civil war between FRETILIN and UDT forces. Among these arrivals were many Portuguese who worked in the colonial administration and a number of soldiers from the Portuguese army. Their exodus from East Timor marked the end of more than 400 years of Portuguese presence on the tiny island. Of the 1,647 Timor-born arrivals on the ships, 672 were Timorese-Chinese; the remainder were mestiço and indigenous Timorese. In addition, a few escaped by air on four planes that carried refugees from Baucau (where the main airport was located) to Darwin (Taylor 1999; Rawsthorne 1994; Thatcher 1991; Morlanes 1991; ETRA 2000). Most who came on these boats have strong memories of the terrifying days leading up to the sea journey to Australia. Carlos, a Timorese-Chinese man, recalls his flight from East Timor as one of the most frightening times of his life:

Oh, it was very bad. I remember the night in 1975 during the civil war, when I had to run with different people to hide. We were hungry for one week, no food, no clothes no nothing. We had only whatever we wore on our body. I left my home. I lost a lot of things, I lost my house, my money, my clothes. First, I ran from my house to a friend's house and we ran to hide in a deep ditch. We had to hide there and next morning we had to run from there to a Church. I didn't know where my sisters and brothers and other family were, but we stayed in the Church that night. Next morning my sister came looking for me. She brought me from the Church to the harbor where we could get on the boat.

We stayed for 3 days on the beach and there was no food, and we saw gunfights and you don't know where you are going, whether you're dead or you're alive. At one stage, there was heavy gun fighting Timorese people were getting killed. So the Portuguese army called us and we had to run. I ran with my niece and my sister. I held my 10-year-old sister in one hand and my niece, who was 5 years old, in the other. Under gunfire, we ran to the barge. I didn't know where my brother-in-law or my other sisters were. We stayed there in the barge until it was full, then they took us to the *Macdili* ship. Fortunately, I found my sisters, and my brother in law, and we went together. On the boat, everybody was seasick. My sister nearly died because she was vomiting so much. But we were lucky because it was only one day and one night.

When we left Dili and we didn't know where we going, but then we woke up in the morning and we are in Darwin. We only knew when someone said "this is Australia here." Everybody woke up from getting seasick, we go off the ship, and they took us to the Army place. We were so hungry. They give us everything like clothes, toothpaste, whatever you need, everything like this for us. And after that, they said, "Now you go and have lunch." I was so hungry. Me and one of my cousins, we nearly ate a whole loaf of bread because there was nothing to eat before I left my country. Probably three days we didn't eat anything. Even in the boat because there was not enough food because there were too many people. They give us only small probably two spoons of rice but it's not enough, we have to feed the kids. (Carlos, mid-50s)

Facing defeat in East Timor, the UDT forces withdrew into West Timor, followed by many civilians. Over the next three months, an estimated

20,000 Timorese were forced, or fled, across the border mostly to the West Timor border region of Atambua (Dunn 1996, 160–61). Many subsequently returned to East Timor, but a large number went from West Timor to Portugal in August-September 1976. This is Julieta's account of her escape to West Timor, when she was just five years old.

the UDT compound in Dili . . . was teeming with UDT families who had fled their homes in fear of their safety. From the compound, we could hear the endless sounds of gunfire throughout the nights. I also remember the night when we had to move from the compound. Under heavy artillery fire, we were told to lie flat on the ground. I was thoroughly disgusted at having to lie on top of stinking urine. I asked my mother what the whizzing sound over our heads was, her reply was, "bullets."
 Then came the long walk to Atambua. I remember the thirst . . . the never-ending thirst. I also remember my eldest sister Madalena explaining to me why I had to eat that horrible fruit that we had been eating day after day. She said that if I didn't eat, I wouldn't have any strength to walk and everyone was already too weak to carry me if that happened. In Atabae, there was a heavy gun battle between the UDT and FRETILIN forces. We were told to lie down. My little brother Jaime (three years old at the time) refused. He wanted to watch the "spectacle"! He was grabbed by the shoulder and forced to lie down by my brother Antonio (thirteen at the time). At one stage, my sister Francisca, my brother Jaime, and I were separated from the rest of the group. We were lost for two days! We were hungry and thirsty . . . I remember my sister in her sky blue dress . . . I remember her collecting dew from leaves into her hands so that my brother and I could have a drink, as we couldn't find any clean water. I also remember our excitement when we heard voices behind the mangroves and they ended up being those of my uncle and his family. . . . we then set out to Atambua where we lived until we left for Portugal in 1976, leaving behind my sister Tina and my brother Anito. Tina had fallen in love with a local man and Anito had been lost in the chaos in Dili. We were not to hear from them until 1980. Tina was married, living in Dili and had two children; Anito had died from malnutrition in the mountains of East Timor in 1978. (Julieta, 27, in Wise 2001, 16)

From 1978, following increasing violence by the Indonesian invaders, large numbers began to leave East Timor. Between 1976 and 1981, a further 2,447 Timorese arrived in Australia, of whom 1,940 were Timorese-Chinese. Six hundred of these arrivals came out under a specially implemented family reunion scheme. A second family reunion program was created following intense lobbying by Timorese and their supporters to bring family out from Portugal. Between 1981 and 1986, 1,404 Timorese were able to move to Australia under this program, known as the Special Humanitarian Program (SHP). During this period, a further 3168 Timorese-Chinese came, mostly from East Timor. The SHP was unique in that it interpreted "family" widely, accepting Timorese understandings of close kin, which includes extended family and informally adopted children. In total, since 1975 there have been four intakes of East Timorese refugees, all under the auspices of special humanitarian programs. The

TABLE 2. Estimates of arrivals from East Timor by year, method, and ethnicity

Year	Method	Timorese/ mestiço	Timorese and Chinese	Ethnicity unknown	Totals
August 1975	SS *Lloyd Bakke* MV *MacDili* RAAF	975	672		1647
1976–1981	Air	507	1940		2447
1981–1986	SHP Program	1404	3168		4572
1986–1990 coming to NSW				1000 (estimate)	1000
1990–1991 coming to NSW	Humanitarian & Special Assistance Program			130	130
1994–1999				1600 (estimate)	1600
Total for group		2886	5780	2730	11396

most recent of these programs, the East Timorese in Portugal, Macao, or Mozambique subclass 208 Special Assistance Category, was specifically designed to reunite families separated in the diaspora. Nancy, a Timorese community worker, recounts her memories of this time:

The family reunion program was good, but for some who weren't approved, many of them were forced to get married to Timorese in Australia.[1] But a lot of these marriages didn't work out in Australia and many of them had to get divorced. It was very hard for them living with the family of your husband in Australia, who are strangers . . . they don't understand you. They can be nice, but they don't understand you. And also for a lot, when they come to Australia it is a shock, and then they don't understand what is going on. So there were a lot of split families like this. The culture shock was very deep. (Nancy, mid-50s)

There was a slowing in the numbers arriving following the cessation of this SHP program. Between 150 and 300 East Timorese people arrived in New South Wales each year between 1986 and 1990. In 1990–91, 282 arrived from Portugal under a Humanitarian and Special Assistance Program. Following the Dili Massacre, a further 130 people arrived after escaping from East Timor. (These figures are from Morlanes 1991, 16–23; Thatcher 1991; see Table 2).[2]

The 1,600 Asylum Seekers and the Sanctuary Network

Between 1994 and 1996, a further 1,600 East Timorese fled to Australia because of fears of persecution, lodging applications with the Australian government for asylum. But by now, the tide had turned in Australian foreign policy and the government line toward East Timorese asylum seekers. Until then, the government had had a fairly sympathetic stance toward East Timorese and the human rights situation in East Timor. The turning point came in 1989, when Australia signed the Timor Gap Treaty with Indonesia, which defined the rights to the oil-rich seabed resources in that area of the Timor Sea that had remained undefined during the years of Portugal's colonial administration of East Timor. In order to begin negotiations, Australia in 1985 extended de jure (legal) recognition to Indonesian sovereignty in East Timor, becoming one of only two nations (with the U.S.) to do so.[3]

With all this high level political maneuvering aimed at positioning to take advantage of these rich oil reserves, Australia began to refuse asylum to East Timorese refugees so as not to cause offense to Indonesia. There was a sense in Canberra that it was time to "put the East Timor issue to bed." When 1,200 refugees arrived in September 1994, Australian immigration authorities took the cynical position that, because the East Timorese held Portuguese citizenship and were not facing persecution in Portugal, they were therefore not entitled to claim the protection of Australia. This was a bizarre and contradictory position, given that Australia had argued forcefully in the International Court of Justice against any claim by Portugal to speak for the East Timorese when the Portuguese challenged the legality of the Timor Gap Treaty; moreover, Australia had recognized since 1985 that the East Timorese were citizens of Indonesia (see Button 1997; Lague 1995).

In 1996, one East Timorese asylum seeker appealed the Refugee Review Tribunal's adverse finding on his claim for asylum. As a consequence of the Federal Court judgment in his favor, in three other East Timorese cases the tribunal deemed that Portuguese nationality was inapplicable and ruled in favor of the East Timorese concerned. However, the Australian government appealed these decisions in July 1997. After deliberately dragging out the appeal process until the end of 1999, the government decided to drop its appeal in the Federal Court against the asylum seekers, opting to return to the normal refugee determination process. By this time, however, the referendum in East Timor had taken place, and this group no longer had any claim to asylum. The legal process dragged on for almost seven years, during which time the East Timorese seeking protection in Australia lived in limbo and faced harsh financial difficulty with no government financial support.

There was a groundswell of public support for the cause of these East Timorese in Australia. A group of Catholic sisters founded the Sanctuary Network in 1995 to protect the rights of the Timorese seeking protection, promising to provide accommodations, food, and clothing to any of the 1,600 East Timorese if they were refused refugee status and threatened with deportation. This act of civil disobedience put those offering sanctuary at risk of six months in jail. By 1998, there were more than 10,000 Australians, Catholic and otherwise, who had contacted the organization to offer to be part of the network by providing a safe house, clothing, and accommodations for the asylum seekers when in need (O'Connor 1999). As it happened, the deportation order did not come through, and the support dissipated. However, in early 2002, these asylum seekers received letters from the Department of Immigration that processing of their applications would recommence now that East Timor had official independence. They were advised that unless they could demonstrate that they would suffer persecution in an independent East Timor, they would have no grounds on which to stand. Once they received official notification that their cases had been rejected, they would have just 28 days to leave Australia.

This was a most unhappy turn of affairs for this group, the majority of whom desperately wished to remain in Australia. Many had been there since 1994, living in limbo, aware that the government could commence proceedings to have them removed at any time. In the years since their arrival, many had gotten jobs, established relationships, and had few ties in East Timor. A number were partway through a higher education program, which they would be forced to discontinue if the government ordered them to leave. Among the group were elderly women whose husbands had been killed in East Timor and who would have no means of supporting themselves on their return. Unlike those East Timorese with permanent residency status, many of whom express a desire to return to East Timor at some point, the extremely insecure status of this group means that they overwhelmingly wish to stay in Australia.

Characteristics of the Community

The first release of the 2001 Australian Census data indicated 9,392 individuals born in Timor residing in Australia, 2,408 of them in New South Wales. There are an estimated 20,000 individuals of Timorese descent living in Australia, approximately 6,000 to 8,000 of these in Sydney.[4] Given that many Timorese were at or near child-bearing age when they came, the estimates of close to 20,000 Timorese can be assumed to be reasonably correct. The most startling statistic to come out of the 2001 census, though, is that, based on "language spoken at home" statistics, more than two-thirds of Timorese in Australia are actually of Timorese-Chinese background (see Tables 3 and 4). However, these figures are by no means clear, as they go by country of birth and language spoken at home. They do not account for descendants born in Australia, nor for East Timorese

TABLE 3. Australian Immigration Statistics, 2001 Census—birthplace,
    East Timor

2001 census: birthplace	NSW	Australia
	2408	9392

TABLE 4. Australian Immigration Statistics, 2001 Census—breakdown of
    residents speaking Hakka (language of Timorese Chinese) and
    Tetum (main indigenous Timorese lingua franca)

2001 census: language	NSW	Australia
Tetum	579	1488
Hakka	1387	7460
Total	1966	8948

who speak English or Portuguese at home. The breakdown may be closer
to 50 percent Timorese-Chinese. The other important fact to emerge is
that as of 2001, it looks as though fewer than 900 Timorese have returned
to East Timor. This may change as Timor becomes more stable; however
the figure is much lower than many commentators expected.

Of those Timorese residing in Australia, many are Australian-born children of East Timorese parents, many of whom have now reached young
adulthood. The first refugees to come to Sydney were the Darwin group
who arrived on the three boats in 1975. Once in Darwin, they were asked
to choose Sydney, Melbourne, Brisbane, or Perth. Nancy de Almeida, from
the East Timor Cultural Centre, was among the group who chose Sydney.[5]

I didn't know anything about Sydney. It was quite funny. I chose Sydney because
before the war, I came to Darwin for a short training course with Qantas. And I
had seen pictures of the harbour. So I chose Sydney because I had always wanted
to see the harbor. (Nancy, mid-50s)

Those who made the decision to come to Sydney were initially sent
to live in two migrant hostels, one in Coogee (in Sydney's east) and the
other in Cabramatta (in Sydney's west). Residents were moved to the
Villawood hostel after the Cabramatta hostel closed. Unlike today, when
Australia has a policy of compulsory detention of "unlawful arrivals,"[6]
newly arrived refugees during the 1970s were housed in hostels where
they were free to come and go. Most Timorese I have spoken with appreciated their time in these hostels, where they were able to learn English,
were given assistance with finding employment and post-hostel housing,
and had access to social workers. Residents report having felt a sense of
community in these hostels during the first difficult months of living in
Australia, and felt that hostel living made their transition to Australia
smoother than would otherwise have been the case.

The location of the two hostels influenced where most Timorese eventually settled in Sydney. Now, about one quarter of Sydney's East Timorese live in the eastern suburbs near the former Coogee hostel, and about half live in the Liverpool/Fairfield area, near where the Villawood and Cabramatta hostels once were. The remainder live in other parts of Sydney, especially around the Penrith, Mt. Druitt, and Blacktown areas in the west. As with many migrant and refugee communities, for many East Timorese it has been important to live in an area where there are other Timorese and to have the company of others who share their history and speak the same language.

There are differences in the makeup of the community. First, there are the differences between those who arrived during the 1970s and 1980s and those who came during the 1990s. The first groups to arrive were primarily educated town dwellers who were socialized under Portuguese rule. The 1980s arrivals often had lived in Portugal for some years before coming to Australia. The 1990s arrivals were often younger and had spent the best part of twenty years under Indonesian rule, the younger ones, of course, having completed their schooling under the Indonesian system. I have concentrated for the most part on the 1970s and 1980s arrivals, because they form the lion's share of the community.

The other very significant cleavage is between the Timorese-Chinese and the Timorese members of the community, made up of mestiço and indigenous Timorese. Those who identify as Timorese-Chinese have formed a relatively coherent community among themselves. They have their own community organization and community events and have little to do with the non-Chinese sections of the community. They rarely took part in political activities, although they have been very involved in charity causes for East Timor, and it is in this context that the most contact with non-Chinese Timorese has happened. The Timorese-Chinese (at least those who identify as such) are generally Buddhist, although anecdotally one in five are Christian. The majority speak Hakka as their first language, while a few speak Tetum as well. They are culturally Chinese yet there are also clear Portuguese and Timorese influences. I explore these differences more fully in Chapter 5.

It is estimated that up to 90 percent of the Chinese population have left East Timor since the Indonesian occupation;[7] most of them now live in Australia. Forming at least half of the community, they are significant in number. The comparatively higher numbers of Chinese fleeing East Timor compared to mestiço and indigenous Timorese can partly be explained by their relative wealth. From the late 1970s until the mid-1990s, East Timor was a closed territory: no one could enter or leave without permission. In Indonesia, of course, this proved fertile ground for corrupt officials to exploit those desperate enough to want to leave, and hefty bribes were demanded in return for exit visas. The Timorese-Chinese were far more likely than other East Timorese to be in a position to raise the money for these bribes, if not from their own funds, then through contributions from family members abroad. Thatcher relates one case that demonstrates the difficulty of the escape process, even if the way is smoothed with finances:

A Chinese businessman . . . claims he paid [AUS] $10,000 to Indonesian government officials for an exit visa for each of his five children. He was subsequently told these visas were not valid and a further $10,000 was demanded to be paid. In spite of these bribes these quite young children still had to leave illegally, travel alone via Kupang to Jakarta and subsequently make their way to Lisbon. Such were the conditions in Timor in 1979, this was judged to be a reasonable proposition. The businessman and his wife (by dint of further huge bribes, this time to a highly placed Timorese Government official, some of which he continues to repay today) were taken by military helicopter to Kupang and their further journey to Jakarta was made by using the personal permit of a high government official. In Jakarta, they obtained Portuguese travel documents through the Dutch Embassy and then travelled directly to Australia. (Thatcher 1991, 20–21)

Nancy de Almeida points out that a great many East Timorese families were in debt because of these bribes, having been forced to repay them once they arrived in Australia, for fear of reprisals against family remaining in East Timor. Many also had to raise money to send to those still in Timor wishing to escape. This placed a great deal of emotional and financial stress on families, often meaning they had to work long hours in poorly paid jobs, which precluded luxuries such as attending English classes or being involved in more hands-on parenting.

There are a number of community organizations set up to help members of the community in need. The Timorese-Chinese Association is the most highly structured of all East Timorese community organizations. It is self-funded and has its own community center in St. John's Park, a neighboring suburb of Liverpool in Sydney's west. It is well equipped with cooking facilities, dance floor, tables, stage, and dining and bar area. There are two other organizations serving other parts of the Timorese community. The Timorese Australian Council, the official body representing the community, receives government funds for community settlement services. This organization is staffed by a manager and a community worker; its primary role is to be the main representative body for the community and to provide services such as counseling referrals, housing advice, help with social security access, and so on. There are a few smaller groups for seniors and a soccer team for youth.

The other organization of note is the East Timor Cultural Centre, run by Nancy de Almeida and her brother Aires. They began in the mid-1980s to promote Timorese culture. In the past, they organized a Timorese choir and taught traditional Timorese dance. They had a small hall on the grounds of a Catholic primary school in Fairfield, where a group of older women, and sometimes their husbands, met most days to take part in a variety of activities such as English language classes, Tetum classes, craft groups, and a regular Wednesday lunch. A few Timorese youth attended after school homework assistance classes conducted at the center by a visiting Catholic sister. The Centre had a good relationship with the Mary MacKillop Institute of East Timorese Studies, an organization of mostly Josephite sisters who work closely with the East Timorese community, providing counseling, social work, and charitable assistance in the area of health and education.

The other main organizations were political in nature. A significant split in the community exists, particularly among the 1970s and 1980s arrivals (especially those who fled the civil war), between those who were supported UDT and FRETILIN. Because of this, certain divisions exist in the community, where events held by one group would not be attended by members of the other. Similarly, as is common with many communities, there are rivalries between the different community organizations, sometimes surrounding perceived political affiliations, sometimes surrounding competition over resources, or simply because of personality clashes. In terms of political groups, there were moves starting in the early 1990s to bring the two sides together for the independence cause under the auspices of the CNRT, which has had some success in patching up the differences, especially amongst the younger members of the community.

Settlement Issues

There are many important settlement issues within the community. Many of the service providers, including East Timorese and non-Timorese social workers, say that the East Timorese community is one of the most traumatized they have come across, and that its members have had significant settlement difficulties with respect to housing, employment, raising children, and learning English, as well as significant physical and mental health problems. In 1994, an estimated 30 percent of the community had poor English skills. The unemployment rate was 23.3 percent, more than twice the Australian national average, and they had low rates of home ownership, 14.6 percent compared with a national rate of 38.9 percent (Rawsthorne 1994).

In terms of housing, many larger families found they had to live in small, overcrowded apartments, often surviving on only one income or on social security benefits. A number of families are supporting family members from the post-1994 "1600 Group," who because of their temporary status receive no social security benefits from the government if they are unemployed. However, a significant number of middle-class families have gained successful employment and have bought their own homes, mostly in Sydney's west.[8] Here, Julieta describes the feeling of confinement at her early housing conditions:

> I remember one of the hardest things to adapt to was living in flats, you feel so confined. Whereas in Portugal—you had your freedom sort of—you could get out easily. And it was more social. Here, in the beginning, we were confined to this little flat on the first floor, and you know, living with nine people in the house. (Julieta, 27)

Ironically, Australia's space and the quiet of suburbia compound this feeling of confinement for some. Julieta describes her first year here:

> Apart from the higher standards of living, I hated everything about Australia in our first year here. We hated the exposed bricks on buildings—in Portugal buildings were cement rendered and painted; we hated the fact that residential streets were so empty of people, that there were no outdoor seating cafes, we hated the flies and the sticky hot weather, but worst of all we hated having to repeat words countless times before the railway ticket seller could understand us. . . . My father on the other hand loved Australia from day one. For the first time in years, he didn't have to worry about where our next meal was coming from.

As Julieta's narrative suggests, Portugal for many Timorese forms a third point of reference to East Timor and Australia and is often invoked in the comparison with "life before." For some, Portugal represents a place of utter poverty and hardship, and Australia compares as somewhere where individuals can get ahead, educate their kids, and have a good standard of living. For others, like Julieta, Australia represents a place of cultural barrenness, unlike the richness of urban Lisbon.

The differences between East Timorese and Australian society have changed the ways families and community members interrelate, something many Timorese experience as a great loss. As Nancy explains, subtle differences can have a major impact on a range of aspects of family and community life:

> In East Timor, whatever we had, we shared. Nobody wanted to see one who was suffering. You would share with close friends, relatives, and children. Then when Timorese came here it was a shock because we don't share anymore. Because now we tend to be more in individual families, just looking after your own. In East Timor, not all, but many large families tried to be together, this is different in Australia. Here, you can't provide for everyone all the time. You work hard here. You work hard, to buy a house, and it is very expensive and you just can't help everybody. Also, because everyone gets social security benefits here, whereas in East Timor you have to depend totally on your relatives. Many family members, once you are married, never contact each other except at Christmas and Easter. Also, because the parents work, the grandmothers end up looking after

the kids at home, so many grandparents end up totally isolated and they don't speak English. They don't think they should learn, so they lose everything, all their independence. In East Timor, you have to say yes to your elders, or they say things against you. But now, the younger ones are more in charge. So there are many changes in family structure.

Age, isolation and financial hardship, and the new changes in the community since the referendum have been particularly difficult for some. One elderly lady in the community explains how these have affected her:

The Timorese community here live far away from each other. Everyone has their own life to live. I am very lonely sometimes. Everyday I just do my housework and sometimes I go out shopping. Staying at home all the time sometimes makes me feel too sad. Everyone is so busy. We only meet now when there is an occasion, like a funeral or a party. Some people like to go out to parties and others are not so interested. We tend to meet more people at funerals. Some people don't like to go out very much, perhaps they don't have a car and travel by train is expensive. People would rather stay home and save, perhaps buy a house, or to make a trip to Timor, or help their families back home. (Louisa, late 70s)

For this woman, the sheer spread of Sydney's suburbia, combined with some of the factors mentioned in Nancy's statement above, translate to a feeling of immense isolation. Moreover, there is a definite feeling of a decrease in community contact since the referendum. Many say they miss the feeling of community they had when there were political meetings, protests, and so on.

There are also significant shifts in class and status. Many experienced a significant change in status from their lives in East Timor, compared to Australia and sometimes Portugal. Some found it quite shocking to go from East Timor's elite to the bottom rung in Portugal.

In Portugal, we had to live in a pensão—a special building where most of the Timorese lived, and you can tell that it is the big poor side of the city. In Portugal, it doesn't matter if you work two jobs, it was so hard to get ahead. For the older people, maybe they don't find it so hard. Mostly they had good government jobs prior to the Indonesian invasion. When they went to Portugal, they have money, they buy a house, or they are a bit more set up. For the younger population it's harder like you don't get study allowance like you do in Australia. If you study, you have to work. And it's sort of like—it's so disadvantaged like everybody just give up study so they can work. (Lihana, 30)

Many more elite East Timorese who came during the 1970s found it quite difficult to adjust to the fact that in Australia they had a standard of living similar to their former servants and underlings. Often those who formerly held good jobs in Timor found themselves working in servile positions, in restaurant kitchens, as cleaners and so forth, a fact that gives much amusement to their former subordinates, many of whom are now able to read and write, hold down a job, and own a home—all of which gives them a feeling of equality with their former superiors. Many have said to me that because everyone can have a job, go to school, and afford a new home, and because there is democracy in Australia, they know now that everyone is equal, and that they don't have to put up with those East Timorese who look down on them and treat them as servants. Conversely, many who were successful in East Timor were unable to reestablish themselves in Australia because of the language barrier and age. Ana, a Timorese-Chinese woman, speaks of the difficulties her own family faced:

We were very wealthy. Dad was a very successful businessman in East Timor, but when we got to Australia, he had to go and work as a process worker or something. He worked in this job, which was very different to before, and they were living in Coogee, he had to come all the way to Meadowbank for work. Every morning he had to leave at about 4 a.m. in the morning, and return after 7 p.m. every night. But he had no choice, because he had to feed the family. My dad never managed to get back to the career level from before we came. They did quite well in picking up the language. I mean—they are not fluent—but they are able to have the day to day. But—no my parents never got back into their original business. Because first of all age, and also capital they had lost everything. I mean here to set up a business is not easy. For them it is a great loss. I mean my parents they worked so hard for what they had in Timor, and it was just lost overnight. And I mean, they lost everything. (Ana, mid-30s)

Missing the Familiar Things

Life in a new culture has many challenges. It is a big shock for many new arrivals to go from a slower-paced, mostly rural place such as East Timor to the fast pace and complex lifestyle of Australian society. Simple things such as dealing with government departments, finding work, negotiating city life—all these are stressful new experiences. Beyond sociological settlement indicators, there is an important experiential realm. So for every statistic on unemployment and English-language competence, there are a myriad subtle experiential ramifications. Perhaps one of the more significant is the feeling of loss that displacement engenders, manifesting itself in what we might call "sensual dislocation" surrounding food, rituals, and special occasions. Nancy describes here her first Christmas away from East Timor, which she spent in the migrant hostel in 1975:

When I came to the Cabramatta Hostel, there were some migrants living there already, but the majority were Timorese, so it was like a small family. The manager, it turned out, had been in East Timor in the Second World War, so he was very sympathetic to our case. He always asked how we were, and provided us with the food that we really wanted. He invited the Salvation Army for our first Christmas in Australia. I remember the first Christmas we spent far away from East Timor. With the music, everyone cried, because they didn't know what was happening in East Timor. There was no news at all. And they cried so much. We went home without having our Christmas that we have in East Timor. That was the saddest Christmas we ever had. (Nancy, mid-50s)

Many East Timorese would share Nancy's feelings about her first Christmas away from home. The first years of life away from East Timor were very, very difficult. It is often missing the familiar things that causes the most sadness—missing familiar food, familiar ways of celebrating events like birthdays, religious festivals, and funerals, for example. Nancy related how the kindness of one of the managers at the Cabramatta hostel made a big difference in the early days. Because individual cooking in the hostel was banned, the Timorese residents would cook some familiar food in secret on the face of an upturned iron, and the manager at the hostel used to turn a blind eye when he smelled their food cooking, knowing how important it was to them. These memories of little kindnesses remain special to former hostel residents even twenty-five years later.

When we arrived in Australia, everyone was very good to us. I remember I went to a shop with my sister and niece. They called me over and gave very nice and expensive jackets to my niece and my sister, and me. Probably cost them $200, unbelievable! And everyone we met would look and say, "You're from Timor?" And they'd give us money. And they really welcome us to Australia. We'd go to shopping and some ladies will say "You're from Timor?" And they would buy whatever they want to give us, bread, lollies, all these things. Freely . . . Give us the money and we were very happy. It made it easy for us to settle here because we know the people love us. They help us to stay here. I was only here for a few days, then I got a job in a factory. I was working with 50 Australian people men and women, every day they teach me English: "This is apple, this is bread . . . eyes, nose." They bring food to me. The ladies bring like a sandwich, every afternoon I go home with a bag full, because they knew I had to look after and feed my little sisters on my own. Each day, a different lady give it to me. I was very very happy. (Carlos, mid-50s)

The East Timorese arrived in Australia just before the big flows of Vietnamese refugees. At that time, Australians for the most part were welcoming and sympathetic toward refugees. By the 1980s and 1990s, national sentiment had shifted. Nonetheless, most East Timorese report quite positive experiences of their time in Australia, perhaps because they, unlike other communities, have usually been represented very sympathetically in the media.

Life in a New Language

I remember when I first came here, I didn't understand any English, and it was so hard. Funny little things would be frightening. I remember seeing a loaf of bread, and it was wrapped, so you can't see what is inside, whether it is white or brown. So I wouldn't buy bread—because I was afraid I would get the wrong one! Yes . . . not knowing the language it was so hard, so hard. (Ana, mid-30s)

For the newly arrived refugee, there are many, many issues to deal with. Learning a new language is the first challenge. Although relatively easy for younger people, it is often difficult for the older members of the community to learn a new language late in life. For those with difficulties learning English, life can be isolating, and many experience this as a loss of independence, relying on children to translate when needed. Older women who in East Timor were strong and independent often find themselves isolated and alone, unable to cope with many of the tasks that others take for granted.

For some of the older women, not having English, they are completely lost. They rely on their children when they get sick, or need help to communicate. But they feel very sad, because when they were in East Timor, they could manage on their own. (Nancy, mid-50s)

Financial demands of looking after extended family meant many had to go straight into jobs and were unable to spend time learning English properly in classes. As Nancy explains:

The husband and wife would both have to work to earn enough money. So those who came here, I think many of them didn't go to learn English they had to go to work. Because back home, there was a demand from the Indonesian government to pay bribes. And if the people back in East Timor didn't ask friends and relatives to send money, they would be killed, tortured, all sorts of things, threatened with death and things like that. So those who came here had to work very hard and send money, and so didn't have a chance to learn English.

With little English, it is very difficult to handle the complexities of immigration, filling in forms, understanding letters, dealing with social security, and so on. This can create an enormous feeling of frustration and sense of powerlessness, which is particularly extreme for older male members of the community, used to being in control of their own affairs. One young woman I interviewed describes her father's experiences:

My dad is just depressed more and more. He just wants to go back to Timor. I mean when I say that my dad wants to go back to East Timor and stay there, it's like, gosh, it's such a like intense feeling. You know, in a way like, I can understand because he, he just hates, he doesn't like this place. He can't speak the language, he hates the fact that Centrelink is always chasing him, the fact that he's not well, and Centrelink wants him to work.[9] I think it's the fact that he's less in control of managing his finances, the fact that he feels that the government is actually controlling him—more than him controlling his life. That's how he sees his life. I think also, like some other men I know, they stay at home while their wives go to work. Because of this, these women can adapt more to the new environment than men can. So, you know that sort of sense of masculinity sort of changes. It is very hard for a lot of men like my dad. (Fatima, 22)

Language difficulties can have profound effects on a person's life. It is difficult to get access to good health care when translators are scarce. In a small community, individuals are often hesitant to use translators because they fear that the translator will divulge information about their case to other members of the community. Often health care workers have had to rely on untrained translators who may not understand something that is being said, such as some specific medical terminology or legal facts, and simply gloss over it. In one particularly tragic case, a Timorese community worker told of the case of a woman who unknowingly adopted out her child in the 1970s when she became a single mother:

There was a woman, she was very sad, and become quite mentally unstable because she had a baby here in Australia. I wasn't interpreting, somebody else was interpreting, and they asked her to sign papers without her knowing what they were. She signed and the papers were Youth and Community Services adoption papers. Once you sign these papers and hand them over, you can't go back on them. I was trying to get them back, I tried hard but I couldn't. So this poor woman, she always had a photo of the baby and she showed it to everyone and she said—this is my daughter. It was really very painful and I couldn't help her. (Rosalina, mid-50s)

Issues Facing Young People

For younger Timorese, a new language can have different consequences. While it is easier for younger people to learn a new language, school can still be difficult. When young people find they are having language-based problems at school, it is often hard for parents to help when they themselves do not speak English or understand the Australian curriculum. It is difficult to seek help for their child, as they are not aware of how best to help or whom to approach. This is compounded by the fact that some parents had little schooling themselves in East Timor, so it is hard to understand the complex demands of Australian schooling, especially once children reach high school. On parenting, Nancy points out that

There is a language barrier between the parents and children. Many parents have only very basic education, and many are not literate. Because of this, the parents cannot help with homework. Maths and Science are international. But parents are unable to help due to language and literacy problems. There are also cultural differences in terms of expectations, assumptions and values. This varies between families, social classes, Portuguese, Indonesian, to Australian society—right? There are communication difficulties between parents and children, which is often very frustrating, especially with those parents who arrived with very young children. The fact that children speak English better than the parents is a big issue, it creates a gap between the parents and children and parents feel that they are losing social control over their children. It is very difficult.

As Nancy attests, growing up in Australia has meant that young East Timorese are fluent and very comfortable in English, using it to communicate with friends outside the family. But this can mean for some, a feeling of living "two lives," or being "two people" at once: the modern, English-speaking person in the outside world making the huge transition to the Tetum- or Hakka-speaking world at home. For many young people, this is very difficult. They feel that they are living in two worlds, split apart, and that their parents don't understand their lives. Sometimes there is a conflict between culturally traditional parenting and the more independent lifestyle of modern Australian teenagers. Again, this can lead to a feeling of estrangement between parents and Timorese teenagers.

Living with the Past

East Timorese people living in Australia do not experience the history of East Timor as some abstract historical fact sheet. It is lived and experienced by them in very real ways. This history is relived through poignant memories of their homeland, and remembered in everyday contexts, at home, at community gatherings. As for children of Holocaust survivors (see Goertz 1998; Hirsch 1992), such memories are almost as real for those born here as for those who had first hand experiences. This history influences the cultures lived, the stories told around the dinner table at night; it influences families and individuals in their life choices and perceptions of the future. These memories are made all the more real through the ever-present worry about friends and family remaining in Timor. There is a constant anxiety about friends and family and, for many, it has meant that it has been difficult to feel settled and to create a strong life here. Paulo describes this experience:

You know, when you come to Australia, it's not like you made the decision, "oh I want to have a better life in another country." It's like you are pushed out. So the feeling is that although we have good life here . . . you have that sense of longing for your country and there are people over there suffering and all these things—it affects you . . . you're not thinking about yourself, you are thinking about the people over there. Maybe because they are suffering—and that affects you. I don't know how to describe it. (Paulo, 36)

The pain of displacement was magnified while East Timor was suffering under Indonesian occupation. Those forced to leave their homelands experience very real feelings of dislocation. Before 1975, virtually no East Timorese had ever migrated to other countries. A large number of East Timorese living here have suffered traumatic experiences themselves or have relatives or close friends who have suffered. Compounding this trauma was the continuing fear for friends and family back in East Timor:

You have to understand all of us here still have our families back there. Here we can say anything about the Indonesian regime and don't feel frightened but it's our families back home that will pay the price. You see the Indonesians don't kill them straight away, they will kill them when everyone has forgotten all about it. They come in the middle of the night like a thief. (new arrival, quoted in Rawsthorne 1994, 36)

This was exacerbated by the fact that there was a continual flow of refugees between 1978 and 1999, each new arrival reminding the community of the situation back in East Timor.

You can see it in their eyes—the fear. Whenever I met someone who has just arrived from Timor, I feel very sad, it reminds me of what is happening to my people and my country. (young person, quoted in Rawsthorne 1994, 36)

Unsurprisingly, the past has always been very much present for East Timorese people living in Australia. It has not been a simple matter of leaving the danger of East Timor and building a new life in new surroundings. People live with the continuing effects of trauma and worry about family in East Timor each and every day. These stresses have had profound impacts in all aspects of life. They form an important thread throughout the community.

And the Future?

As I alluded to earlier, there have been significant changes in the community since the referendum. For some this has, ironically, created a new sense of loss: people miss the belonging they experienced when attending protests and community events centered on the independence struggle. Many of the key leaders in the community, the motivated individuals who would organize community gatherings and events, returned to East Timor to take up positions in the new government and with international NGOs. This has left something of a vacuum in the community, and many complain that there are fewer parties to attend.[10] For some, there is a feeling of happiness that East Timor is free, but there is also a sense that the community is shrinking and that people are now in limbo, deciding whether to return. Many have family and friends who have gone back. However, prior to the end of the Indonesian occupation, many Timorese felt unsettled and unable to think about the future when their country was suffering so greatly.

Displacement and living with the awareness that your homeland is occupied is undeniably difficult. It can mean for some, a feeling of being thrust into the world, without roots or direction. For many, the great burden of uncertainty has been lifted now that East Timor is free. Although it will take a long time to recover, the stress of the Indonesian occupation has finally ended. The opportunity to look to the future has returned for this community, and perhaps the weight of the past will become lighter.

Chapter 3
Nation, Transnation, Diaspora: Locating East Timorese Long Distance Nationalism

> Together, we will fight for peace, for justice, for freedom and for the right of all the peoples of the world.
> Long live East Timor!
> —Xanana Gusmaõ (1998)

At first sight, Fabiola looks unremarkable. She is an ordinary young woman who lives in a small apartment in suburban Fairfield and works as a clerk in a retirement home. We have shared many everyday jokes, laughed together about her latest Australian boyfriend, and chatted in the usual way about "everyday" things. Her small stature and amiable character belie her extraordinary personal history. The contents of the bookshelf in her small study room are the only hint of her bigger story: a myriad independence campaign texts in English, Portuguese, Bahasa Indonesia, and even Japanese.

Fabiola, thirty-five, came to Australia in 1992 sponsored by the United Nations High Commissioner for Refugees (UNHCR). She escaped East Timor via Jakarta, where she was a university student heavily involved in the East Timorese student resistance. From Jakarta, she bribed her way out of Indonesia, making her way to Bangkok, where the Southeast Asian office of UNHCR is located. While awaiting the outcome of her application for refugee status, Fabiola spent time on the Thai-Burmese border with Burmese activists, sharing strategies and resistance stories. Following the months she spent with this group, she came back to Bangkok to help establish a Thai-East Timor solidarity group before flying to Japan to develop solidarity networks there. When her application for asylum was finally accepted, she made her way to Australia.

Once in Australia, Fabiola became active in resistance and community politics, becoming the Australian representative of the East Timor Democratic Socialist Party, which has strong links to the Australians in Solidarity with Indonesia and East Timor (ASIET). CNRT sponsored her escape from East Timor, and she was part of José Ramos-Horta's Diplomacy Training Program. Now that East Timor is independent, she feels that she would like to continue to live in Australia for the foreseeable future. Despite this, she still has a long-term boyfriend in East Timor and has made several personal and work visits back since November 1999. It does look as though Fabiola's future will continue to be "of two places."

Fabiola's story epitomizes many of the complex transnational and political trajectories of East Timorese "long distance nationalism" (Anderson 1998, 73), as well as the deeply localized aspects of her life here in Australia.

There are two striking features about the East Timorese diaspora: the extent to which the collective fight to free East Timor from Indonesian occupation has figured in their collective imagination, and the number of symbiotic political alliances developed with the "outside." By symbiotic, I refer to dialectical or dialogic forms of alliances that are both mutually constitutive and mutually beneficial. Diasporas are, like nations, imagined communities (Anderson 1991). Imagined communities require "imaginative resources" (Appadurai 1996) to create and maintain a sense of collective identity. Diasporic identity, Stuart Hall has argued, is constituted not outside but within representation. Cultural representation is therefore not a "second order mirror held up to reflect what already exists." Instead, it is able to constitute us as new kinds of subjects, "and thereby enable us to discover places from which to speak" (Hall 1990, 314). The implications are profound.

These enabling spaces from which to speak pose both limits and possibilities. The imaginative resources available to a diasporic people have an impact on the shape of their collective imagination and consequently the kind of subjects identifying with it. It is therefore extremely important to lay out the elements of this representational regime in order to understand how and why a diaspora group identifies in a certain way. In the case of the East Timorese refugee diaspora, the collective imagination has focused strongly on the maintenance of a long-distance nationalism, creating an overwhelmingly homeland-focused identification. But this long-distance nationalism is no simple replication of the nationalism taking shape in East Timor itself. The transnational and intercommunal connections involved in creating and circulating the "cultural texts" of East Timorese diasporic identification mean that it is fundamentally important to understand how the discursive sites of national imagining "hail into place" and "enable" certain diasporic identities. Put simply, the collective diasporic imagination is shaped by three things: the imaginative resources available, the discursive environment, and the prevailing enabling structures. These enabling structures might be discursive or institutional, or stem from particular alliances and relationships.

As Anderson has famously pointed out, communities are imagined because a nation's members will never know all their fellow members, yet in the mind of each lies the image of their communion. The foundation for imagining national communities, Anderson argues, was the spread of technologies of print production, which created unified fields of exchange and communication (1991, 44). Anderson's notion of imagined community requires a complex unpacking of the processes through which this "community" is imagined.

Because East Timor has been cut off until recently from those in exile, there has been little of the "usual" transnational diasporic flows such as money, letters, movies, photos, visits, and so on (see Basch, Schiller, and Blanc 1994; Appadurai 1996; Steen-Preis 1997). Because there is no commercial cultural production in East Timor, Timorese is predominantly an oral culture, and there was widespread suppression of any creation or display of East Timorese culture by the Indonesian occupiers, the raw material for imagining the East Timor homeland and the diaspora as a collectivity has been political in nature. So rather than by watching Bollywood movies and engaging in visits to relatives, the re-creation and maintenance of the diaspora have occurred through a different set of flows, predominantly through the promotion of a long-distance East Timorese nationalism. The diaspora has been active in developing a highly dynamic and vibrant diasporic public sphere built on important alliances with the Australian and international communities and the circulation of political materials.

People Moving Through Different Spaces and Places

Somewhere in the vicinity of 20,000 East Timorese people have come to Australia since the Indonesian occupation, more than 10,000 to Portugal, and a few to Macao, Mozambique, Canada, the United States, Ireland, and other parts of the world. The early 1975 refugees came to Australia by ship from Dili to Darwin in Northern Australia. Later arrivals came via Portugal, often spending a number of years there before applying to come to Australia to join family and be closer to East Timor. Some later arrivals after the 1991 Santa Cruz Massacre in Dili were students in Jakarta, taking a complex route out or entering embassy compounds there. Others, such as Fabiola (introduced at the beginning of this chapter) came via places such as Thailand. Although small, this diaspora group has maintained strong transnational ties with their national and international counterparts.

All these routes put sets of diasporic relationships in place. The strongest links are between those in Australia and Portugal, with much shuttling back and forth, particularly by those who were involved in the political sphere. East Timor was virtually closed to the world until 1989, making visits home and the maintenance of social, cultural and family ties extraordinarily difficult. In the 1990s, visits began to be possible, following the policy of Indonesian "reformasi."[1] Transnational human mobility and social ties have been a central point of reference for transnational studies (see, e.g., Smith and Guarnizo 1999; Basch, Schiller, and Blanc 1994). In the East Timorese case, the flows of people until recently have been directed from East Timor to the diaspora, and followed by a circulation of people within the international diaspora.

Luis's Story

I interviewed Luis in October 1999. Luis's narrative reflects a series of transnational relationships stretching from those established under Portuguese rule to more recent ones developed after Indonesian occupation. Not only do these relationships affect his identity within the diaspora and the decisions and life patterns he has followed, but his travels and those of other Timorese also have created a transnational web that has had an impact on the shape of East Timorese diasporic nationalism.

Luis, forty-eight years old, came to Australia in 1986. He left East Timor in 1971 on a scholarship to study in Portugal. At the end of his studies, the civil war broke out, followed by the invasion, making his return unsafe. He remained in Portugal for several years, eventually migrating to Mozambique with his wife, an East Timorese refugee he met in Lisbon. They moved there to find a life similar to that in East Timor and to get away from the urban slums of Lisbon. Mozambique, a Portuguese-speaking nation, was attractive, as they felt comfortable with the Portuguese language and culture, and they expected they would be happy there. Luis and his wife eventually had two children in Mozambique. However, when the children were school-aged, the family made the decision to move to Australia to provide a "better life" for the children and to be closer to East Timor.

At that time, Luis spoke only textbook English learned in school and Macasae, his Timorese local dialect. He learned Tetum, East Timor's "national language," after leaving East Timor. His parents are indigenous East Timorese and his extended family still live in the village in East Timor. Luis feels that he has never really laid down roots in Australia, as he always expected that East Timor would be freed one day. He told me he always "put off 'home' feelings until East Timor is free." He went back to East Timor for the first time in 1995 and saw his family for the first time in twenty-five years. For him this was a very emotional journey, particularly since his elderly father was unwell. At the time we talked, he planned to move back to East Timor some time in the near future, as his father wanted him to come back before he dies. His wife was already working there on a six-month contract with a large NGO, the Christian Children's Fund. His adult children (both heading for university; one wants to be an army nurse) decided to stay in Australia. He says that his daughter would like to help East Timor in her work, although not live there.

Luis's narrative shows us a number of things, not least the extent to which Portugueseness and the fraternity of ex-Portuguese colonies figure in the mobility patterns of East Timorese refugees of Luis's generation. In contrast, Fabiola (introduced at the beginning of the chapter), who grew up under the Indonesian regime, lives largely through a different transnational social field, influenced by the sociocultural circumstances into which she was born. Her mobility and language patterns are linked to Asia, while Luis's social field is largely influenced by the European metropole and its colonies. In other words, patterns of mobility, and cultural identification, are generationally influenced, and influenced by the culture of the colonizer.

However, as is common for many migrants, issues such as where to bring up children also greatly influence mobility decisions. In Luis's case, this meant that his children grew up in Australia and have lives well and truly anchored there. In contrast, Luis and his wife remain focused on Timor. This means that they have had to develop a complex bifocal outlook on the future, one that is, like Fabiola's, "of two places." This has required him and his family consciously or unconsciously to negotiate their combined life trajectory, for example, through such means as taking six-month contract work in East Timor, with plans to return to Australia for a short period before taking another contract. His children too, have adjusted their outlook, planning careers that will allow them to work in both places.

This kind of bifocal outlook is not uncommon in the East Timorese community. In part this has to do with the highly homeland-focused nature of their diasporic public sphere where the primary texts for collective imaginings are politically focused. This public sphere has created an enormous moral pull toward the homeland.

The Circulation of Political Materials

Cultural products, including dance and music, as well as pamphlets, books, speeches, meetings, and rallies, formed the primary communicative strategies for creating the symbolic space for the long-distance nationalist project. Most material originated with or was circulated by the various East Timorese political organizations that had bases in Sydney. With the exception of the post-referendum protests calling for the intervention of a peacekeeping force, most of these activities ceased after the 1999 referendum.

The various political organizations based in Sydney were the key routes through which material was circulated. There were four key political organizations operating in Sydney during the independence struggle: the East Timor Relief Association (ETRA), the National Council of Timorese Resistance (CNRT), FRETILIN, and UDT.[2] ETRA was the primary East Timorese organization in Sydney, formed in early 1992 following consultation with Xanana Gusmão in East Timor. Ostensibly neutral, its stated mission was to provide resources to the East Timorese community in Australia to campaign effectively about their cause in the wider world community. They were also involved in raising funds for humanitarian relief efforts for East Timorese living under Indonesian occupation, which were used for medicine, clothing, and food. ETRA organized many community gatherings and rallies. In addition to advocacy and liaison with governments, international bodies, aid groups, UN bodies, and church groups, it carried out education campaigns about East Timor among the wider Australian community through providing speakers to charitable, cultural, and education organizations.

FRETILIN and UDT both had branches in Sydney with significant followings, which came together following the formation in 1988 of the CNRT coalition for the collective fight for East Timorese independence.[3] The CNRT brought together the political and military arms of the resistance to fight under a collective and neutral banner. These organizations were quintessentially transnational in nature. The leadership was spread across Australia, Portugal, Macao, and Mozambique, with ambassadors assigned to countries such as Brazil and Angola. Regular communications were kept up and meetings and conferences were held when possible.

Unlike many other migrant communities in Sydney, the East Timorese had no specific community media outlet that was not political in its aims and content. This has enormous ramifications if we take up Anderson's (1991) argument about the role of print media in "imagining communities." The range of communication practices that provided the raw symbolic material for imagining the East Timorese diaspora in Sydney were primarily political in nature and homeland-oriented. The resulting collective imagination was one that emphasized a collective exilic identity.

There were a range of means through which these messages were communicated and, importantly, many with significant transnational dimensions. These include performances at community gatherings, photos and tapes smuggled from East Timor, pamphlets, Web sites, radio programs in Tetum, and a special East Timorese section in the local

Portuguese-language newspaper. Donations from the refugee diaspora and solidarity supporters circulated through these organizations through donations, redistributed as humanitarian relief or spent on political campaigning.

Performances were held at most community gatherings, political rallies, and other large events. These included the East Timorese Youth Choir and the East Timor FRETILIN Dancers, who performed traditional dance. The choir would sing songs in Tetum, with strong homeland and resistance themes. One favorite patriotic resistance song performed, and sung along to at most gatherings and rallies, is "O Hele O" (Small Streams). Sung in Tetum, the words translate as

Streams flowing together become rivers
Refrain:
O hele o, o hele ole, o hele le,
O hele o, o hele o hele, le hele o
When rivers unite, what can oppose them?
So must the Timorese unite
Unite to resist the wind that blows from the sea
The wind that blows from the sea whips the Kabala
Whips our eyes, whips our backs
Makes our tears roll down, our sweat flow down.
Sucks the fat from our earth, the fat from our bodies.
Streams flowing together become rivers
When rivers unite what can oppose them?
Timorese united, let us sustain our homeland.

It became an anthem for the movement, audiences at protest events frequently singing along with great passion (many in tears). The affective quality of the music has proven a very successful strategy in bringing a sense of emotional collectivity to the cause. With its traditional melody, it is a song that reminds East Timorese of home. Its use of landscape metaphors has strong emotional pull, and its message of solidarity and strength in unity has a strong effect when sung in a large group.

Traditional dance was also a common feature of most gatherings. The FRETILIN Dancers consisted of young East Timorese, mostly children of parents who were politically active. The dancers wore traditional costume consisting of the *tais* dress and headdress and played traditional drums. A dance performed frequently, the "Rice Dance," is interesting in that it provides a window into the "inventedness" of tradition (Hobsbawm and Ranger 1983, 1), and the transnational links political versions of tradition often contain (see Figure 4).

I have seen the Rice Dance performed on many occasions. It is a simple dance, with drums and a choir singing the background music while four young women in traditional dress perform planting and harvesting movements. What is interesting about this dance is that an East Timorese man in Mozambique composed it in 1970. The dance is a romantic portrayal of peasantry and highlights the political context in which it was conceived, the nascent left politics of pre-independence East Timor and the influence of East Timor's "colonial sister," Mozambique. Indeed, the anticolonial movement in Mozambique at that time—the Front for the Liberation of Mozambique (FRELIMO)—is said to have been one of the models on which FRETILIN based itself. The author of the song was probably there either in exile or to fight for the Portuguese military in the Mozambique independence struggle.

So here is a dance, ostensibly traditional and valorizing the pure and good "East Timorese peasant culture." It was written in exile under influence of the Mozambique anticolonial struggle and performed through the years in East Timor as a resistance to Portuguese and then to Indonesian occupation. Finally it was exported to Australia and performed frequently as a key display of the traditional East Timorese culture for which, among other things, the community was fighting.

Most work about diasporic transnational networks shows how diasporas often maintain links with the homeland through letters, phone calls, photographs, and so on. In the case of the East Timorese, the occupation of East Timor meant that communication with family was difficult,

Figure 4. Traditional East Timorese dancers in tais costume. Photo courtesy Mary MacKillop Institute of East Timorese Studies.

and that the messages, photos, and so on that did make it out were often to help the resistance cause. There are many examples of photographs of East Timorese being tortured by Indonesian military (taken by soldiers but stolen by independence infiltrators) being smuggled at great risk from East Timor, put on display at community gatherings, and sent out to solidarity groups for use in political campaigns.[4] So in place of letters from "Aunty Fernanda" or "grandma" were long letters from Xanana Gusmão addressed to the diasporic community as a whole.

Before his capture and imprisonment by the Indonesian military in November 1992, Xanana would record political messages of solidarity and requests for help onto tapes, which would then be smuggled to Australia and copied many, many times to be distributed within the community. I noted that several of my interviewees had a number of these tapes on their bookshelves at home. In addition, each year there would be a New Year's message from Xanana, usually published in the ETRA newsletter, *Matebian News,* and other places. Gusmão, causing great embarrassment to Indonesia, would constantly smuggle these messages out of his Jakarta prison cell following his capture. The message is clear; the diaspora is as much a part of the resistance as those in Timor. His 1995 New Year message, for example, signed off thus:

To all of you we send the love of our people, the embrace of the FALINTIL fighters, and a "Hai amigos" from all the East Timorese political prisoners. HOMELAND OR DEATH! THE STRUGGLE CONTINUES ON ALL FRONTS! TO RESIST IS TO WIN! (FETWA 1995)

A similar example of this kind of "knitting in" the diaspora to the cause is a story that was popularly told among FALINTIL fighters in East Timor, and that Xanana has since repeated in press conferences in Portugal and Australia. The story, as Xanana and members of FALINTIL recount it, goes like this.

Xanana and his men were on their camp, somewhere on a mountain of East Timor. There seemed to be no enemies around so some men were sitting quietly by the fire while others were resting on the tents. Suddenly one of them— who was listening to the radio—came out, jumping and shouting "we are alive, we are alive." All the other men come running to see what was going on, but all he could do was keep on repeating the same words "we are alive, we are alive." Xanana finally managed to calm down the man and he explained, " I heard it on the radio, we are alive." "What do you mean? What did you hear on the radio?" Xanana asked, and his answer was "I did not understand it because they were speaking in English but I understood one word: EAST TIMOR," and all the other men joined him in a cry of joy. (Melo 2001)

Xanana, at a press conference in Lisbon in 2000, argued that if it weren't for those who fled East Timor and devoted a big part of their lives to the independence cause, the world might never have known the truth. He has been quoted many times as saying that the diaspora is as much part of East Timor, and as important to the cause, as those remaining there. The story has come to symbolize the transnational field of the independence cause. It has become a metaphor for the important link between those who stayed and those who left.

Many of the messages outlined above were published in the various available pamphlets, Web sites, and newsletters. The main source of news was the newsletter *Matebian News*, published monthly by ETRA updating the community on ETRA activities, East Timor news, and community issues, particularly relating to asylum seekers. The title of the newsletter is interesting in itself—Matebian being East Timor's largest mountain, the most sacred place on the island. In addition, there was a range of Web sites for FRETILIN, CNRT, ETRA, Free Timor coalition, and most of the solidarity groups. ETRA's site (2000) was an extraordinary resource listing events, a history of East Timor, and information about women's issues, the diaspora itself, and youth, just to name a few examples. Pamphlets were another frequent form of communication with the community. Often the pamphlets were written by Xanana Gusmão, sometimes outlining particular issues, sometimes just emphasizing the importance of the diaspora in the struggle. One interesting pamphlet tells the story of Xanana Gusmão's then wife, Emilia, and her escape from East Timor. The story emphasizes the extent to which those inside East Timor relied on the diaspora to promote their cause. It also highlights the strength of the links, from the highest level, between East Timor and the diaspora in Australia, and the transnational flow of political ideas from other parts of the world.

Emilia (whom Gusmão married in 1970 and split from in 1999) fled to Australia with their two children (now adults) in 1990. The pamphlet was written by Xanana (Gusmão 1996) and distributed throughout the diaspora and among solidarity supporters. One scene describes Emilia leaving East Timor. According to the pamphlet, hundreds of school children lined her route to the airport, heads bowed in respect, in defiance of the Indonesian military. When her plane landed in Bali, she found a crumpled note in her pocket, which had obviously been put there by a member of the crowd before her departure. It read:

> You leave us not forever
> We do not forget,
> You have helped Timorese women keep their dignity and hope,
> Xanana remains and is not alone,
> So you can leave us. Go!
> Shout like Winnie Mandela!

Here, in one small pamphlet distributed throughout the diaspora is, again, a story of the strength of the connection between those in exile and those in East Timor. It shows the level of reliance the resistance had on the diaspora to "get the story out." The reference to Winnie Mandela shows a high level of awareness of global political discourses as well as the transnational flows of ideas from similar political struggles. This is an important example of how globalizing processes provide the structuring conditions, or the "opportunity structures" of contemporary political discourse, which in turn are taken up by localized causes and, in the case of the East Timorese, fed back into the shape of the diasporic public sphere.

In addition to newsletters, there were two local community radio programs broadcast in Tetum each week. Highlighting the often splintered nature of the community in Sydney, one was produced by ETRA while the other was ostensibly UDT. Reportedly each program was listened to only by its own constituency. Most of the content was news from East Timor, East Timorese music, and announcements about community and political events.[5]

The other key mode of communication was through the two pages of the Sydney Portuguese-language community newspaper, *O Portugues na Australia*, that were devoted to the East Timor community. Mostly the items were news stories about East Timor and community announcements. This newspaper provided a significant sense of "fraternity" with other Portuguese-speaking peoples. It has pages for the Mozambique, Brazilian and Macao communities, for example. One of my informants said, "you will not find a Timorese house without a copy of this newspaper on their coffee table." This statement needs to be qualified, however. Those speaking Portuguese are largely the section of the community who came in the 1970s and 1980s, mostly over thirty-five, and also Australian- or Portuguese-born children of East Timorese parents.

Rallies and community gatherings were a major part of life for the East Timorese community in Sydney. Rallies began in 1978 and were held on a regular basis for the next twenty years. They started out with a small base but gained much larger community support from 1991 after the Dili Massacre. The last major rallies were held in 1999 to call for the intervention of an international peacekeeping force. The vast majority of rallies held over the years were organized in coalition with solidarity groups. There were also political meetings meant primarily for the East Timorese community, held mainly for planning resistance strategies, fundraising, and communicating issues, as well as dealing with community politics.

Mass rallies, in contrast, were often large, dramatic, and sometimes the subject of national media reports. For example, each year on the 12 November anniversary of the Dili Massacre, protest rallies and church services would be held around the country. Protest vigils were also held outside Indonesian consulates. Potent symbols were important at these rallies. FRETILIN and CNRT flags were common sights, and at a number of Dili Massacre commemoration rallies the participants carried large crucifixes, up to two meters in height, painted with the words "Dili Massacre East Timor."[6]

Ties to Religious and Solidarity Groups

Church organizations have been key solidarity partners in the cause and important centers for East Timorese community activity. These organizations are seen as neutral, beyond UDT/FRETILIN party politics, and therefore provide one of the few spaces where members of both constituencies are comfortable taking part in group events. There were several church organizations set up as solidarity groups for the East Timorese cause, such as the collective Christians in Solidarity with East Timor (CISET) and the Mary MacKillop Institute for East Timorese Studies (MMIETS). The latter are mostly Josephite nuns, based in the suburb of St. Marys in western Sydney, who work with the community in Sydney in a variety of ways and continue to provide health and education services in East Timor.[7] MMIETS was established in 1994, following a visit by East Timor's Bishop Belo to the Josephite Chapel in North Sydney. The institute was set up after the bishop's appeal to the sisters for help, and following consultations with the East Timorese community in Sydney. Among their aims are "to assist the East Timorese people to preserve and develop the Tetum language so that they can express their culture and identity in today's world" (MMIETS 2000). This is an important point: Tetum was described by FRETILIN as the "vehicle of nationhood." However, although most East Timorese in Sydney speak Tetum, in East Timor there are several widely spoken dialects in addition to lingua franca Tetum. Some Timorese in Australia learned Tetum there, and young people born in Australia or Portugal were given classes at the East Timor Cultural Centre. Catholic churches in Australia and East Timor were strong supporters of using Tetum as a strategy of cultural resistance. The Mary MacKillop Institute, for example, produces Tetum teacher education kits and children's books, which were and are used widely in East Timor.

As pointed out earlier, the 12 November Dili Massacre commemoration ceremony has been held each year since 1992 at Sydney's St. Mary's Cathedral. The service has taken an unusually hybrid form, blending traditional East Timorese song and dance and rituals with a Catholic

Mass. Large numbers of East Timorese and many members of the solidarity movement have attended each year. The mass, conducted by the local Timorese priest and the archbishop of Sydney, has always had a strong protest edge in addition to its spiritual dimension. As of 2003, it was still being held, although becoming progressively smaller in scale. The Church-Timor link was further enhanced by the vocal support of Sydney's Catholic archbishop for East Timor, and several Catholic nuns from the above organizations became prominent supporters of the cause, speaking at most protest rallies and public events. The two East Timorese priests in Sydney and many in the East Timorese community would travel some distance to attend the mass, which is held in Portuguese (even though it is held in Tetum in East Timor).

Another important project was the Sanctuary Network. Run by Christians in Solidarity with East Timor (CISET), it was set up in 1996 following attempts by the Australian government to deny asylum to the 1,600 refugees who came in 1995. CISET organized a network of Australians who would hide the refugees should the order to deport them come through. It is a good example of the kind of work carried out by solidarity and Christian groups. Unsurprisingly, such groups are held in high esteem by East Timorese in the diaspora.

Church support for the East Timorese cause extended from the Vatican to Australia and elsewhere in the Catholic world. The Vatican gave Bishop Belo the special post of apostolic administrator. Under Indonesian rule, the bishop of East Timor should technically have been an Indonesian bishop. In order to make an oblique statement that the Church viewed Indonesia's occupation of East Timor as invalid, Belo was appointed bishop of a dormant Italian diocese, unused for more than a century and with no territory attached to it. He was then appointed Apostolic Administrator of East Timor as a "back door" means of creating an independent East Timorese Church.

As I pointed out in Chapter 1, when the pope visited East Timor in 1988 he laid the crucifix from his neck on a pillow on the tarmac, and kissed it, rather than the ground, as is his custom. Most agree this was a statement about not wanting to validate Indonesia's sovereignty over East Timor. This story became legendary among East Timorese both there and in Australia, repeated frequently when meeting people in religious contexts. It was seen as an enormously important symbolic gesture from the highest level of the Catholic Church, which communicated that East Timor "belonged to God" and not to Indonesia.

The impact and implication of the Church-East Timor relationship could be summed up as follows. First, the church provided a widely recognized "language" in which to empathize with the East Timorese cause and through which the community was able to understand itself and its plight. Second, the Catholic Church is a phenomenally influential transnational organization. It provided the resources through which the East Timorese cause was able to endure. In addition, the nuns working in and for East Timor, such as those running the Mary MacKillop Institute, acted as "conduits" for information. They often provided news of conditions back in East Timor and news of friends and family remaining there. Finally, the church provided a "moral" dimension to the resistance.

In addition to religious groups, Australian and international solidarity groups also played an extremely important role in bringing the East Timorese cause to the attention of the non-Timorese community. These groups consisted of non-Timorese who were sympathetic to the East Timorese cause. This category includes core members of the group who worked as volunteers, and also those unattached to any particular organization but showed support through attending rallies and so forth.

There is a whole range of organizations, from large international ones served by sophisticated Web sites to national, state, and community groups. Of the more significant in Sydney were ASIET and the Australia East Timor Association (AETA). These organizations, sophisticated networks of mostly non-Timorese working in consultation with the East Timorese communities, held regular meetings, distributed monthly newsletters, had Web sites, organized talks and rallies, and participated in coalition activities with other groups. Although outwardly neutral, most solidarity groups had strong sympathies for FRETILIN and were often left-leaning politically. ASIET, for example, had links to the Australian Socialist Party and the *Green Left Review*. AETA was less political, but FRETILIN-oriented and to the left, nonetheless.

However, I support Goodman's (2000, 33) view that one of the key reasons for the diaspora's success in garnering support from the wider Australian community, including solidarity and church groups, was its ability to orient campaigning to broader cultural values and aspirations instead of asserting an overtly political stance. The language of the campaign was shaped by contemporary discourses on peace and self-determination, such as those put forward in the United Nations Declaration on Human Rights. These are discourses that have wide circulation among transnational NGOs, activist networks, peace advocates, and the United Nations. The language has significant sway among nations such as the United States, Portugal, Canada, the UK, and Australia. It is also an idiom that fits with the language of the Catholic Church and the kinds of discourse arising from the South African resistance to apartheid exemplified by Nelson Mandela and Desmond Tutu. This meant toning down the more anticolonial rhetoric derived from FRETILIN's earlier relationships with the Mozambique independence movement.

Solidarity groups have also played a major role in "domesticating" the

East Timor issue in Australia, selling it as one with particular relevance to Australia because of Australia's role in East Timor in World War II and its subsequent recognition of Indonesian sovereignty in East Timor, and appealing to the broader notion of Australian "mateship" (Goodman 2000). In addition, these groups were active in raising money to be sent to East Timor and to assist ETRA. Examples of fundraising efforts are the several CD music compilations with songs donated by Australian artists such as Midnight Oil. These solidarity groups were also part of an international network, with groups around Australia, and local groups in Thailand, Japan, the US, Canada, Ireland, Indonesia, Germany, the UK, Holland, Norway and New Zealand to name a few. It was an extraordinary grassroots network, often harnessing the internet to disseminate information (Figures 5–7).

Interestingly, during the course of my research, I discovered that none of the very active solidarity groups operating in Sydney's inner city had an interest in the welfare issues facing the East Timorese in the diaspora. The focus was completely on freeing East Timor, and any contact with East Timorese in the diaspora was with this goal in mind. The only time these groups had any welfare-oriented involvement with the East Timorese in Australia was to assist with newly arrived refugees. The Timorese

Figure 5. Protest in Canberra. 1989. Photo courtesy Australians in Solidarity with Indonesia and East Timor.

東チモール

抵抗するは★勝利なり

青山森人
Aoyama Morito

社会評論社

Figure 6. Cover of book about the independence struggle published by a Japanese solidarity group to promote East Timor's cause in Japan.

Figure 7. Some of the many T-shirts produced during the campaign. Photo by author.

community live predominantly in the working-class outer western suburbs of Sydney. There are few settlement resources available to them as a group, and there were (and still are) significant needs within the community. Issues relating to parenting, schooling, language, trauma, poverty, domestic violence, youth, unemployment, and so on have been the day-to-day realities of this group. But the importance of settlement for the East Timorese community in Sydney seemed not to figure at all in the priorities of the solidarity groups. In the year I spent working in a community center for East Timorese in Fairfield, not once did I meet anyone from the solidarity movement.

Relations to Larger Processes of "Transnationalism from Above"

Writers such as Guarnizo and Smith (1998; see also Mahler 1998) separate what they term "transnationalism from below" from "transnationalism from above." Transnationalism from below refers to what might be termed grassroots politics, which nevertheless are part of transnational coalitions. Transnationalism from below can also refer to the processes by which nonpowerful actors build spheres of interaction that cross borders.

The term is often used to describe the ethnoscape of migrants. Transnationalism from above, on the other hand, refers to processes and organizations that are global in outlook and scale. These might include, for example, multinational corporations, the United Nations, large NGOs such as the Red Cross or World Vision, or global mediascapes and the CNNs of the world. There are considerable overlaps between "above" and "below" flows. For example, transnational grassroots organizations sit somewhere between the two. The East Timorese "diplomatic circuit," too, appears to be somewhat of a categorical anomaly, if we apply the separation too stringently. It is important to understand how transnational processes are negotiated on the ground, and to see how the transnational refracts and shapes the local. Specifically, I want to understand how processes that might be deemed "from above" apply to the forms in which East Timorese came to imagine themselves and their cause in the diaspora.

The operation of East Timorese long distance nationalism relied heavily on securing the support of the international community for its cause. Indeed, it may be argued that this was the most important and successful dimension of the independence project. This meant that the nationalist discourses circulated by the East Timorese independence campaigners needed to be palatable enough for the international community to empathize with. The implication is that there occurred a process of subtle change in the public sphere of images, rhetoric, and motives for an independent homeland. The Declaration of Human Rights and its language of peace and self-determination, for example, became a key touchstone for the East Timorese independence movement. International discourses provided a kind of "opportunity structure" that shaped the kinds of messages circulated about the homeland. The international media, of course, allowed the world to become aware of a range of popular political struggles, which in turn fed into the ways in which the East Timorese independence movement has shaped its language, points of identification and political strategy.

An interesting example of this comes from one of Xanana's Christmas messages sent out in 1995. In a string of references to the end of apartheid in South Africa, the Middle East peace process, the disputes in the former Yugoslavia, and the political situation in Haiti, Gusmão positions East Timor's struggle within this field of international affairs and makes liberal reference to humankind's universal principles of freedom, justice, and peace. "East Timor," he says, *"is a small example of this general struggle"* (FETWA 1995, my emphasis).

The international diplomatic circuit also became part and parcel of the East Timorese cause. Nobel Laureate José Ramos-Horta is an example of someone with exceptional strategic talent for international diplomacy. Ramos-Horta spent his time in exile from 1975 to 1999 traveling the world, lobbying governments and the United Nations to recognize East Timor's cause. His prime targets were Australia, the United States, Portugal, and the United Nations in particular. To gain an ear, he had to master the language and discourse of "international peace" and "universal principles of justice and democracy."[8]

During his years in exile, he set up his Diplomacy Training School in Sydney for East Timorese in the diaspora. This program provided training in such topics as diplomacy, the language of the United Nations and international human rights, how to communicate with high-level politicians and officials, how to communicate the cause in a way the international community could identify with, how to dress, and how to write letters. The Diplomacy Training School was an extraordinary example of the extent of awareness among East Timorese of the need to bring their cause into the international arena and to adjust the language of independence to suit.[9] The diplomatic missions undertaken by Ramos-Horta regularly included working parties of East Timorese from the local community—community leaders, postgraduate students, and so on. Missions included making representations to the United Nations in Geneva and New York and to various parliaments, including Portugal and Brazil. The community in Sydney would usually be quite aware of these missions and take part in official pre- and post-trip discussions, through supermarket and kitchen table debate at the local level. The separation between "community" and "high diplomacy" and politics was very much blurred. Indeed, Ramos-Horta lived among the community when in Sydney, at his mother's modest suburban home in Liverpool. This meant that his day-to-day life was very much knitted into the fabric of life of the Sydney East Timorese.

Another example of the link between international discourse and Timorese long-distance nationalism was the empathy between the East Timor cause and internationally popular causes such as the anti-apartheid movement. A little-known transnational dimension of the struggle was Nelson Mandela's support for the East Timorese cause. In a fascinating transnational exchange, Xanana Gusmão sent a letter on 15 May 1994 from his Indonesian prison cell to Mandela, congratulating him on the end of apartheid. The letter reads in part:

Your election as the first President of a united, democratic, nonracial South Africa is an inspiration to the fight of oppressed people everywhere, the fight of the victims of repression, injustice and crimes committed by totalitarian regimes. Humanity has taken another step forward toward Human Freedom and the Freedom of Peoples. Today, the suffering Maubere People have yet another reason to carry on, and to keep the flag of freedom flying. The oppressed people of East Timor have been encouraged even more to make the sacrifices needed to defend their rights, to uphold freedom and justice, and to attain peace. . . .

we are also certain that the successful restoration of law, justice, freedom and peace in South Africa cannot be complete while, in other parts of the world, repression continues to create victims, and while governments of many countries contemplate with indifference the crimes being committed by the powerful. LONG LIVE UNITED, DEMOCRATIC AND NON-RACIAL SOUTH AFRICA. LONG LIVE THE JUST STRUGGLE OF OPPRESSED PEOPLE THROUGHOUT THE WORLD! (Gusmão 1994)

Mandela subsequently became a strong supporter of the East Timorese cause, finally visiting Xanana in prison in 1997. The two figures have obvious political parallels and developed a strong mutual bond and respect for one another's struggle. Following the meeting Mandela regularly sent emissaries to visit Gusmão in prison. Interestingly, Mandela raised the East Timor question with Indonesia's president Suharto. This is significant, given the long relationship between Indonesia and the anti-apartheid movement. Mandela reportedly made reference to Indonesia's support for South Africa's struggle in his representations to Suharto. Mandela's prominence and the public recognition of his own imprisonment and struggle against oppression created a powerful point of identification between the two causes, one that gained international resonance. In a final twist, Xanana Gusmão became known as the "Mandela of South East Asia" (Human Rights Solidarity 1999; Havely 2002).

Werbner has argued that "when British Pakistanis claim equality as citizens or when Muslim women in Britain say with utter conviction that Islam posits the equality of men and women, they are expressing the *zeitgeist* of the times, rather than simply the truth of Islam at its foundational moment" (1998, 26). So too the East Timorese connection to these broader political discourses. The text of Gusmão's letter creates an affinity with the South African struggle and brings it into a wider struggle for the "Freedom of Peoples," under whose banner East Timor also fights. Rather than a localized struggle for ethnic independence, the fight for the homeland became a struggle for universal "Human Freedom."[10]

Extending Anderson's thesis (1991) regarding the role of media technologies in creating the imagined community, this anecdote illustrates a couple of important points. The East Timor homeland cause, to be successful, had to speak a language accepted internationally. Mass media has saturated the world with stories of Mandela's anti-apartheid struggle and Bishop Tutu's peace and reconciliation model. These images became a kind of ready-made model for translating the East Timorese cause, which in turn offered an internationally empathetic audience for this kind of "peace talk." As a result, this means that the stock of images that fed into the diasporic public sphere for imagining East Timoreseness in exile became shaped by processes and discourses "from above." Tapping into these discourses was a most successful strategy for the East Timorese independence movement. It created empathetic alliances and harnessed international solidarity from an array of nations, in a way that, for example, the Sri Lankan Tamil struggle has never been able to achieve.

Local Experience of Transnationalism from Above

In the case of the East Timorese diaspora, there is an uncanny "collapse" between traditionally separate spheres: public and private, global and local, political and personal. The "out there" of nation building and international politics is well and truly experienced "in here," "on the ground," in living rooms, shopping centers, community groups, and church.

Over coffee one afternoon in 2001 with two East Timorese friends, both from Liverpool, the conversation turned, as it frequently does, to East Timor. I asked if they knew what the new East Timorese flag might be and when independence might be declared formally. (These were issues subject to heated debate by those at the highest level in East Timor.[11]) One coffee companion didn't know, but replied, "Oh, I'll just ask Mrs Ramos-Horta. I always see her at the shops in Fairfield. She'll know." My companion pointed out that she always stopped for a chat with her, and that Mrs. Ramos-Horta often had news and gossip about the latest CNRT politics, UNTAET, and what her son José was up to.

It is possible to see from this quite extraordinary anecdote the extent to which the East Timorese community in Sydney experience at the level of the everyday a sense of direct connection to the "homeland" in a nation-building sense, and linkages to transnationalism from above. There is a high level of awareness, evidenced in snippets of everyday casual conversation in Liverpool kitchens and at the vegetable market in Fairfield, of processes that are normally confined to a privileged elite of transnational political actors. In a way this brings to the East Timorese in Sydney a particularly strong sense of closeness to East Timor and a feeling of connectedness and relevance to the creation and future of the East Timorese nation.

In early 2001, I was chatting with a group of ten or so East Timorese young people, mostly between ages fifteen and nineteen. We were discussing whether to invite José Ramos-Horta to open a community event we were planning. Again, what struck me was the level of awareness they showed of the community politics around such a decision. One girl said to the group, "Come on guys, we are all FRETILIN kids here," and talked about how having Ramos-Horta would upset other members of the community, who would avoid the event. The group proceeded to discuss how upset they were at Xanana for letting the militias come back to East Timor, and their anger that he had apparently made some comments perceived as anti-FRETILIN. Throughout the conversation, there was a casual slippage between discussing their everyday lives in Sydney and talking about politics in East Timor as if it was in fact as much a part of their lives as their local community politics. Several young people at the table had one parent now working in East Timor; two had fathers who were part of the government. Yet none of the young people anticipated moving to East Timor, having grown up in Australia.

In a way, the social space occupied by these young people collapses the two worlds—public and private, Australia and East Timor—into a single transnational social field, allowing them to move between the two. Their lives are oriented around both Australia and East Timor. Life in Sydney is deeply interwoven with events in Timor, not through exiled longing for homeland, but as part of the fabric of everyday life, in casual living room discussions, in how the community identifies one another, around the dinner table. They give meaning to this seemingly fractured world precisely through perceiving it as all part of the same social field. Through dinner table discussion, involvement in the political sphere, increasing contact by telephone, and so on, the space between these worlds apart contracts and knits into everyday life in Sydney.

Theorizing the East Timorese Diasporic Public Sphere

As a refugee community, not simply a migrant one, questions of displacement, return, and longing for homeland are paramount. However, there is no automatic relationship between displacement and a sense of collective exile. There is no built in reason that this group should have become so committed to their exile identities, fighting for the freedom of their homeland. The homeland-focused diasporic identity derives in part from the primarily political nature of the imaginative resources available for their collective identification.

Collective identification has to be *worked at*. This means that there is a process of boundary maintenance, of creating, defining and perpetuating East Timorese "culture." Indeed, communities, as Anderson has famously argued (1991, 6), are to be distinguished, not by their falsity/genuineness, but by the style in which they are imagined. In the East Timorese case, this imagining has occurred primarily in the diasporic public sphere. Werbner defines this sphere as "a space in which different transnational imaginaries are interpreted and argued over, where aesthetic and moral fables are formulated, and political mobilisation generated" (1998, 11).

For this refugee diaspora, the core strategy of imagining itself has been one of political symbiosis. As we have seen, the East Timorese diaspora successfully garnered significant international support for its cause through well established transnational connections cultivated over twenty-five years. This meant that East Timorese long distance nationalism was shaped by a focus on international diplomatic efforts and their success at building strong alliances with church and solidarity groups. So although refugee diasporas such as the East Timorese have a specific homeland-oriented imagined community, the East Timorese imagined community has been aided very much by transnational flows between the diaspora and their homeland and between the diaspora and sympathetic outsiders.

As Gupta and Ferguson argue, cultures should be imagined as fundamentally interconnected rather than as separate and discrete entities. That is, we need to explore the "production of difference within common, shared and connected spaces" (1997, 45). This approach emphasizes the need to examine the clusters of interaction within which displaced populations such as the East Timorese construct and maintain meanings of "homeland" and "community." What I am arguing is that it is crucial not to fall into the trap of treating the diasporic space and its attendant transnational cultural flows as being bounded within itself. Rather, seeing the East Timorese diaspora as imagined through connection allows us to see the importance not only of flows that originate and circulate within the bounded diaspora grouping (if there is such a thing), but also of how interactions in a sociohistorical context shape the consumption of these flows, and how flows from elsewhere are taken up and given meaning.

Indeed, one of the interesting things about the East Timorese case is the fundamentally porous and hybrid nature of its diasporic identity. The strategic alliances and symbiotic relationships developed with the outside, the filtering through the enabling discourses of religion, human rights, and Australian values of mateship and loyalty (vis-à-vis the World War II soldiers), for example, have had a significant impact on the way in which the diaspora has been able to imagine itself. That is, the diasporic public sphere emerges dialectically with other spheres (see Werbner 1998, 26).

In sum, there are two important theoretical points highlighted by the East Timorese case. First is the issue of *interconnection*. Transnational flows do not necessarily originate within the diaspora, and even if they do, they are not conceived or received in isolation from "outside" the "homeland" and "diaspora." Gupta and Ferguson (1997, 46) have argued that, rather than juxtaposing preexisting differences, we need to explore the construction of differences in historical processes. If we apply their logic to the case of the East Timorese, it emphasizes the need to locate the diaspora group, and the transnational flows through which they imagine themselves, within a grid of interrelated difference. There are many interconnections here. These might be connections that create a sense of difference, such as the colonial encounter and the relations that follow it. Another set may be ideas picked up "from outside"—such as the influence of the anti-apartheid movement or Africanist anticolonial discourses on East Timorese politics. Or they might be the connections established with international human rights discourses or relationships to the wider Australian community. I have tried here to map some of the more important of these transnational and intercommunal flows in terms of how they are indigenized within the diaspora, how they interact with one another, how the context counts, and how these things go on and create the "shape" of the kinds of meanings the East Timorese diaspora makes of itself.

This leads to the second point: that we need to locate the symbolic practices of diasporas such as the East Timorese diaspora within space and within sets of interactions. In this way, we can see that diasporic processes are anchored in space. They are not "global"—they do not transcend spaces and operate identically everywhere. Context imposes both limits and possibilities. So, although these processes flow across borders, they are nevertheless experienced in located space.

Third, therefore, we need to understand how particular kinds of flows, particular sets of interconnections and clusters of interaction, have a bearing on how the East Timorese diaspora makes meaning of itself. These things will shape the stock of ideas and images available to the diaspora grouping in collectively imagining itself and its homeland in exile. Appadurai convincingly argues that the power of the "imagination in the fabrication of social lives is inescapably tied up with images, ideas and opportunities that come from elsewhere" (1996, 471). However, flows do not simply occur within a diaspora grouping. We need to take into account the hybridizing encounters that have an impact on the shape in which a collectivity imagines itself. As Ang (2001, 87) points out, "the encounters *between* peoples are as constitutive of who they are as the proceedings *within*." This stance requires us to locate the diaspora's imaginative resources within clusters of interactions; it is about locating the wider discursive environs that enable and inscribe the diasporic imagination. This means locating the diasporic imagination within the kinds of "enabling discourses" that circulate within the location of diasporic consumption. We need, therefore, to recognize that in cases such as the East Timorese, so reliant on local alliances and connections with other groups, there are significant hybridizing processes at work (see Nederveen Pieterse 2001).

In addition, three very significant characteristics of the East Timorese diaspora need to be emphasized. As we saw earlier, one of the core distinguishing features of this group is the extent to which the collective fight for "homeland" has figured in their diasporic imagination. However, unlike many contemporary refugee diasporas, this group has widespread links to and support from outsiders: the Australian community, solidarity and church groups, the international NGO sector, Portugal, and so on. In many ways, even if there was little "real" day to day activities associated with "community," the links with these outside supporters brought the imagined community to life. This is the key departure point, in terms of their sense of imagined community, between the East Timorese in the diaspora and the East Timorese at home.

This brings me back to Fabiola, introduced at the beginning of the chapter. How might her particular biography and self-perception be situated within this wider story? Fabiola's story shows the importance of mobility patterns. Her trail through Indonesia and Southeast Asia left sets of solidarity relationships in place that are an enduring feature in her life-world. All the people and cultures she met along the way had an impact on how she imagines herself, her cause, and her homeland. She made friends with many in the solidarity movement and was influenced greatly by the left politics of ASIET and the Australian Socialist Workers Party. She has also had poetry published in a prominent feminist publication in Australia. Her meetings with the editors of this magazine and feminist support groups for East Timor translated her sense of self. Her involvement in Ramos-Horta's international diplomacy program set her within a transnational political context completely removed from anything she would have experienced growing up in the village in East Timor. Through this program, her sense of herself and her cause has given her a decidedly confident and international outlook.

All these connections have structured how she experiences and uses her "East Timoreseness" in exile. She grew up speaking Indonesian and feels little affinity with the Portuguese "old guard." Her points of identification lie with those she worked with in Indonesia in the student resistance (both Timorese and Indonesian), those in the underground movement in East Timor, and her friends and political compatriots in Australia. Feminism has created a space for her to identify as a strong woman fighting for a cause. She has worked with the sisters at the Mary MacKillop Institute developing traditional East Timorese stories into children's books. This has helped her imagine herself, her cause, and her homeland in highly affective cultural-religious terms. She has worked on temporary contracts as a translator for UNTAET in Timor (translating war crimes testimonies), but was registered and paid as a foreign national. However, living in Australia has also to some extent knitted her into place, creating an extended social field that encompasses both Australia and East Timor. She is both "here" and "there," but her life in Australia has been very much structured by "the cause," East Timor.

One important outcome of my research was an increased awareness that East Timorese long distance nationalism is not a simple replica of the nationalist processes in the homeland.[12] It is an obvious point, but one too frequently overlooked. The vast majority of the material written on East Timor and its years of resistance and fighting for a free homeland perpetuates a casual slippage between East Timor and the people, ideas, symbols, and politics coming out of the diaspora. This (predominantly journalistic) material on East Timor never differentiates, in terms of either content or motive, between the nationalist project in East Timor itself and that occurring abroad.

This work takes for granted that the nationalism put forward by those in the diaspora represents East Timorese nationalism in general. None of this work has attempted to unpack the complex relations that bring nationalisms to life. It is, however, imperative not to conflate the two because, when it comes to questions of "return" and developing an independent East Timor, a whole set of extraordinarily complex issues and contradictions arise. Indeed, this has already begun to occur in East Timor. There have been huge splits between returnees and those who remained in East Timor. The splits are generational, and center on aspects of cultural identity, language, the flag, political ideals, cultural identification, and so on. Understanding the modes through which deterritorialized identities are created and imagined allow us to anticipate in advance the fact that "return" is no simple process. It is not simply that refugees change and acculturate to the host society. Rather, the whole range of diasporic cultural experience is created in and through a different set of connections and needs to be seen in its specificity as occurring within particular social, cultural and historical junctures.

Hall has argued that "far from being grounded in a mere 'recovery' of the past, . . . identities are the names we give to the different ways we are positioned by, and position ourselves within, the narratives of the past" (1990, 225). This impels us to be aware of the ways in which the "past" has been created and imagined in context and has gone on to position East Timorese in the diaspora. In other words, we need to see how this past has structured the possibilities available to position themselves within it. This theoretical stance, emphasizing the connectedness of identity, means that the deterritorialized identity of the diasporic imagination is a different "East Timor" to those remaining at home.

The distinction between home and place of exile is blurred because of the extent to which transnational and intercommunal links have fed into the way this community imagines its homeland. But this means that there is no easy separation between their "western" and "traditional" identities, which becomes starkly apparent when visiting home. On the one hand, they have been exposed to and influenced by Australian culture. On the other, the extent to which their everyday lives in Australia have been focused on maintaining their state of exile and freeing the homeland means that there is often a high degree of guilt and ambivalence attached to their perceived loss of culture and ambivalent feelings about returning to East Timor.

And the future? There have of course been some dramatic changes for the diaspora since independence. Many changes we are yet to see, but those that have taken place already have had extraordinary impact on the shape of the community. Many of the key organizations referred to in this chapter, such as ETRA, have closed, lie dormant, or become aid projects for East Timor. The two radio programs in Tetum have been put on hold. Now there is only one, running irregularly. The presenters of the other show have returned to East Timor. Indeed, although only a small minority of the general community have moved back to East Timor, the majority of the key leaders in the diaspora have returned, many to take up prominent government posts. Many families have been fragmented. Many returning to take up jobs or government posts have left wives, husbands, and children behind in Australia indefinitely. Some are continually shuttling back and forth between East Timor and Australia. Many families that have been split up in this way plan to move the "Australian half" to Darwin in order to make this shuttling process faster and more economically viable. Younger people are worried about loss of family in this way, and most do not want to go to East Timor to live.

There are no longer large political rallies and protests. Many with whom I have spoken miss them. Solidarity groups have become focused on East Timor rather than diaspora, turning into aid projects and offering political support to East Timor. There has been a shift to fundraising for reconstruction. There has been a move from aspirational human rights discourse to the messy and often divisive reality of real-life politics, bringing up old political divisions within the community and creating new ones. There is widespread anger at the way the Australian, NGO, and international communities began "riding the East Timor bandwagon," taking over and not listening to the East Timorese. There is anger that those from the outside who were enlisted to help the cause seemingly took over running the reconstruction process. Many feel that, although the diaspora needed outside help to gain independence, these supporters should pull back now and let East Timorese run the country for which they fought. There is anger at the Catholic Church's increasing conservatism in East Timor, particularly surrounding gender issues. In East Timor itself, there has been widespread anger at returnees taking East Timorese jobs. Many returnees are afraid that those in East Timor have not appreciated their importance in the struggle, and are worried that they won't be needed anymore. All these changes, some of which are deeply traumatic, are just beginning to have an impact on how members of the diaspora are experiencing their collective identity, on the imaginative resources for imagining themselves and their homeland.

Chapter 4
Embodying Exile: Embodied Memory and the Role of Trauma, Affect, Politics, and Religion in the Formation of Identities in Exile

This Maubere consciousness, the historical identity, proper and genuinely Maubere, does not bow before massacres, persecution, banishment or torture. It is for this identity that the struggle is affirmed, with blood and death.

—Xanana Gusmão (2000)

Suffering in common unifies more than joy does. Where national memories are concerned, griefs are of more value than triumphs, for they impose duties, and require a common effort.

—Ernest Renan (1996)

Its been very difficult. Um . . . especially when you come to Australia, it's not like you made the decision "oh I want to have a better life in another country." It's like you are pushed out. So the feeling is that—although we have good life here—um . . . that sense of um . . . longing for your country and there are people over there suffering and all these things . . . it affects you . . . you're not thinking about yourself, you are thinking about the people over there. Maybe because they are suffering—and that affects you. I don't know how to describe it. It affects you, you know?

—Paulo, interviewed 2000

Each of these opening quotations emphasizes the significance of shared pain and affect in the formation of collective identities, and, as Xaviér's story shows, these also have a very real impact on individual lives. Xaviér is an East Timorese man in his mid-thirties, living in Fairfield, whom I interviewed one afternoon in January 2000. He fled to Portugal from East Timor in 1986 with his family, and eventually all came to Australia under the special family reunion program. As with most East Timorese I have met, Xaviér had suffered the loss of family and witnessed many traumatic events in East Timor. His mother, older sister, and two brothers live in Fairfield. I have met his sister and brother and know that they suffer terribly psychologically and physically resulting from their traumatic experiences.

Xaviér, who has has ambitions to be an actor, worked with a theater company in Sydney and performed in Timorese plays. The interview took place at the home of a mutual friend. The small apartment in Fairfield, was on the second floor, and the interview was held around a table in a front room overlooking the street. Although I hadn't met Xaviér before, he seemed very easygoing, if a little timid, and was very eager to be interviewed. We chatted informally for a few minutes, but he became very nervous when I turned on the tape recorder. I offered to turn it off and take notes instead, but he insisted that I record the interview. He began to relax a little, and we talked for about half an hour.

Then, unexpectedly, we heard sirens screaming. Two fire engines pulled up just outside and firemen jumped out, running toward our building. We could see and hear all this from the room we were in. Xaviér became extremely anxious—in fact, completely terrified. It was quickly established by his friends in the apartment that there was no fire. The neighbors had tried to hold an open barbecue on their balcony, and someone had called the fire brigade because of all the smoke. While the rest of us thought this was really quite funny, I realized that Xaviér was still terribly frightened. His whole body was trembling and he seemed to be having some kind of panic attack. When I looked at him, it was almost as if he was not quite there—as if he had been transported back to some terrifying moment in the past. Even after 20 minutes of calm reassurances from his friends, he was still in a state of high anxiety. By that time, it was close to sunset. He noticed it was getting dark and began to panic again: "I have to get home—please, please, I have to get home. It's getting dark." I offered to drive him home, as he was afraid to walk (although it was only a short distance). We went to my car; our friend sat in the front and Xaviér in the back. I could see him in the rearview mirror, sitting but curled down as far as he could shrink himself, as if trying not to be seen from the outside, or perhaps not wanting to look outside and see the dark. We finally got him home and inside, where we made some coffee and he calmed down markedly once he felt back in his safe space. What I hadn't known about Xaviér before our interview was that he had been diagnosed as suffering from post-traumatic stress disorder (PTSD)[1]. He often had flashbacks and had a fear of the dark that was so severe that he rarely left his home after sunset. For Xaviér memory is an embodied, felt experience, and his reaction can be seen as a reexperience of traumatic sense memories.

We decided to end the interview that day, but the following afternoon he telephoned me and asked if I could come to his house to try another interview, as he had some important things he wanted to share. I was hesitant in the second interview with my questions, as I wanted to avoid anything that might bring up painful memories for him. What he wanted to tell me about was his dream to start a theater group for East Timorese youth in Sydney. The group could play sports and "do" culture and music, but most of all he hoped (although it was still just a dream, he said) they would write and perform plays about East Timor, especially about its history and the wars and occupation.

You know the struggle was important. But you know, it is slipping away from our everyday life. There is a lot of story—not only in 1975, but in 1945—a lot of East Timorese died. So in theatre, we can try to live, to live again these stories. Not just to read about, but to live again these stories—it is important for young people to live these, because they don't know. . . . And is good for me to, umm . . . to get familiar to the younger generation . . . so I can feel myself integrated into that Timorese society. (Xaviér, mid-30s)

My interview with Xaviér was a major turning point in my research. It forced me to think deeply about questions of body, affect, memory, and sensory experience in relation to traumatized refugee communities and their diasporic identities. Inspired by this small window into Xaviér's life, my mission in this chapter is to explore some of the processes of social belonging and affective connection to the homeland within the East Timorese refugee community. The impetus for this focus arises from the three defining characteristics of the East Timorese refugee diaspora in Australia. First, in addition to the tragedy of displacement, large numbers of the community suffered severe trauma in East Timor. Second, large numbers in the community have seen themselves as temporary exiles in Australia. Third, the majority of collective activities and circulation of news within the community before independence was focused on the struggle for an independent East Timor.

How, then, have the combination of trauma, the ongoing problems in East Timor, and the modes through which the independence struggle was enacted influenced the construction and experience of a particular affective Timorese refugee diaspora identity and moral community? Put differently, in the context of the struggle, *how have the bodily and sensory experiences brought about by displacement and trauma been reexperienced and channeled into affective diasporic identities?* Conversely, how do the "language" and particular modes of performance used in the struggle influence how East Timorese in the diaspora make sense of, experience, and feel their identities, their trauma, and their displacement?

Exile, Settlement, and Trauma in the East Timorese Community

For community service providers, the traditional mode of approaching settlement issues regarding refugee communities, such as the East Timorese, is through traditional sociological indicators of settlement, such as employment, housing, education, language, and levels of trauma. While not disputing the importance of such indicators, I am interested in exploring what lies "behind" these objective factors, usually expressed in statistics; the kinds of processes at work, the qualitative "thickness" beyond these more commonly attributed causal factors.[2] There is no doubt that compared to other groups in Sydney, such as the Sri Lankan, Cambodian, or some of the Balkan communities, the East Timorese community has had problems with settlement. In all the areas outlined above, such as language skills, unemployment and levels of education, the East Timorese community has had higher than average levels of difficulty (Rawsthorne 1994). The Service for the Treatment and Rehabilitation of Torture and Trauma Survivors (STARTTS), the main trauma counseling service in Sydney, which has worked for years with the East Timorese community, reports that many East Timorese have seen themselves

as temporary exiles in Australia rather than as refugees or migrants [and that there] has been little attempt amongst the Timorese community in Australia to establish independent lives in Australia. Consequently many Timorese have not attempted to address the psychosocial needs of themselves or their community and the traumatic experience they have faced. (Tang 1999)

My own research substantiates this picture. There do seem to be a high number of East Timorese in Sydney who have seen themselves as temporary exiles.[3] However, although this seems to be overwhelmingly true for indigenous/mestiço Timorese, it is not at all true for the Timorese-Chinese population, even though they suffered similar levels of trauma and came to Australia at the same time and mostly in the same way. Anecdotally, moreover, although Timorese-Chinese (especially those who came in 1975) experienced similar levels of trauma as non-Chinese,[4] post-traumatic stress disorders are less present. Aside from socioeconomic and educational factors, I would like to propose there is something *cultural* at work here. Something cultural that *works on, through,* and *from* the body, something cultural that feeds into the realm of *affect.* Something cultural in the way trauma is experienced and the way it articulates with certain cultural identities. Something cultural that creates a certain kind of affective exile identity, which has its roots in the way the struggle for East Timor's independence has played out in Australia.

While pondering these questions, it struck me that of all the material from cultural studies and anthropology on diasporas, I had seen virtually nothing that has dealt with the question of trauma, and very little on questions of affect and sensory experience, as they pertain to contemporary forced migrants. When you consider that refugees make up a large proportion of diasporic peoples today, it becomes patently clear what an enormous omission this is. Yet my experience with the East Timorese community in Sydney tells me that the effects of trauma play a very central part in day-to-day life, in political identification, in feelings toward other community members, in "trust structures," in orientation toward the homeland. Indeed, the word "trauma" is familiar currency in the community. Many times I have heard community members explaining someone's behavior as so and so "has trauma." Every person, every family I met, has directly experienced traumatic events or has close friends who have. The symptoms of post-traumatic stress are present throughout the community. It quickly became apparent to me that any study of diasporic identity within a refugee community that omitted such an important issue is seriously deficient.

Theorizing Strategies of Intensity and the Role of Affect

We take for granted that there is such a thing as "diasporic identity." Anthony D. Smith (1991, 23) has argued that ethnies such as the Jewish or Armenian diasporas persist even when long divorced from their homeland, through an intense nostalgia and what he terms "spiritual attachment" to the homeland. The question remains, however, how and why do subjects imagine themselves into a particular community or identity? What processes play into such imaginings? The answer, I believe, lies partly in the question of affect. Understanding processes of affect (see, e.g., Noble 2002; Grossberg 1998), defined at the simplest level as bodily emotion associated with an idea or set of ideas, is an important dimension of any attempt to understand why individuals or community invest themselves in a particular identity. The imperative must be to understand the processes that inspire and produce an affective relationship to a particular cultural identity. The body, of course, is central to this relationship, because emotions are experienced in the body; it is the site of feeling, of affect.

At this juncture I want to explore in a more comprehensive way how and why political protest and the struggle produced spaces of social belonging for East Timorese refugees, and consider what benefits participation in such activities might have had for those Timorese involved.

Ghassan Hage's (2002) work on Lebanese migrants, focusing on nostalgia, homesickness, and affect, provides some important insights. In a very interesting essay, Hage theorizes the ways Lebanese migrants in Australia were differentially implicated by reading news from Lebanon and experienced it with varying intensities. He argues that migrants (and people in general) actively engage in strategies of *affective intensification.* While focusing on Lebanese migrants and their news reading practices, Hage argues that an analysis of differential implication in, and intensity of, the experience of a particular reality may be applied to many aspects of social life. Hage deploys these two notions as analytical tools for measuring a person's *affective* and *symbolic* "distance" from the Lebanese news.

Intensity, as Hage conceptualizes it, has to do with the extent to which a reality is involving and affecting, but it is also an intense *relation* where the person's engagement in a reality contributes to its intensity (2002, 193–94). This important point frames his analysis of Lebanese migrants, where he pays particular attention to the bodily movements and responses of the migrant reader to the news from Lebanon, such as slapping the newspaper or spitting on the floor in anger in response to various news items. These utterances, interactions, and bodily movements are termed *strategies of intensification.* The employment of such strategies is aimed at "narrowing the physical and symbolic gap between news and reader and in the process, augmenting the intensity of this reality for that reader" (200). In other words, we can see this in terms of the body doing work to increase affective engagement with the topic at hand.

The desire on the part of migrants to be implicated emanates from what Hage terms "migration guilt." Such guilt derives from the disruption of a moral economy of social belonging, whereby members of a community are indebted to that community in a reciprocal gift-exchange relationship. This debt is incurred by the individual in receipt of the gift of community belonging and social life. In this reciprocal relationship, according to Hage, one repays the gift of communality through lifelong participation in the communal group. He argues that for this reason migration is a particularly guilt-inducing process. This guilt-inducing state of indebtedness is most acute when the community (a family, religious group, village, or nation, for example) is going through a hard time and the person is not there to help. In this way, "when you do not share the fate of the collectivity which gave you social life, you are guilty of letting others pay alone for a debt you are collectively responsible for" (203). The use of affective modes of intensification and affective language is important in these strategies of intensification. The more intense the mode of being implicated, Hage argues, the more "debt" is repaid in this symbolic moral economy, which is also a physical moral economy, based on bodily performance.

Hage also points out that the desire to be more implicated in the homeland cannot be taken for granted, and is not felt equally among all migrants (204). He argues that such excessive attachment to the homeland can be seen to some extent as a strategy of compensation for one's life not turning out as hoped for in the new country. In the case of the Lebanese migrants in Hage's study, this hope is primarily centered on the level of social and economic achievement experienced in the host country. In the case of the East Timorese refugee diaspora, although these are important determining factors, I believe there are also others at work. These have to do with, first, the rupture of forced displacement; second, the levels of trauma in the community; third, the fact that the homeland has actively "called up" repayment of the moral debt to the nation; and fourth, and perhaps most important, the fact that protest strategies have all, in different ways, been modes that tap into East Timorese bodies and emotions, creating an incredible affective pull into a sympathetic community of suffering.

I believe Hage's approach offers a potentially fruitful path for understanding many of the processes I have seen at work within the East Timorese community. This excerpt from one of my interviews with Fatima is representative of views I have heard many times over during the course of my research:

I was involved in Timorese cultural dancing. I would go to protests—I would go to different like events—Just to make everyone aware of the Timorese people. I wanted to go there—and sort of be part of that for myself. Because I think I saw for my parents, and I saw for my uncle—and the suffering and . . . [drifts away for a few moments] . . . and I wanted to be part of that. And I think, in a way, like, I became more Timorese when I got involved with this stuff.

Fatima's words demonstrate very clearly the relevance of the notion of migration guilt experienced in the face of the suffering of those remaining in East Timor. Fatima describes how in her case this translated into a desire to participate in the political struggle. Beyond the obvious political benefits, her participation in cultural dancing and protests also gave her a sense of belonging as an East Timorese person, and eases her guilt about the suffering of her family and those in East Timor. When she danced, "I became more Timorese." Cultural dancing is an embodied activity that generates affective identification with Timoreseness. As she says, "and the suffering . . . I wanted to be part of that." To share their suffering means also to share in being East Timorese, to share in the moral community of East Timor, and to repay that debt of belonging. Perhaps many of the protest events for the East Timorese struggle represented spaces in which East Timorese refugees were able to participate in strategies of intensification. For many East Timorese, participation in these events provided an opportunity to share in, and reproduce, the moral economy of East Timoreseness and to appease feelings of guilt arising from the sense that they had fled their war-ravaged homeland to save themselves and their own families, leaving the majority of (particularly poor and uneducated) Timorese back in East Timor to suffer alone.

Religion, Ritual, Crowds, and Protest

As for many former Spanish and Portuguese colonials, Catholic ritual is an extremely prominent feature of social life for East Timorese in East Timor and in the diaspora. For East Timorese refugees in Australia, ritual and commemorative practices played a paramount role in public expressions of grief about the situation in East Timor. These practices also brought them into a global Catholic moral community of martyrdom based on displays and performances of both bodily suffering and suffering bodies.

Rather than static texts, such as the newspaper to which Hage refers, I suggest that the bodily character of these specific modes of protest set in motion a particularly dialogic process with the participants. The story of the Catholic mass and protest held in Sydney each year to commemorate the four hundred or so Timorese who died in the 12 November 1991 Dili Massacre is a classic example of the mixture of protest forms used in the struggle.[5] The 1996 mass was one of the more spectacular and probably the biggest, as this was the year in which José Ramos-Horta and Bishop Carlos Belo jointly won the Nobel Peace Prize. Somewhere in the vicinity of five hundred people attended a large peaceful protest march to St. Mary's Cathedral that immediately preceded the mass. At the head were around two hundred East Timorese marchers, and at the very front were three pairs of young East Timorese men, each carrying a crucifix approximately ten feet long and five feet wide. Roughly fashioned from unfinished logs, the crucifixes were carried on their shoulders in a Christ-like walk toward the place of crucifixion, emulating Christ's journey to Golgotha. Behind them were a group of around one hundred East Timorese, mainly women, each carrying a smaller, white crucifix, perhaps twenty inches long and ten inches wide. On the front of each crucifix, along the crossbar, was written the name of a person who had died in the Dili Massacre. All the East Timorese in the protest, both marchers and crucifix carriers, wore a tais scarf around their neck. The tais is the traditional cloth of East Timor, as recognizably East Timorese as the sarong is to Indonesia or the sari to India.

The march continued slowly through the city toward St. Mary's Cathedral. Upon arrival, a rally formed outside with banners and speeches, after which the audience/congregation filed in. At the front of the church were the East Timorese youth choir, singing a mixture of protest and religious songs in Tetum. The mass, too, was a mixture of protest and religion, robed clergy sharing the stage with East Timorese in various forms of traditional dress. In a curious juxtaposition, traditional East Timorese drummers led the procession toward the pulpit, while the Catholic nuns had given rousing speeches to the protest crowd before the service (Figures 8–10).

In light of the highly religious aspects of much East Timorese protest, as the above example demonstrates, it is important to note that the percentage of the East Timorese in East Timor identifying as Catholic rose from less than 30 percent before 1975 to more than 90 percent during the period of Indonesian occupation. This rise is attributed to the fact that the Catholic Church in East Timor provided sanctuary and protection from many of the worst atrocities of the Indonesian military. It was also a form of cultural resistance, as the majority of Indonesians are

Figure 8. Protest in 1997 featuring a cross. Photo courtesy Mary MacKillop Institute of East Timorese Studies.

Figure 9. Protesters entering St. Mary's Cathedral for the Dili Massacre mass in 1997. Photo courtesy Mary MacKillop Institute of East Timorese Studies.

Figure 10. Protest in 1997 with image of Kamahl, a young Australian student killed in the Dili Massacre. Photo courtesy Australians in Solidarity with Indonesia and East Timor.

Muslims, and Catholicism provided a powerful point of cultural differentiation. In addition, the Church openly promoted the maintenance of East Timorese cultural traditions in the face of the onslaught of "Indonesianization" policies. In the context of the enormous suffering forced upon the population, many people found great comfort in the meanings they were and are able to derive from Catholic Christianity.

In the diaspora, everyday religious practice was not quite as universally adopted, but Catholicism was still an extremely important dimension to the collective meanings and practices of the community. The levels of participation ranged from a committed core group of practicing Catholics to those who, although not deeply religious generally, still attached a distinctly Christian meaning to the sufferings of East Timor, especially during protests and the St. Mary's mass. Many people I have spoken with see East Timor's independence as resulting from the intervention of "God."

There were so many deaths in East Timor. I truly believe the power for independence come from God, not from human beings. (Felismina, 40)

There were several committed groups in the community specifically focused on just such an intervention. On the 8th day of every month, for five years, a group of East Timorese women and a Josephite nun visited the tomb of Mary MacKillop to pray for East Timor's freedom and the safety of family and friends. The prayer vigil would last for more than an hour, with the women kneeling before the tomb. Kneeling is a symbol of humility, but also evokes embodied suffering, interpolating the kneeler into the moral economy of discomfort and affect.

When I first met Sister Josephine she would pray, she said she wanted to place East Timor in Mary MacKillop's care—on her tomb. She believed that Timor's independence would be through Mary MacKillop. So that is how I started to have a devotion to Mary MacKillop. The sisters took me to her tomb alone. Then I kept visiting the tomb. Then she asked me to get the old ladies to go with me to the tomb and we started to pray to Mary MacKillop for her miracle for Timor to be independent. So then I started the elder group—maybe 6 or 10 or something. We used to go every month on the 8th. She died on the 8th of August. Every month we went. Then it grew bigger and bigger. That is how it started. So I was involved when the Bishop came the first time. We went to the Mary MacKillop tomb with him. Then the sisters took me to different Churches, and social justice groups—to talk about East Timor. (Nancy, mid-50s)

On the eve of the referendum vote in 1999 this group, along with around one hundred East Timorese community members, congregated at the Mary MacKillop Chapel in Sydney's western suburbs for a midnight mass and an all-night prayer vigil to pray for a peaceful and successful vote. The mass included a procession where the entire congregation filed one by one to light candles for East Timor. Prayer and singing lasted throughout the night. They filed out at dawn and made their way across town to the voting place. Such demonstrations of the connection between religious faith and the will for peace in East Timor continued in subsequent protests against the post-referendum violence that broke out in East Timor. Many East Timorese joined protests, prayer vigils, and sit-ins outside the Indonesian embassy in Sydney. Those who joined the vigil outside the embassy, which lasted some weeks, brought candles, held prayer sessions, sang, and sat with crucifixes in protest at the violence.

It is clear that religion permeated the struggle in many different ways, from practical assistance to the symbolic framing of the morality of the struggle to actual protest events in which the boundary between religious ritual and political protest is blurred. These and other performative protest strategies might be characterized as active processes that contribute to the creation of a kind of "somatic belonging."

The creation of a somatic belonging is illustrated well by Anne-Marie Fortier (1999, 47; 2000, 133) who relates her experience and response to her own migration and sense of displacement. Fortier recounts how, following her migration from France to Canada, she found a sense of belonging in a Catholic church in Montreal, despite having renounced her Catholicism years before.[6] She found "homely comfort" in the "habitual space" of the church and its rituals. Fortier reports that she was experiencing some deep-seated sense of selfhood that had sedimented into her body. The reappropriation of these bodily rituals became a strategy for creating a feeling of embodied belonging. As Fortier points out, memory and cultural identity are deeply embodied and always incorporated through iterated actions.

Catholic ritual, as has been well documented (see, e.g., Mellor and Shilling 1997), is a deeply embodied practice. The coupling of religion with trauma and the homeland struggle in the East Timorese case can be seen as a process by which a sympathetic community is created, and which in turn articulates with exile identities. The embodied nature of Catholic ritual provides a potent ground of sensorial identification for a traumatized community, especially through the invocation of the powerful imagery of Christ's tortured body. The central symbol of Christianity is the figure of the tortured man. Stephen Moore argues that "God's forgiveness is extended to the sinner over the mutilated body of his Son" (quoted in Axel 2001, 147). The torture of a man's body is the expiation that puts the world right. In the East Timorese case, identification with the moral suffering of Christ becomes enhanced through the creation of the kinds of sensual solidarities which often manifest in collective ritual and crowd processes.

Mellor and Shilling argue that Catholicism harnesses the sensual volatility aroused through ritual and carnival to stimulate "effervescent" encounters with the "sacred," to encourage collective identification that binds people together in a co-presence (1997, 29). In this way, the "sacralisation of embodiment is simultaneously the creation of a sacred, communal expression of sociality." This emphasizes that "individuals are not bound together simply by shared beliefs, but through effervescent experience of having bodies which become incorporated into the Body of Christ" (67). Extending Michel Maffesoli's argument that such sensual solidarities are a process of people "keeping warm together," Mellor and Shilling argue that the recognition of the sacred is more than "keeping warm together"; it is also the "heat" of getting "burnt" together and even "burning" others (176).[7] In this way, an important sympathetic relationship is created between the sensorial community of religious East Timorese and the idea of Christ as the ultimate representative of moral suffering. The once isolating rupture of unruly pain and emotion associated with individual trauma becomes part of a corporeal, sensorial collective narrative, which is made meaningful through sympathetic identification with the suffering of Christ. It in turn becomes channeled into the warmth of a moral "community of suffering" (Werbner 1997a, 235), and offers a sense of martyrdom in the name of the struggle, thus giving a sense of repaying that enormous debt owed to the homeland.

Reminiscent of Martin and Kryst's work on American pilgrims to a site where apparitions of the Virgin Mary are said to appear (1998, 224–25), this is not merely a process of identification with certain representations. Rather, the performance is *enacted* and *lived* through the experience of the participant's body. The enactment of these dramas in places other than the everyday, their spatial specialness, adds to their potency. In this context, such analysis should be extended beyond Catholic ritual to incorporate the highly ritualized protest crowds, and also forms of ritual performance such as street theater and even singing and East Timorese cultural dance in the protests. Drawing on Bachelard, Kalpana Ram (2000, 8) argues that dance and singing have the capacity to create an embodied sharing among the audience, tapping into the "aliveness" of the performance, to give presence to an entire set of emotions that are somehow inherent in the patterns of performance.

Song, Dance, and Theater: Performing Affection for the Homeland

Like the Church, East Timorese choirs were a ubiquitous presence throughout the protest movement. The choirs were comprised of mostly young East Timorese under twenty-five who were often the children of parents active in the movement. The songs are mostly in Tetum, with the lyrics a mixture of strong nationalist sentiment, nostalgic longing for the landscape of East Timor, and religious messages. A few songs have become especially popular favorites at rallies, protests and other gatherings, and one in particular, "O Hele O,"[8] became an anthem for the movement. Below are some lyrics to other popular protest songs.

Come Back
Come back to your land!
Come back to your land!
Come back to your land, truly yours
Timor is our land, yours and mine.
O come and return to Timor Loro Sa'e
Timor Loro Sa'e, our Timor.

Every Night
Every night, every night
I sit by myself,
I think of my homeland,
My own homeland Timor Dili
I called out, I called out
I called out to you;
No one answered
Your feelings are my feelings
Are always there.
My beloved ones and my suffering
That's what is there.
Return to me with happiness,
My precious beloved ones.

There were two main choirs in Sydney. The earlier one was the youth choir Hananau Kore A'an (Singing for Freedom), a mixture of mostly younger asylum seekers who had arrived in the 1990s. Formed in 1995–96, the choir grew out of an earlier youth theater project, Steps to Freedom, where some youth developed performances to illustrate their experiences in East Timor, and of leaving and coming to Australia. The choir performed at both East Timorese and non-East Timorese gatherings and at political rallies. The second choir was the Mary MacKillop East Timorese Singers, formed early in 1997. The stated mission of that choir was to celebrate East Timorese culture by singing at religious and cultural gatherings using mainly Tetum. All the members of the choir were East Timorese. They performed at rallies and community gatherings and recorded a CD. Their repertoire had a more religious focus than Hananau Kore A'an, with a sister from the Mary MacKillop Institute in the role of choir leader. Both choirs were disbanded following independence.

Highly melodramatic performances were very common. A typical example was a performance in 1996 that formed part of a larger East Timorese performance program and art exhibition that toured Australia. Called Tuba Rai Metin (Firmly Gripping the Earth), it was performed and exhibited at the Museum of Contemporary Art in Sydney, and at the Casula Powerhouse Arts Centre in western Sydney. As a creative protest event, Tuba Rai Metin was a spectacular success and is one of the most remembered by the community and by solidarity activists. The centerpiece was a life-size replica of a traditional East Timorese lulik house.[9] As part of this performative protest, a famous tais weaver living in Australia was employed to weave a long tais cloth (nearly fifty feet long, by the standard width of about five feet). Painstakingly woven into the black, red, and white tais were the names of all those known to have died in the 12 November Dili Massacre.[10] The weaving was partly done in public to form part of the performance. Once ready, the tais was wrapped around the lulik house, where it remained for the duration of the exhibition.

Following that initial performance, prior to the referendum, this tais was used in all key protests as a central piece of imagery. It was usually carried by the front group of protest marchers and held up to illustrate the number who had died in the massacre. At another large protest, the Dili tais was set up outside the New South Wales Parliament house in Sydney, draped over a giant crucifix, with a sign "In memory of those massacred by the Indonesian Military at Santa Cruz cemetery on November 12, 1991." This tais is one of the most remembered objects from the protest movement in Sydney (Figures 11–13).

Theater performances were also held as part of the Tuba Rai Metin project. Performed by East Timorese youth, the short plays reenacted the Dili massacre. They included the use of replica guns, boys in uniforms representing Indonesian soldiers, and screaming "victims" at the center. At the Museum of Contemporary Art performance, there were also cultural displays of dancing and singing, and a fair-like set up with stalls selling tais cloths, Timorese crafts, and books and videos about the situation in East Timor. Because of its western Sydney location, the Casula Powerhouse performance was the most highly attended by the East Timorese community. Many of the older women in the community attended, with a number dressing up in traditional East Timorese dress. Such plays and performances featuring traumatic stories were commonplace in the Sydney community and formed a central part of the independence movement, functioning as a kind of witnessing technique. In fact, street theater performances about the situation in East Timor were performed regularly at East Timorese protests in Sydney since at least 1984 (Figures 14–17).

The Role of Ritual Objects

Ritual objects were a distinctive feature of the East Timorese struggle in all of the protests. Examples of the ritual objects used are the Dili Massacre tais, crucifixes, other tais cloths, traditional drums, traditional East Timorese ritual objects in churches, memorials made from a crucifix with stones representing the dead, and the life-size model lulik house. In this context, objects are not merely signifiers in the semiotic sense. The context and materiality of ritual objects in protests function as important mnemonic devices which elicit sensory and affective responses from participants. As Nadia Seremetakis argues,

The involuntary circuit of the senses reveals that embodied performance is in part constructed out of the cross-communication of senses and things. . . . The sensory landscape and its meaning-endowed objects bear within them emotional and historical sedimentation that can provoke and ignite gestures, discourses, and acts. (Seremetakis 1996, 7)

Although individual objects carry the sediment of their own history, the combination of objects made use of in the highly dialogical space of protests cross-reference one another, discursively meshing the history of the objects (religious, cultural, connected to family and homeland) with

Figure 11. Weaving the Dili Massacre tais at Casula Powerhouse. Photo courtesy Mary MacKillop Institute of East Timorese Studies.

Figure 12. Dili Massacre tais set up with cross in Sydney. Photo courtesy Mary MacKillop Institute of East Timorese Studies.

Figure 13. Replica lulik house outside the Museum of Contemporary Art in Sydney, as part of Tuba Rai Metin. Note the Dili tais around the house. Photo courtesy Mary MacKillop Institute of East Timorese Studies.

Figure 14. Timorese theater performance as part of Tuba Rai Metin, this time at Casula, near Liverpool. Photo courtesy Mary MacKillop Institute of East Timorese Studies.

Figure 15. East Timorese children at a protest in Sydney around 1991. Photo courtesy Australians in Solidarity with Indonesia and East Timor.

Figure 16. East Timorese street theater at Sydney airport with performers dressed as Indonesian police portraying scenes of police abuse in East Timor.

Figure 17. Street theater scene acting out military abuses. Photo courtesy Australians in Solidarity with Indonesia and East Timor.

the affective connection they arouse in those connected to them, in turn meshing with the overall discourse of the struggle. In the case of the Dili Massacre tais, for example, Timorese refugee bodies and emotions are pulled into the performance through witnessing the very physical, sensuous act of the public display of the Timorese weaver painstakingly weaving into the cloth each of the 400 or so names of those who died in the massacre. In every East Timorese home I visited in Sydney, the tais cloth is the first thing to meet the eye upon entering.

The evocative power of cloth in Southeast Asia is a well-documented form of identity construction (Niessen 1993), and in East Timor it has an especially powerful role in evoking East Timoreseness. Particularly evocative are cloths woven in the traditional back-loom. Produced through the women's bodily suffering during the weaving process, their very materiality evokes this suffering. East Timorese tais have patterns often representing the region in which they were woven, bearing symbols of importance, such as the crocodile, or representing local agriculture. Some patterns also represent the family tree and ancestral stories. Special ones are kept for use at important events such as weddings and exchanged as gifts at important occasions. They are often handed down through generations and many families managed to escape East Timor with their family tais cloths. Following Seremetakis (1996), the cultural meanings of objects such as tais cloths ignite the senses and emotions, provoking a sense of connection to the cloth and its meanings, and crossing over to the context of the Dili Massacre and the homeland struggle.[11] This in turn connects bodies, memories, and senses into an affective relationship via the objects, to the cause. Similarly, as David Parkin argues:

under conditions of rapid and sometimes violent flight and dispersal, private mementoes may take the place of interpersonal relations as a depository of sentiment and cultural knowledge. . . . They are like ancestral memorials encoding continuity between and across the generations. (Parkin 1999, 318)

In the East Timorese case, the use of such material objects in political protests has a dual function, at once encoding and igniting continuity with family and cultural traditions in East Timor, and translating this generational continuity into the East Timorese national imaginary.

Trauma and Witnessing Strategies

The use of distressing images of torture and trauma was a central and deeply moving aspect of the independence struggle. There is no doubt that it had a profound public impact. Coupled with strong solidarity support, the images of human rights abuses were a key to the success of the campaign. For example, the worldwide broadcast of the film footage of the Dili Massacre, smuggled out of East Timor by a British journalist, is widely held to have been the major turning point in the independence struggle. In the years following the broadcast of this groundbreaking footage, the campaign built on this increased awareness of human rights abuses through the use of graphic material aimed at shocking the world into recognizing the truth of what was happening in East Timor. For example, there were several protests that featured detailed photographs of East Timorese victims of torture. Displayed on large boards set up in prominent city locations, the photographs featured horrific and extremely graphic images of Indonesian soldiers inflicting various forms of torture on East Timorese captives, of women being gang-raped by soldiers, and of dead bodies with appalling torture wounds.

A number of the stories and images featured elements of religious sacrilege. One particular example published in one of the major books on East Timor and widely distributed throughout the movement was a photograph of the dead body of a young girl (Aubrey 1998), lying naked in a concrete torture cell, covered in cuts and horrific wounds. Various profanities written in Bahasa Indonesia are written on her body, and a crucifix has been drawn on her stomach. Stuck to the wall just above her head is a picture of Jesus Christ, and at her feet is a sign in Bahasa, paralleling the death of Christ on the Cross, which translates as "If you really are God, come down and bring her back to life." The photograph is part of a series that were widely distributed, showing two young girls being subjected to rape by groups of Indonesian soldiers, having cigarettes being burned onto them and nails being hammered into their bodies. Shocking as they are, these images were just a small number among the many hundreds I have seen used in the campaign.

Such images were circulated throughout the world among solidarity supporters and the East Timorese diaspora on Web sites, in newsletters, and at exhibitions. Some were also published to illustrate a number of books on the political history of East Timor, which were widely read within the movement. Many of the images, videos, tapes, and reports of torture and severe human rights abuses were smuggled out of East Timor through the Timorese clandestine resistance movement, at great risk to those involved. The powerful impact of these images cannot be denied. Such methods are common among movements as diverse as the Tamil Tigers and Sikh nationalists. They perhaps have their roots in the "witnessing" that took place following the liberation of the Nazi concentration camps of World War II.

The influence of post-Holocaust techniques of commemoration and witnessing is also evident in publications such as the two widely known collections of East Timorese "witness stories." Michelle Turner's *Telling East Timor* (1992) was the most important and best known, while Rebecca Winters's *Buibere* (1999) also had quite an impact. The Turner book is very well known in the solidarity movement and the East Timorese community, and the author herself was well known to Sydney's East Timorese people. As the granddaughter of an Australian World War II veteran who fought in East Timor, Turner was inspired to write the book as a gesture toward "repaying the debt" many of these veterans felt Australia owed the people of East Timor. The book was researched in Australia and in East Timor. It consists of a compilation of oral histories from East Timorese people relating their experiences of war and occupation over the years—from World War II to the Indonesian invasion. The stories are extremely graphic and deeply moving, detailing in a very personal way the full extent of the horrors faced by those living under the Indonesian occupation. The book was produced with the assistance of some members of the Sydney East Timorese community. Interestingly, one member of the community told me (and requested anonymity) that she had heard that those telling their experiences to the author exaggerated a few of the stories. There was obviously an awareness of the political currency of these terrible stories. Also, because of a fear of the Indonesian military it was difficult for Turner to meet people in East Timor who felt able to tell their stories, so the East Timorese contributing in Australia felt that they had a responsibility to provide material that would make a great impact.

The circulation and consumption of such imagery is both bodily and performative. The use of such torture imagery, combined with bodily and ritualistic commemorative practices such as the use of Catholic ritual in protests is reminiscent of the Filipino *payson* form, which Vicente Rafael refers to as necropolitics (2000, 2002). The *payson*, described by Filipino historian Reynaldo Ileto (1979), is a vernacular form of Catholic ritual performance surrounding Christ's passion, appropriated to promote Filipino revolutionary politics. According to Rafael, the *payson* performance centers thematically on "innocent lives forced to undergo humiliation at the hands of alien forces; of unjustified deaths both shocking and public; of massive responses of pity and prayer that would, in mobilizing alternative communities of resistance, finally drive away forces of oppression and pave the way for some kind of liberation" (2000, 209–10).

The use of testimony, commemoration, and witnessing such as the *Telling East Timor* collection, the display and circulation of torture images, and the collective commemoration of traumatic events such as the Dili Massacre are significant means of bodily and affective cooptation. For the participant, the appeal of such acts of public remembering lies in the way they permit a personal bodily and emotional connection with events of which they were not directly part. In this way, an event is made "to feel more like a memory" to the participant, by borrowing the memories of others (Engels quoted in Humphrey 2000, 10). This characteristic makes such practices highly successful spaces for achieving a sense of intensification (Hage 2002) in participants to enhance a sense of belonging to the homeland and the struggle, and therefore repaying the moral debt owed by those who fled.

In this way, hearing traumatic testimony, viewing horrendous images of torture, commemorating massacres, and so on not only work to "move" the wider community emotionally into action for the East Timor cause. They also function to retraumatize the East Timorese community in a way that taps into the bodily nature of trauma, and work to rescript their narratives of self into affective identification with the cause. Most important, it is the convergence of the bodily nature of trauma with the bodily dimensions of torture images, drama, performance, ritual, and images of the tortured Christ that generates the most powerful sense of affective belonging and identification with what is being witnessed, commemorated or testified to.

The effectiveness of all these protest strategies as spaces for intensification is enhanced by the fact that they are bodily performances that bring the participant into a bodily and affective relationship with the struggle, and therefore to share in East Timor's fate. The symptoms of forced displacement and the effects of either directly experiencing severe traumas, or being closely related to those who have, have a great impact on the level of affective intensity such practices induce. Partaking in strategies of intensification such as protest activities has therefore had a enormously important role in creating a space for social belonging in the moral economy of East Timor and pacifying the kind of migration guilt Hage describes (2002). For East Timorese individuals who have suffered, and continue to suffer, the effects of trauma, affective investment in the protest movement provides a mode through which the renarration of traumatic memory can be translated from meaningless terror and pain into something meaningful. It gives a sense that a person's trauma is no longer a private pain, becoming instead part of the greater struggle of East Timor and the universal Catholic imaginary of martyrdom.

Trauma, Affect, Narrative

All members of the East Timorese refugee diaspora have experienced trauma in one form or another. They might be categorized, therefore, as a "traumatized community." Every person I interviewed had experienced traumatic events, had lost loved ones during the occupation, or was close to those who had. To illustrate the extent to which such memories permeate the community, these are just a few examples taken from my interviews.

Julieta remembers being a four-year-old and along with her family being caught by FRETILIN during the civil war and narrowly escaping death. She remembers being caught in a gun battle. She remembers walking for more than a week through the mountains to escape to West Timor, and the endless thirst and near starvation. She tells of the sadness at losing her brother when they fled, and subsequently learning that he starved in the mountains in 1978 during the famine. Paulo tells of his recollection of being a thirteen-year-old and the terror of watching an Indonesian soldier parachute into his backyard during the invasion, and remembers a FRETILIN soldier holding a gun to his head, only to be rescued by a cousin moments before the trigger would have been pulled. Fatima tells of discovering a schoolgirl by a river. The child was near death, torn apart and disfigured from being gang-raped by Indonesian soldiers. She remembers the night the soldiers came and took her brother away, never to be seen again, and remembers holding the body of her best friend, shot by Indonesian soldiers in front of her at a protest. Maria tells of the terrible task she had of comforting the children of a close friend. Her friend's husband, who was planning to join her in Australia soon, had been brutally murdered by Indonesian soldiers. One day after hearing the news, the woman hung herself, unable to cope with her grief. Felismina tells of the horror at seeing bodies washing up on the beach in Dili, and the never ceasing torment of her memories of the time she was horrifically tortured and raped over several weeks in detention for allegedly colluding with the independence fighters.

I could easily relate twenty more such stories, so common are they. These individuals carry the weight of these experiences with them each and every day. I don't mean to repeat such stories as a gratuitous shock tactic. What I want to illustrate is the extent to which such stories permeate the very fabric of the Timorese refugee diaspora in Australia. They float around, whispered in explanation for "strange behavior"; they live beneath the surface among friends and family, rarely spoken about, especially in the first person, but all in the community know about such stories or have stories of their own.

Exacerbating the primary trauma, the effects of trauma and loss are often experienced more intensely under the kinds of conditions of isolation, loss, and displacement that forced migration entails. An example of such trauma is illustrated by Hoffman (interviewed in Zournazi 1998), who relates her parents' reexperience of trauma in the process of migration to Canada. As Holocaust survivors, Hoffman felt that her parents embodied, in very real ways, the horror and suffering of that period in history. As new arrivals in Canada, they relived these formative experiences in a bodily way, through the isolation and shock of immigration. Hoffman reports that her parents felt extremes of insecurity, anxiety, depression, and loss. In Poland they were able to cope because of a broader sense of spatial, familial, cultural, and sensory belonging. Migration reignited the feelings because of the profound isolation and loss they experienced at that time.

As with many children of Holocaust survivors (see Goertz 1998), many younger Timorese born in Australia, even if they have never been to East Timor, experience what we might term "trauma by proxy," growing up in the difficult context of living with parents who had suffered and in the shadow of constant reminders of the situation in East Timor. Moreover, large numbers of those in the diaspora had close friends and family left in East Timor and there was always the constant worry about their safety. People in Sydney were reluctant to criticize the Indonesian regime for fear of brutal reprisals against family back in East Timor. What is more, constant new arrivals fleeing East Timor served as an ongoing reminder of what was happening there. As one young person pointed out,

You can see it in their eyes—the fear. Whenever I meet someone who had just arrived from Timor I feel very sad, it reminds me of what is happening to my people and my country. (young person quoted in Timorese Australian Council Settlement Report, Rawsthorne 1994)

Trauma, then, comes in many forms, through direct experience in East Timor, through stories of the suffering of family and friends, through the experience of loss and displacement, through the guilt of fleeing, leaving loved ones behind, through ongoing worry about the fate of those who remained, through seeing constant new arrivals in the community freshly escaped from the horrors of what was happening, and more broadly, through living day to day where such stories permeate the very basis of family and community life.

The effects of such trauma are many. According to the trauma counselors and social workers who work with the East Timorese community, trauma frequently turns to anger or is turned inward. There are extremely high levels of domestic violence in the East Timorese community, not only by husbands against wives, but by mothers against children and sibling against sibling. Basic trust structures break down. There are high levels of anger, suspicion, and distrust within the community. There are several groups with long-held hostility toward one another (see Tang 1999; Rawsthorne 1994). Minor disagreements frequently turn into resentments where the parties won't speak for years to come. For many, any sense of future or hope is lost, resulting in high levels of poverty, unemployment, depression, and general sense of atrophy. And there are many cases of post-traumatic stress. The sad irony of the East Timorese diaspora is that one of the principal characteristics of the community is the extent to which it is permeated by mistrust, disunity, and anger. With the many fractures and simmering disputes at the grounded day-to-day community level, community belonging and a sense of shared purpose were to be found mainly in the homeland cause. Here, the angers of everyday life could be set aside for the more abstract and comforting moral community of exile.

Theorizing Trauma and Narrative

At the center of homeland projects is a sense of imagined community, on the one hand, and, on the other, individuals whose sense of self, self-narratives, and affective identification have some kind of "fit" with this identity. At the simplest level, identities are the stories we tell to, and of, ourselves. Work on post-traumatic stress disorder (PTSD) (Caruth 1995b) has shown that one of the principal characteristics of trauma is the way the traumatic event somehow ruptures the narrative self.

Although there is currently much debate about the over-diagnosis of PTSD (see, e.g., Bracken 1998; Summerfield 2001), there are nevertheless some generally recognized symptoms often present in survivors of trauma. These are usually delayed responses to the traumatic event and include hallucinations, intrusive thoughts, recurring dreams, thought or behavior that stem from the event, and a feeling of numbness that may have begun at the time of the trauma. They can also include an increased arousal to (and avoidance of) stimuli recalling the event (Caruth 1995a, 4). Caruth argues that the most salient feature centers on the reception of the actual event. The original event is not assimilated or experienced fully at the time, but only belatedly, when it possesses the survivor in the form of traumatic memories. In this way, she argues, the traumatized become themselves the symptom of a history that they cannot entirely possess (5).

The inability to assimilate the experience at the time of the event is a kind of protective response in some ways. However, because it is a protective mechanism, the weight of the trauma is such that the individual is often unable to take control of the memory and make meaning of it at the level of self-narrative, even long after the event. Traumatic memories also shrink time because they are so embodied. Such memories have a "presence" that gives them a feeling of being closer than other memories. In this way, the shrinking of time brings the memories into the immediate present, at least until the memories are narratively integrated. For East Timorese, this in a way can function to bring the homeland ever closer.

Mastering these traumatic memories requires the integration of the event into some kind of meaningful narrative. The telling of the event is one step in this process of renarrating the self. Their particularly bodily and sensory character, however, exacerbates the difficulty of integrating these memories. It is not easy for a trauma survivor to tell in a way that communicates all the complex bodily and sensory dimensions of the experience. The conventions of spoken narrative exclude the possibility of expressing "all there is to say, all that I have felt, all that I saw, felt, smelled, heard," and so on. Charlotte Delbo, a Holocaust survivor (in Culbertson 1995, 2), distinguishes between "sense memory," a kind of "deep memory, and "thinking memory," the rational, ordered, and clear memory of narrative. It is possible to have a sense of the latter when you hear a trauma survivor speaking about the traumatic events in unemotional tones. This presents what Delbo calls "external" memory, which is socially constructed. It skates along the surface of words, engaging only the intellect, not the body's reexperience, which cannot be known in words, only in the body (3). The implication, then, is that the unrepresentability stems not from the extremity of the trauma event, but from the "split between the living of an event and the available forms of representation with/in which the event can be experienced" (Van Alphen 1999, 27).

It is difficult to find words that carry the full somatic, sensory, "skinly" feeling I want to convey when writing of bodily and sensory experiences. Without implying that these are beyond representation, they are nonetheless beyond the realms of spoken expression. I have therefore employed italics in the text at points throughout this chapter, to indicate where I want the reader not just to read but to "feel"—on the skin, in the senses, inside the body, in the stomach, in the bones—psychologically, proprioceptively, proxemically. Imagine the difference between "Xaviér was afraid," and "Xaviér was *afraid.*" It is the difference between just reading that Xaviér was afraid and taking that in as an abstract piece of information, and actually feeling, with your whole body, what it might be like for Xaviér to be *afraid*. In this sense, affect is communicative. So in the interview with Xaviér his fear was communicated to me through his bodily responses, which in turn caused an affective response in myself and others in the room—hearts racing, stomachs tightening—in turn invoking a sense of affective empathy with him.

With this discussion of the body, trauma, and narrative in mind, I want to reflect back for a moment on Xaviér's story, introduced at the beginning of the chapter, to consider the particular conjunction of trauma, strategies of affective intensification, belonging, and struggle. I would like to suggest that Xaviér's desire to set up a youth theater group is not just about wanting to educate East Timorese youth about history. Nor does he simply want to organize youth activities as a community activity. Because East Timorese identity is a *bodily knowledge*, what he hopes for, and what I think comes through in his words, is that he would like East Timorese youth to share, to live, to feel, to experience through their bodies, the past that he carries with him, a past, as we have seen, that has such immanent somatic presence for him. For Xaviér ("you know, it's slipping away from our everyday life") there seems to be something isolating—in a very physical, sensory way—about young East Timorese who have not experienced the war, and who "know" abstractly, but don't "know" in the way that he does. During the struggle, a kind of somatic community was enacted through protest performances and religious vigils, which many people like Xaviér have actually missed.

There are two major impulses driving Xaviér and by implication others like him. First, Xaviér has a need to reintegrate his trauma into the wider meaning of the homeland struggle. This is an outcome of the isolating nature of traumatic memory, the need for some kind of meaningful reintegration of that experience, and the drive of the "migration guilt" introduced earlier. Second, he wants his memories to be shared, to create a sense of belonging to a community that somatically shares his isolating experience. Performance, singing and ritual in particular, taps into and ignites a sense of collective somatic belonging among participants.

In this way, and this is the core of my argument, the hyper-performative and bodily nature of many of the core independence activities—drama, singing, dance, religious icons, using religious spaces for the cause, and commemorative strategies, torture images, and stories of trauma—provided a compelling milieu in which experiences of trauma were rendered meaningful in a very embodied way. One of the important outcomes of trauma is the way that it ruptures the self, ruptures the narrative of memory. For Xaviér, theater provides an effective (and affective) means through which his trauma can be bodily invoked, reexperienced, and rescripted in a way that deisolates him, allowing him to share, or renarrativize, or reintegrate his individual pain with the larger homeland project.

For this reason, the sensorial character of traumatic memories, and indeed bodily memories generally, might be characterized as raw emotional nerve endings that lie in the body, vulnerable to ignition in contexts that tap into this extralinguistic realm of sense memory. The corporeal and sensorial nature of the performance repertoires of the East Timorese struggle has functioned as mnemonic devices that induce the bodily sensations of traumatic memory in members of the refugee diaspora and funnel them into the discursive framework of the homeland cause, thus rescripting traumatic memories into a broader collective project. For example, the physical act of young people acting out scenes of military abuses, or the physical and emotional effects of viewing images of torture and then walking in a protest carrying a crucifix, singing songs of longing for the homeland, all tap into powerful yet undefined bodily memories of trauma, creating a powerful affective catharsis that meshes with other bodies in the crowd and is actively invested in and pulled into the fight for the homeland. Coming back to Hage's notion of "intensification," for refugees suffering intensely from migration guilt, the affective pull of such processes that tap into the full force of bodily memory can also offer a sense of satisfying redemption. That is, these protest strategies create both an affective and a moral pull toward the homeland, which is satisfying in many ways for the participant, because these processes also function as spaces in which the refugee can be implicated in the homeland through engaging actively in modes of affective intensification.

The Community of Listeners

In Chapter 3 I discussed the mutually constitutive nature of symbiotic alliances between the East Timorese community and solidarity supporters. In that discussion I pointed out that the East Timorese political project in Australia did not operate on "neutral" territory, that the relationship with solidarity groups and international discourses played an important role in shaping the struggle for independence.

Similar processes are at work in the issues discussed in this chapter. The protest strategies outlined here can generally be defined as testimonial, witnessing, and commemorating techniques. The important point is that these are always "heard" by a community of listeners and that this "listening" always takes place within a cultural frame. Certain codes and narrative forms will have resonance for certain listeners. If testimony takes place in the context of a political project, then those aspects which achieve most resonance with the audience of "listeners" will be those which achieve the greatest effect. In other words, retelling stories, especially stories of trauma, requires sympathetic interlocutors.

These are an important set of ideas for understanding the impact of the political techniques discussed in this chapter. Antze and Lambek (1996) make the significant point that the right to establish authoritative versions of testimony never rests with the individual alone. In order for a survivor to reintegrate the memories through meaningful narrative, there needs to be a process of "witnessing" by a community of "listeners." Meaning is social. Therefore, testimony or narratives are meaningful in the social and cultural context of those who "hear." As Humphrey (2000) points out, testimony is always engendered by the cultural milieu in which the witnessing occurs. Remembering, telling, commemorating, and witnessing are therefore always constrained by conventions. Who is hearing, who is validating what is told and the messages contained in the commemoration? What kinds of "ears" are listening? How do these shape the retelling?

In the East Timorese case, the important communities of listeners were the solidarity movement, the Catholic church, and the broader Australian "listening" public, all of whom needed to be present for the struggle to succeed. These groups provided meaning frameworks or enabling discourses that "heard" certain kinds of narratives and were responsive to certain kinds of identities. It does seem that they were most receptive to a certain kind of East Timorese diasporic identity that emphasized the suffering of exile as a particularly moral state of being. This community of listeners offered a very particular set of narrative possibilities. This is an especially important point because of the prominence of the political struggle, religious discourse, and solidarity support, coupled with the bodily and affective nature of Timorese protest and the fact that there were few other communicative outlets for the diaspora.

It could be argued that these listeners shaped the ways in which members of the diaspora made meaning of their experiences of trauma, their status as exiles, and their relationship to the homeland. These enabling discourses filtered the reexperience of trauma and the flow narratives, into which these memories are reintegrated into meaningful "fictions of self." Indeed, these narratives give meaning to life—"who am I, where have I come from, where am I going, how has my past caused my future, what is the meaning of past events in the course of my life, how are these valued in the world, what is the meaning of the 'me' who has suffered this trauma?" That is, such discourses frame the moral path of the refugee's future. They also shape what might be termed *trajectories of hope*.

For East Timorese in the diaspora, this moral path leads firmly toward East Timor, and therefore invests absolute moral authority in those who remain as exiles, futures resolutely trained on the homeland.

Victims are frequently objectified and homogenized in contemporary Western societies, masking the reality that the experience of trauma is context-dependent. The iconographic "victim" often becomes a politicized, commodified category (Humphrey 2000, 23). As Sturken (1999, 241) and others have shown, during the twentieth century in the West, trauma victims such as war veterans and Holocaust survivors came to carry enormous cultural weight and were awarded a great deal of moral authority for their experience. East Timorese in Australia were invariably portrayed as representatives of the struggle, invoked as iconographic victims, freedom fighters, or representatives of Timorese indigenous culture.

In many ways, solidarity groups were the key driving force behind the public face of the Timorese community in Sydney, and they placed great moral value on the involvement of East Timorese people in the struggle. It seemed that to be considered a genuinely good and committed East Timorese, you had to be involved in the struggle. I heard a number of stories of activists berating members of the East Timorese community for not being involved enough. In one instance a solidarity activist actually visited one of the East Timorese organizations in Western Sydney to insist that they had a responsibility to become more active in the struggle. To be admonished thus was very troubling for those East Timorese who chose not to be involved. Although equally well meaning, Catholic solidarity groups often invoked similarly naive frames of representation. Here, East Timorese were constructed as Christ-like in their pious innocence and suffering. They were spoken of as small, gentle, cultured people, represented as "gentle singing Pacific islanders," inherently peaceful and good, culturally pure underneath the layers sullied by centuries of colonization. This was also a particularly gendered discourse: wives, mothers, daughters, children were the ultimate icons of moral victimhood. It seems fair to say that East Timorese refugees in the diaspora were only invoked as a means to support the cause.

East Timorese in Australia were rarely represented as full human beings who had lives and families in Sydney, who had dreams for the future, who might wish to settle there. These images would have undermined the power of the political cause. Instead, East Timorese were invoked as representatives of the nation of East Timor, as representatives of the group whose sole aim it was to free the homeland and return. East Timorese in the struggle had to show that they were worthy of outside support, that they were representatives of those suffering oppression by the occupier, that they were innocent and peaceful victims. While I am not arguing in the least that these things were not true, the political struggle drew on powerful discourses such as those described to give resonance for the community of listeners. These discourses invested particular meaning and worth in remaining culturally pure and oriented toward exile. In this way, the struggle had a homogenizing effect on East Timorese identities in Australia.

In making this point, I am by no means dismissing the genuine support offered by Australian solidarity and church supporters. They consistently demonstrated real empathy with the suffering of East Timor's people, and their support was central to the success of the cause. Most East Timorese are grateful to them for their tireless efforts, and these groups continue to do useful and important work in fundraising and other charitable activities in East Timor. However, I argue that the discourses that were useful in advancing the independence struggle and were important to its ultimate success also had unintended effects on the ways East Timoreseness is imagined and experienced by East Timorese refugees living in Australia.

*   *   *

I have argued in this chapter that the affective pull toward the East Timor homeland results from the traumatized nature of the community and the way the struggle was conducted in Australia. The ritual and dramatic form of this protest, and its liberal use of dramatic performances and commemoration of traumatic events, created a kind of embodied connection with the political struggle. The discourses of the struggle provided an enormously meaningful narrative for those who have been traumatized by the situation in East Timor. Rather than the emotionally isolating experience of unspoken trauma, the dramatic playing out of trauma through the protest movement invested traumatic events with meaning, which tied members of the community into a warmness of sensual, affective collectivity with a cause.

Being heard was deeply empowering for many East Timorese people, and it was heartening for them to have public recognition for their cause and to share their pain with others. To be part of a strong protest movement gave a sense of power and action. I do not mean to deny any of this. Yet, although it has been all these things, although it may well have been a kind of healing practice, it also created a very specific moral "East Timoreseness." Affect and morality are analytically different; affect operates at the level of the individual and morality at the level of community. The fact that the two get connected in these processes is what makes the pull so strong. So while spaces of affective intensification are useful to appease the guilt of migration, to give a sense of repaying the debt owed to the homeland, the movement was such that East Timorese generally were able to engage in available modes of intensification, in this case the strategies of the independence struggle. Thus, the modes of intensification, the appeasement of guilt, make a person feel closer to the homeland in a *particular way* and offer only *certain* moral trajectories of belonging. The discourses of the struggle were and are not "value free." They invested significant moral value in East Timorese remaining as temporary exiles. The struggle for Timorese independence relied upon the support of the East Timorese diaspora, a "call to arms," if you like, requiring East Timorese refugees to repay their moral debt to their homeland.

All this had very specific implications for the way in which the community in Australia imagined itself in place. Now that East Timor is independent, it also has vast implications once the difficult realities of actually returning home are faced. These are issues I pick up on and examine in more depth in the final chapter. In the following chapter, I move away from the public discourses of Timoreseness toward exploring the messy reality of quotidian Timoreseness. As I will show, the homogeneous constructed political identity discussed in this chapter belies the complex, hybrid, shifting, and often contradictory patterns of Timorese identities in Sydney.

Chapter 5
Locating East Timoreseness in Australia: Layers of Hybridity, Anchored and Enmeshed

> We have a cue to explore the movement from culture to multiculture and the other openings created by culture's routine and irreverent translocation: something that is all the more precious now not only because it repudiates the claims of raciology but also because it is incompatible with the arcane desires of the butterfly collectors of alterity who prefer their cultures integral and like their differences to remain absolute.
> —Paul Gilroy (2000)

I'd like to open with a brief look at Fatima's story because it highlights many of the issues I explore in this chapter. Fatima is a young East Timorese woman in her early twenties whom I interviewed in 2000. Her parents fled East Timor to Portugal in 1976, and Fatima was born there in 1978. Of her five siblings, only one was born in East Timor. She arrived in Australia in early 1993. Her parents are well known and very politically active in the community, and her mother, father, and elder brother all have a fervent wish to return to East Timor as soon as it is practical. She has been studying international law at a university in Sydney and worked for a period as a community worker with an East Timorese community organization. After her arrival in Australia, Fatima became involved in an East Timorese dance and cultural group performing dances at protest events, and she also actively attended protest events with her family.

The most striking thing about Fatima is the extent to which she feels and values her Portugueseness. She is troubled that she is not recognized as Portuguese in Australia. Portugal is where Fatima feels she belongs, and the place to which she is most culturally attuned. Fatima explained to me that her identity was less questioned in Portugal. She took comfort in being able to say she was born in Portugal and felt that her identity was less confusing there because people knew by her looks that she had East Timorese background. In Australia, however, she feels that because of her dark-skinned "Asian" appearance she is not able to say that she is Portuguese, and feels a certain emptiness in being denied this recognition of her Portugueseness. As she says:

I think more and more in Australia I feel like I can't say that I'm Portuguese. Because there are a lot of different cultural backgrounds. And they see me as what they see—like I'm from Asia. In Portugal it was different. Um . . . they knew that I was from East Timorese background. But because of my accent they could see that I was born in Portugal. Like that person who said—oh "that's ok—you were born here. That's ok. You are Portuguese." . . . In Portugal it is more acceptable to say it. But when I come here it is such a variety and they see me as what they see . . . like Asia—Asia—Asia.

Fatima explained to me that she actually has "Indian," "Chinese," "Portuguese," "Indigenous," and "some other Asian" "in" her. Her mother's side is a mixture of Chinese and Indian, and her father's side Portuguese and indigenous Timorese. However, she experiences the pressure of being over identified as "Asian" in Australia quite negatively, so much so that she pushes to the back of her mind those other possible identities, such as Indianness and Chineseness, in favor of Portugueseness.

Fatima's hybridity is not a free-flowing place of creative cultural exchange, as hybrid identities are often made out to be. Instead, her "inbetweenness" gives her a distinct sense of insecurity and disorientation. She expresses this as a sense of profound emptiness:

How can I explain this? How could I claim [East Timor] as my home when I was not born there? But when people ask me where I was from—I say that I'm Portuguese . . . I'm totally like contradicting myself that you know—I'm saying that [East Timor] is my homeland [but] when people ask me where I'm from I say that I'm Portuguese. And the fact that people say that I'm not East Timorese because I was not born there in Timor—and that I'm not Portuguese because I don't look like Portuguese you know its like two different things—extremes just pushing pushing against each other—and there I am in the middle and I don't even know where I stand you know? It's like just—I'm empty.

Moreover, perhaps because of the way East Timoreseness under the political cause has been defined by indigeneity, connection by birth to the land, and indigenous culture, she also feels that it is difficult for her to claim an outright East Timoreseness.

I know I definitely can't say that I'm East Timorese because I was not born there and I'm stealing the rights from other people who were born there.

Ironically, she also seems very aware that her *situation* in Australia, that is, the way that her ethnicity is *situated* within Australian ethnic relations, forces her into a certain identity—East Timoreseness.

When people ask me that question [what is your background?]—I always go "Portuguese." And then they always come with "But . . ." So it seems like—even though they don't say "but"—I feel myself like saying—I have to say that I'm Timorese.

Fatima's story demonstrates that East Timoreseness is not simply a birthright. There are several identity possibilities for Fatima, and those available to her, to a large extent, depend upon the context and a range or combination of discourses in that context that allow or exclude certain of those possibilities. In other words, identity performances depend on contexts of reception—for example, between Lisbon versus Sydney. If she went to Thailand, for instance, she might be expected to be "Indonesian." These context-related constraints are also about embodiment and physical stereotypes. As Gillian Bottomley has argued, identities "are the dialectical interplay of self-identification and identification by others, and of perceptions and structural forces" (quoted in Noble, Poynting, and Tabar 1999, 31).[1] Moreover, even within the category "East Timoreseness" there is a range of ways this is understood and experienced by different individuals, influenced by many intersecting factors, such as class, cultural capital, age, background, and personality factors.

As opposed to the more overt political identities on which I've concentrated in previous chapters, here I direct my attention to the everyday experience of "relational" East Timoreseness in the lived context of Sydney. Taking Clifford's notion of *location*, defined as "an itinerary rather than a bounded site—a series of encounters and translations" (1997, 11), my aim is to locate East Timoreseness in space and time. As Loretta Baldassar points out,

What is presented to, or perceived by outsiders as a coherent, homogeneous group identity is, in fact, characterized by competing and contrasting discourses and practices both internal to the group (including age, gender, class and personal experience) as well as external to it (including state and government policies, wider community perceptions, media representations and so on). Any community, whether local or national, which posits its own group identity is characterized by contestations of power masked by powerful, malleable and resilient unifying symbols which are often interpreted differently by its own constituents. (1999, 293)

Following Baldassar, I consider some of the power relationships involved, on the one hand, in the struggle between various hybridizing processes brought about by colonization, mobility, education, and migration, and, on the other, the homogenizing impulses of the independence struggle.

Showing the situated nature of a vulnerable refugee community is fraught with difficulty. As a refugee diaspora fighting for independence from 450 years of Portuguese and then brutal Indonesian colonization, the imperative to establish a strong public East Timorese identity could not have been more powerful. Anticolonial struggles throughout history have so often relied on claims to ethnic tradition. In the East Timorese case, individuals in the diaspora have often been caught in the center of several competing claims to East Timoreseness, confused by competing struggles for East Timor's anticolonial fight, the need for identity and belonging in Australia, and the necessity to be accepted and valued as the hybridized East Timorese many have come to be—that is, to be East Timorese in their own way.

The political basis for this chapter is therefore not to show claims of homogeneous East Timoreseness to be fake or manufactured or to demonstrate that East Timorese have simply been "Westernized" or become "Chinese," "Portuguese," or simply "hybrid." Nor is the point to prove that somehow all claims to a single homogeneous East Timorese ethnicity are automatically bad, and that highlighting hybridity offers a liberatory path. As Werbner argues, hybridity is not automatically the panacea for homogenizing ethnic claims. In her view, the measure of how "good" or "bad" an ethnicism is depends on the extent to which members of that group have "the ability (and right) . . . to engage in reflexive self-critical distancing from their own cultural discourses, and hence also to recognize the potential validity of other discourses/communities of language" (1997b, 14). It is not at all clear that this ability is unavailable to the East Timorese represented in this chapter. However, at this important juncture in the community's history, there will certainly be some working out of what it is to be *postcolonial, post exile, East Timorese.* It is in the context of this process—the strategic "working out" of the imagined future of postcolonial East Timoreseness—that I hope this chapter will make its contribution.

Theorizing/Localizing Hybridity

It has been argued for some time that diasporic identities reflect the condition of displacement and require us to disarticulate the link between people, place, and identity, on the one hand, and to rearticulate or resituate these identities within relationships of the new locality, on the other (see Clifford 1994; Gupta and Ferguson 1997; Hall 1990). Moreover, the shift toward localizing identities in this way precipitates a recognition that identities are hybrid. Recognizing the hybridity of diasporic subjects, however, should not take us into the uncritical terrain of "happy hybridity" (Lo 2000, 153), the form of hybridity talk that evacuates all specificities of power, history, and politics. More recent accounts of hybridity remind us that it is imperative to move beyond a naive and unquestioning celebration of the hybrid in order to explore the concrete ways in which hybridity is experienced on the ground. We need to ask, what are the specific regimes of power and boundary marking at work, and what are the different registers and modalities of living hybridity? (see Ang 2001; Werbner and Modood 1997; Bloul 1999; Brah 1996). In other words, we need to consider hybridization as process (Werbner 1997b, 22).

One useful approach is to focus more closely on how hybridity is experienced in the context of shifting boundaries, and on the related concepts of recognition and difference. This approach flags the centrality of understanding how a politics of recognition meshes with lived identities. Nederveen Pieterse (2001) reminds us that boundaries are provisional and their meanings are by no means constant. While some boundaries disappear, change, or shift in meaning, others remain and new ones arise (239). Nederveen Pieterse is pointing to the relationship between boundaries and the politics of recognition, whereby recognition is "a function of the available categories of knowledge and cognitive frames in which self and others are identifiable" (219). Thinking through the implications of encounters between hybridity and boundaries takes us beyond previous conceptualizations of the hybrid that give little sense of the tensions conflicts or contradictions (Lo 2000, 153) that are so often present in intercultural encounters.

The East Timorese case is unique in the extent to which relevant boundaries have changed and are shifting due to a layering of contexts from Portuguese to Indonesian colonization, from life in East Timor, to Portugal, to exile in Australia, to the independence struggle, and finally, to the possibility of return itself. Each of these historical contexts implies boundaries that may have had currency at one time, or in one place, but may have subtly shifted or changed altogether as each new context is layered on. Hybridity, as Fatima's narrative makes clear, comes about as much through slipping between the cracks of these shifting boundaries and codes of recognition, as it does through cultural intermixing.

This theoretical approach requires a careful mapping of the mutually constitutive relationships between cultural and material factors, which combine in different contexts to position or make available certain identities. Members of the East Timorese community live through and in relation to cultural encounters between hybridity, present and past boundaries, and certain codes and discourses of recognition. In this case, these include: the intersection, for example, between Portugueseness, Europeanness, Asianness, and East Timoreseness; between class, cultural capital, and colonial relationships; between Chineseness and East Timoreseness; between Australianness, multiculturalism, appearance, and belonging; between age, youth and gender; and between Australian institutional influences such as state multiculturalism and ethnic community organizations. I consider these "entangled tensions" (Clifford 1994) by way of a series of case studies based on individuals interviewed for this research. Following are four characters who, in one way or another, have a particular experience of East Timoreseness or Timorese-Chineseness. I explore how for each of them their sense of East Timoreseness is to some extent the outcome or intersection of particular sets of relationships as described above. In some individuals one factor, such as class, may have more influence on their sense of East Timoreseness. However, the point is not to imply that all those of a particular class (or gender, age, or whatever) will have a particular understanding of their East Timorese identity. Rather, I argue that particular constellations of factors (gender, place, colonial experience or individual psychological characteristics, for example) come together to articulate how that person both acquires and ascribes meaning (Brah 1996) to their East Timoreseness.

Lihana's Story

Lihana is a young woman at that time in her early thirties. Our interview took place in the living room of her tiny apartment above a shop in Fairfield. She is an attractive young woman, and seems very strong and forthright in her views. Yet at the same time, during our interview, she would often ask if she was answering in the right way, eager to get it right. During that conversation, she shared with me her pride that her family was a strong female one and told me that this had made a big difference in her life in Australia. Her mother is indigenous East Timorese from the mountainous region of inland East Timor. Her father was of indigenous and Portuguese background. She describes her family as not assimilated into Portuguese culture. In East Timor, they followed East Timorese culture and would have been designated "unassimilated mestiços" by the colonial administration. They speak mainly Tetum at home, and she is also able to speak one of the dialects from Maubara, where her grandparents were from.

During the Indonesian invasion, her family fled their home to return to Maubara, at that time occupied by FRETILIN. They lived there for three years before their capture at the end of 1978. Following this traumatic experience, the family lived in Dili, where Lihana attended an Indonesian school and afterward a Portuguese school (which was eventually closed down following the 1991 Santa Cruz massacre). The family finally escaped to Portugal in 1987, where seventeen-year-old Lihana had to redo her secondary schooling at a night school for mature students. Her father died in Portugal, and Lihana, her mother, and sister eventually came to Australia in 1992. Lihana and her husband, an East Timorese man, mix largely with other East Timorese. Her sister was very involved in the independence struggle, Lihana less so. She works long hours as a nurse and sees herself as a strong young woman, with more freedom because of the female-dominated family from which she comes. As is common among many East Timorese women in the diaspora, she made the conscious choice to keep her own family name when she married, rather than take on her husband's.

The title of this chapter, "Locating East Timoreseness in Australia," is meant to designate both physical and metaphoric location. Beginning with physical geographies, how has location figured in Lihana's sense of her own identity? As for Fatima, introduced earlier, this is perhaps one of the most significant factors influencing Lihana's experience of East Timoreseness. For Lihana, her sense of displacement from East Timor goes beyond simply family and cultural aspects. For her, there is a certain embodied dissonance in her displacement.

I miss the ocean so much. You go every time to see the ocean. And I was like from Maubara—you could see the sea from where we lived. And even in Dili—you know it's on the seaside—and you can always see mountains as well. I would say back home you are always wondering what's on the other side of the mountain. But here [in Fairfield]—it's all flat. So you can see everywhere. I know it's funny—but like you know—what's on the other side—you get another mountain . . . ! It's really exciting. [laughs] Because it's an island—you always get to see the ocean. I always say that I would be really happy if I could get a house in the mountains you wake up and you can see the ocean. It doesn't matter if you are not close to it—just seeing it. So I really like ocean and mountains. I don't know—somehow—if I could get those two together. [laughs] It's very relaxing.

Unlike some East Timorese in Sydney, Lihana's family were not cosmopolitan city dwellers in Dili. This makes a big difference in her sense of community with other East Timorese. There are many dialects and cultural differences among the different districts in East Timor. These differences are more sharply felt by those who grew up outside the city.

Because I spent most of my time—inland in the mountains. We were not city people you know. Like it's really even your neighborhood is different. You know almost everybody. And when we went to Portugal—and you have strangers—you have other Timorese that you don't know before. In a way you feel unprotected.

This experience was perhaps most strongly felt during her years in Lisbon, Portugal. Lisbon is a city much more spatially divided than Sydney in race and socioeconomic background. Many East Timorese, including Lihana, tell how difficult their years in Portugal were, living in large slum areas in crowded *pensões*. These marked the residents out as "foreign," and life in these *pensões* was very difficult.

The financial status was so hard. Like, in Australia, although you sort of tend to not assimilate—but the standard of life is almost the same (for everyone). In Portugal you have to . . . mostly we had to live in a *pensão*—a special building where most of the Timorese live—you can tell that it is the big poor side. It doesn't matter if you work two jobs.

The notion of "assimilation" comes up frequently in conversation with East Timorese, who often compare their experiences in Portugal to life in Australia. Lihana considers four things key to her sense of difference, her "not being assimilated" in Portugal: the physical separateness of the *pensões*; the fact that, financially, there is an enormous difference in lifestyle (including where one lives) between rich and poor in Portugal; the fact of physical difference (Lihana felt that East Timorese were forever marked as foreign in Portugal, particularly those with darker skin); and the fact that Portugal is perceived by East Timorese as a monoculture, so that many felt permanently outsiders. However, "assimilated" mestiço East Timorese who adopted Portuguese culture were able to achieve a sense of belonging.

I find it easier here [in Sydney]. Because there—you are always thought to be from somewhere else. Um . . . more in the way like I believe because they are more Portuguese. They are not a multicultural country—so you still feel like you don't have any other people to support you—like outsiders—and also the culture I think is different. You had to pick it up a few years after being there. In Australia—it's a multicultural country and there are laws going towards helping in this way. It's not so—um . . . it doesn't show—maybe it's just the way I feel. Like if you get someone to talk to they are from somewhere else and then you find that you have someone to talk to about feeling like you—you weren't born here—or something like that.

Not surprisingly, her sense of belonging in Sydney lies not so much in feeling a part of some "Australianness," but rather, that there are many others in a similar position, "from elsewhere." This gives her a feeling of belonging in the sense that it is all right to be from somewhere else. Moreover, even those "from elsewhere" are able to have a comparatively high standard of living, and there is not an enormously obvious difference in living standards between rich and poor. However, in many respects Australia's multicultural framework provides an ambivalent sense of belonging for Lihana. On the one hand, there is a feeling of acceptance of being from elsewhere. On the other, a degree of ethnic overdetermination takes place in this context, with a perceived lack of some broader space to feel some sense of belonging to:

I think it's important [to teach our children about East Timorese culture] because living here, it is a multicultural society. But it is a shame that Australia doesn't have its own culture.

This is a sentiment I have heard more than once from East Timorese who formerly lived in Portugal—that "it is a shame that Australia doesn't have its own culture." This possibly derives from an ambivalent sense that in Portugal, even if it meant bracketing one's East Timoreseness, there was a "culture" to belong or assimilate *to*. In a multicultural society like Australia, while there is definite appreciation and support of being able to maintain one's own ethnic identity, there is a sense that this always positions those designated "ethnic" as outsiders, as there is no other space of belonging available. In other words, because East Timorese were, in East Timor, versed to some extent in Portugueseness—its food, dress, bodily disposition, and so on—it was possible for many to move between being Portuguese and being East Timorese. "Australianness" is perceived as something so amorphous as to be impossible to learn and take part in. Referring to the invisibility of whiteness in Australia, Schech and Haggis (2001, 151) lightheartedly point out that while "ethnic" Australians have their ethnic identity and can dress up as multicultural Australians, Anglo-Australians "have nothing to dress up as" on multicultural days at school. They argue that, in this way, whiteness emerges as lack.

Other factors play an equally important part in Lihana's sense of identity. Gender, for example, is one of the more important. Being a woman has been a mixed blessing. On the one hand, coming to Australia was more frightening for her and her mother and sister than for her husband.

I think that—like I told you my mum was a widow. I had to help my mum in financial ways—and in a way I was feeling insecure as a woman—not having close relatives by our side. But I always have my mum—I always live close to my mum and my sister. On the other hand, my husband—he came here by himself. And I would say that—I believe he was spoiled in a way—not spoiled—but had people working for them in Timor—probably it was hard, it was difficult for him as well—coming here to stay by himself—and his brother and sister do everything for him.

For Lihana, although it was terribly frightening to make such a move without her father's help, she feels that her family background (not terribly privileged) made them stronger and more self-reliant than her husband, who came from a well-off mestiço family with servants, making it a much bigger transition for him, especially arriving alone without family. Moreover, she believes that the experience of having to negotiate living in a new country, and the fact that the women in her family had to work to support themselves financially, has been a source of strength for her as a woman. This experience has given her a sense of herself that would never have been possible in conservative East Timor.

In East Timor, gender is just a culture thing—usually the male have the most benefits and power. Like my brothers—for example back home—like my grandpa he always says oh—you know—let's say the house—it's going to be for your elder brother or you know—respect your brother he's the eldest—listen to him. It doesn't matter if like he's naughty or whatever. But in other ways—my mum is quite—you know is different—because we have to work all this time—like my brothers and myself—we work the same and also my dad died a long time ago— so we have like a female dominant household. So it is quite different. Quite strong like, as women, because of having to support ourselves, and make a life in Australia without our father.

Unlike many other East Timorese to whom I have spoken, Lihana does not equate breaking traditions, such as those surrounding gender, with becoming more "European." Although Lihana's father had both East Timorese and Portuguese heritage, their family hold dearly to the fact that they were not "assimilated," but remained "true" East Timorese. She resents the fact that others, noting her light color and the fact that she is "modern" and educated, label her mestiço.

It's just the color. If you are mixed like Portuguese—they call you a mestiço. It depends on the situation. If you have a good relationship—if you have money or whatever and you help people. Like in the case of war, or whatever, they always call you mestiço—they call you mixed. They will say you are not true Timorese or whatever. It is up to you to defend—I was born here—I'm Timor- ese, I eat the way you eat, I walk the way you walk—you just have to tell them that you are Timorese. There is no one to tell me that I'm not. You know. They have no right to say that.

Lihana's narrative shows the importance, once again of embodied ex- periences and markers of difference and identity: they eat like she does and walk like she does. For Lihana, and for many other East Timorese, simply being proud enough to put your hand up publicly and say "I'm East Timorese" without being challenged is terribly important. Under both the colonial regime and the Indonesian occupation, indigenous East Timorese were seen as inferior. It is an important act of resistance to say "I'm proud to be East Timorese." When I asked Lihana what it means to her to be East Timorese, she replied:

It depends—if you ask for someone living in the city—they probably say—you know—all the Timorese—they'd say they eat different things—more like Por- tuguese style. But then for those people that left before the Indonesian invasion. Its like a mixed culture in there. But now they also have assimilated to Indone- sian culture. But for myself—being East Timorese—you speak the language—

you know the dialect—you know people that you know. And small things—how you help each other—or if someone dies—what you do, like ceremonies. . . . Also just being proud—like when I ask you where you come from—you say, I'm from East Timor. Like . . . from which area you come from. Just a little bit of knowledge—that you know you are East Timorese.

She flags a very important issue here, that there are those who feel that the most distinctive thing about being East Timorese is the influence of Portuguese culture, which is what marks them as different from, say, Indonesians or West Timorese. Then there is the simple fact that many younger East Timorese grew up under the Indonesian occupation; they were socialized into many aspects of Indonesian culture with no connection to Portugal. Finally, there are those, like Lihana, for whom markers of indigeneity, such as speaking a traditional dialect and knowing traditional ceremonies, are the most important indicators of their East Timoreseness. Nevertheless, the most common response from the majority of East Timorese in Sydney to the question, "Are East Timorese in East Timor different now?" is one that uses European markers of space and manners as the central point of differentiation. I asked Lihana how they have changed:

I think they've changed a lot. In a way—the way they think, the violence, even the way they walk!! I would say. And manners. Manners are gone. They have no personal space—they crowd into you . . . And also- you take it like a society too. Before the Indonesians, if you throw something in the street—everyone would just stare at you. Now, they don't care if the streets are filthy. So society there changed this way.

Lihana's reflection on the meanings of Indonesian cultural influence in East Timor reflects a widely held sentiment of many East Timorese in the diaspora. "Manners" are an important marker of identity and differentiation. In this instance, it is almost universally agreed among Sydney East Timorese that under Indonesian rule, East Timorese have "lost their good manners." Manners are valued by the vast majority of East Timorese in the diaspora as a positive influence from Europe, inherited via their Portugueseness.

Felismina's Story

Felismina is an educated East Timorese woman of forty. Her family are "assimilated indigenous" Timorese. Her father was a nurse, expelled from his job for refusing Indonesian citizenship. She arrived in Australia in 1995 after thirteen years in Portugal where she attended a university to study in the humanities and subsequently became a teacher. She was quite involved in the independence movement, helping the CNRT and publishing articles in Portuguese newspapers. She has not worked in Australia, although in recent years most of her time has been taken up caring for her aging mother, with whom she lives in Fairfield.

The interview with Felismina took place in the study of a friend's apartment. Felismina came across to me as a gentle, rather shy, but highly intelligent woman with strong views on East Timor. She was interested in my work because she seemed to have very fond memories of her own university studies. We got along very well because of this mutual interest, and we got together socially several times during the following year. Because of our similar backgrounds, our conversation during the interview often hovered around our shared experience as university women. Like many educated East Timorese over thirty, she feels very strongly about the importance of the influence of Portuguese culture on East Timorese people.

Now we call ourselves East Timorese. But that describes a national identity, not our traditional culture. But in reality, we have two nationalities. Portuguese and East Timorese. As soon as we became independent, we say we are East Timorese. But we must recognize how important our Portuguese nationality is in us. We still have Portuguese identity, because Portugal's influence goes a long way back into our history, and also has been important to us during the history of the struggle.

This position has caused some difficulty for her in her political life. Felismina feels that traditional East Timorese have much to learn from European culture, and this is not a popular view within FRETILIN. Following the 1999 referendum, Felismina was asked by FRETILIN heads in East Timor to write an article on the future of education there. Her views on the importance of promoting Portuguese culture to future generations of East Timorese were unpopular with political leaders in Timor.

I wish that East Timorese weren't so narrow in their idea of their culture—in our culture. I'm not saying that they are ignorant or anything. But they don't want to learn. If they learn a little bit more about other cultures, such as Portuguese culture, it would be good, because it helps to give them an understanding of history. When I was asked by the national resistance in East Timor to write an article about how education should be in East Timor in the future, I told them, it's very hard to write an article about education because I'm going to say the truth that East Timorese need a concept of education that helps to civilize them. To have a successful nation, to develop, the Timorese need to civilize their emotions and their minds. This is what I have learnt studying in Europe. But the national resistance people, they don't agree with me. They would just say . . . "—well—we are civilized people, we are not backward." And they may kill me if I wrote those things. So it was safer for me to tell them that it's impossible for me to write this article.

In many ways, paradoxically, Felismina's East Timoreseness rests on her pride in Portugueseness. However, conflict inevitably arises when in contact with East Timorese who remained in East Timor, who to some extent have fashioned an anticolonial politics that rests on the primacy of recultivating indigenous East Timoreseness, rejecting all signs of cultural colonization—including Portuguese and Indonesian influences— as a tool to claim sovereignty over East Timor and to highlight the illegality of Indonesia's occupation. Felismina's views also reflect a curious throwback to pre-1975 East Timor, where for the most part there was little in the way of widespread anticolonial politics and no attendant rejection of Portugal and Portuguese culture. Fleeing East Timor in 1975, Felismina formed an anticolonial politics that both rejected Indonesian cultural influence and tapped into former Portuguese or European systems of categorization based on ideas of European superiority and the uncivilized nature of indigenous as well as Indonesian manners. Importantly, East Timor's double colonization marks a fundamental ambivalence in postcolonial East Timorese identities, which is even more marked among those in the diaspora such as Felismina. The usual trajectory of anticolonization struggles has been by-passed in this instance. There has been little need to eject Portugueseness, because it is no longer the enemy. Indeed, their Portugueseness is seen by many as the primary signifier of their *difference* from Indonesians.[2]

In many respects, Felismina's time in Portugal, especially her years at the university, were her happiest. The reasons are complicated. In part they have to do with the social life she was able to have there, and her newfound independence. But they also have to do with a feeling of belonging she gained from having a single "monoculture"—Portuguese— into which she felt she was able to successfully assimilate, while at the same time being able to maintain her East Timoreseness in private.

In Portugal, I had to bracket my East Timorese part in a way. Yes. A lot, a lot, in everyday relations, in everyday relations with Portuguese people. I felt like every day I was breaking with my Timorese culture and putting myself inside of Portuguese culture. But I was happy. I was happy in a way that I learnt my new culture. I liked my degree, I liked the Portuguese language and I liked the knowledge I gained in Portugal. All of these things helped me to grow up—I felt good about myself. My self-esteem was very high there.

That Felismina highly valued her time in Portugal is clear. However, because she had become used to Portuguese culture, it was quite a shock to come to Australia and experience the strong emphasis on "ethnic community" that exists in multicultural Australia, and in the context of the independence struggle. For the first time, she felt pressure to focus on an East Timoreseness with which she didn't completely identify. On the one hand, she feels that Australia's promotion of multiculturalism created a good environment for East Timorese to unite for their political purpose of achieving independence for East Timor. But at a personal level it was really very difficult to be expected to be "East Timorese" all over again. Like Fatima, she experienced the emphasis on mixing within a bounded ethnic community as closing her off from other identity possibilities.

Multiculturalism is really important here in Australia to make an East Timorese community because it helps to promote our East Timor nationality—not necessarily our Australian nationality—but East Timor nationality. In Portugal the problem is it is different because their policy on culture is different. They don't support ethnic communities. Portugal is a mono-culture. In Portugal we had a sense that we are East Timorese but every day because we meet with Portuguese people we speak Portuguese language and we mix so much with them. So sometimes, like myself, when I came to Australia, I had great difficulty in mixing within East Timorese community! Because there was a sense that I'm Portuguese! Yes—I had become more Portuguese. In the way of thinking, sitting and eating—even still today I have many problems with my Timorese brothers and sisters. And sometimes I have to think and to accept the reality that although I am expected to be Timorese, I don't fit in.

The institutionalization of multiculturalism, which emphasizes boxing individuals into single ethnic communities, forces Felismina into the difficult position of feeling a degree of alienation because although she has been greatly influenced by Portuguese culture, she is not free to identify as Portuguese. Nor does she feel particularly East Timorese. Or rather, the sense in which she imagined or experienced her East Timoreseness in Portugal does not have the same currency in Australia. This has caused a painful sense of being somehow divided:

When I arrived, it was a great shock for myself. Because I was coming with the Portuguese culture and now I find that I have to mix with the East Timorese community. I feel sometimes that it's a completely new community for me, like having to learn a new community for myself again. I was thinking about my friends in Portugal—oh my dear, my god, I cried so much thinking back to my life in Portugal. Sometimes I have to try to be strong because I can't—because I really want to be near East Timor and to join with the national resistance here to work for East Timor. It's hard. It's kind of something that I have to struggle against—I have to try to come back to my culture—but at the same time, I still try to mix with Portuguese people because I don't want to lose my Portuguese culture, because I love, I love the Portuguese culture. I feel myself divided. Even now, I'm still feeling divided, I don't want to go one side, Portuguese culture, and on the other side, I don't want to lose East Timorese culture. But—like I said, I wish that East Timorese they don't close so much in their culture—in our culture—that they would accept other cultures into them.

In a sense, the highly compartmentalized multicultural landscape of western Sydney has the curious effect of keeping her within the East Timorese community. In Portugal, the cultural map was much simpler.

She was an East Timorese surrounded by the Portuguese culture into which she enjoyed assimilating. The perceived amorphous nature of "Australian" culture, especially that of middle-class, educated Australians, does not provide a solid ground on which she can stand. While there are Portuguese in Sydney, they are simply another "ethnic group," relating to whom, although pleasurable, doesn't provide the same sense of self-esteem and belonging to the (European) national cultural space that it did in Portugal. Moreover, Felismina is having to cope with the fact that her outward identification with Portugueseness, once a source of pride in Portugal, holds less value in this new cultural context. She is faced with the expectation that simply because she is East Timorese, she will naturally fit in with other East Timorese in Sydney. But in reality her different life trajectory has created an East Timoreseness that doesn't necessarily "fit" with East Timorese who came straight from East Timor or spent only a couple of years in Portugal before coming to Australia.

On Portugueseness, Asianness, Class, and Colonialism

Fatima's and Felismina's stories highlight one of the most striking features about many East Timorese in the diaspora: the extent to which Portugal and Portugueseness, and indeed Europeanness, figure in many people's sense of self, providing a very important point of identification. This experience of Portugueseness shapes, in different ways, the experience of Australia for many East Timorese. Life in Australia is frequently compared to Portugal rather than to East Timor. Although there is a sense among many East Timorese that life is easier in Australia because they are able to enjoy a much higher standard of living there—many still feel they fitted in much more in Portugal. Many East Timorese (especially educated city East Timorese) feel proud of their Portuguese heritage and are proud of the fact that they appreciate Portuguese culture, enjoy its art, food and way of life. Many, especially those who were schooled in Portugal or attended a university there, see Australia as a dry, flat, cultureless place, far inferior to the continental ways of Europe (see Thatcher 1991, 133).

Nicolau, for example, feels that, although he likes the lifestyle and people in Sydney, Portugal is his home because he loves the European way of life. This does not translate into a dislike or disdain for what he sees as East Timoreseness. Rather, as for many East Timorese, this very Portugueseness reinforces the value of East Timorese identity, in that this is what differentiates the East Timorese from mere "Asianness."

This Portuguese culture, it is very important to Timorese people. Being part of that social way of life. People tend to look at the European style. And it is good for us. It helps a lot of people to be more creative. When people say to me that I am one of the Asians . . . so I say to them like—our way, the way we are living is similar to Portuguese. We are different to Asians. The way we are living is different to Asians. Our social life is more to European. We are totally different. We are more in the Europe way than the Asian way. I heard Xanana's comments on TV—he was saying that the Portuguese language has set East Timorese people aside culturally. I agree with everything that he is saying. And I agree with every decision they take [in East Timor] that has a connection to Portugal. I believe that if we stick with Portugal we'll be the best country in Asia. (Nicolau, 33)

I believe that this convergence between a sense of East Timorese national identity and Portugueseness is actually something relatively new, and ties in with who it is East Timorese need to see as the "other" at a particular point in history. That is not to say that valuing Portugueseness is only a recent phenomenon among East Timorese people; quite the opposite. As we have seen, before 1974, Portugueseness was the marker that differentiated one from being too "native" or too "East Timorese." The meshing of East Timoreseness with Portugueseness is a recent response to the history of Indonesian occupation, a way of divesting the Asianness in East Timoreseness, of marking a core difference from Indonesianness. One of the most common occasions when this manifests itself in everyday speech, as we saw with Lihana, is when diasporic East Timorese speak about manners in the new "Indonesianized" East Timor. Nicolau explains what he sees as the difference:

People in East Timor are different than they used to be. The Indonesian way of living—they are a bit rough. The young ones who were born in Indonesian era, they are into Indonesian society. Like—if I was in a group and we were talking. This is an example. You know. What you *should* do is one talk, one listen, one talk, one listen, you know? Or if you want to talk, you say excuse me. You know—stop him, and excuse—you know—politely. But no—with the Indonesian way—no. We talk, one talk, blah blah, we all talk—and by the end, we don't know which one is which, who say this, who say that. And we are used to driving like here—decently. In your lane, when you change lane, you give people notice. Blinker. But there, they don't give any notice. Like here—if you change lanes—you do it politely. And if you get hit at a red light, you get out of your car and say excuse me, what happened? But there—they get out of the car and say "ef" this and "ef" that. That's how I find it there. (Nicolau, 33)

This sense of Portugueseness remaining intact in diasporic East Timorese, while it has been lost in those who remained in East Timor, is most poignantly felt in those who have visited East Timor and found they no longer fit in with family and friends.

Home for me now is in Portugal.[3] I've been back to Timor in 1997 and I feel like I'm a stranger to them. Not my family no, but to my friends I'm a stranger. Like those I used to go to school with—they look at me as if I'm the Nuno that they knew—but they treat me as if I'm not Timorese, they don't see me as Timorese anymore. Because the way that I used to be before I left is different from what they are used to now. I can see it in their expression. When I talked to them—I could see that they all feel like I'm higher than them now, more superior because I'm not Asian like them, more like a European. (Nuno, 33)

This is not an uncommon experience. Thatcher's research showed that in 1991, more than 75 percent of her East Timorese and mestiço respondents over age thirty-eight identified themselves as Portuguese, while their younger counterparts identified themselves as East Timorese or Timorese-Portuguese (1991, 219). Interestingly, in my own research ten years later I did not meet one East Timorese (of any age, mestiço or otherwise) who identified simply as either Portuguese or Timorese-Portuguese. Although some, like Fatima, say they feel Portuguese, they don't feel they can or should identify as such. Most proudly identify as East Timorese. However, as we have seen, for many their sense of East Timoreseness is tightly bound up with, or reliant on, some sense of inherent Portugueseness. Quite a number would call Portugal home. While proudly identifying themselves as East Timorese, it is an East Timoreseness that is very much reliant on Portugueseness.

I have heard numerous anecdotes from members of the community about the shock many of the early elite East Timorese (mestiço and assimilados) felt when they arrived in Australia. Used to being respected for their Portuguese "manner" and proud of the fact that they were recognized by the colonial authorities as being assimilated into Portuguese culture in East Timor, they based their sense of self on the extent to which they were *not* seen as East Timorese (that is, following native East Timorese ways). They were troubled and confused on their arrival in Australia when Australian authorities and the wider Australian community called them East Timorese. They felt that they were being lumped in with the East Timorese "natives." According to Thatcher (1991, 254) they also resented being treated the same as the East Timorese-Chinese, whom they considered socially inferior. As one of Morlanes's participants noted in her study of the Darwin Timorese community:

When I first came to Australia I thought that the Timorese was the *pes descalos* (the bare footed native, the Timor). When I was living interstate I attended University. There I said I was Portuguese but nobody could believe that I could be from Timor and be Portuguese. So I found that it was easier to say I was Timorese than to say that I was Portuguese, thus, from then on, I never again mentioned I was Portuguese. (Morlanes 1991, 187)

And another respondent:

I always thought that I was Portuguese. If I had come here before the conflict, and somebody had asked me about my nationality, I would have answered that

I was Portuguese. It's only here in Australia that people started to say that I am Timorese. The problem is that when we were in Timor we did not have to label ourselves as has happened here. In Timor we all were Portuguese. (186)

It is readily apparent from these anecdotes that class and cultural capital (Bourdieu 1994) intersect with ethnic identity in complex ways. For those with aspirations of upward class mobility, under Portuguese colonialism that meant divesting oneself of all traces of indigeneity and becoming Portuguese. However, such meanings no longer apply in Australia, where the politics of recognition have forced those in the diaspora to resituate themselves within East Timoreseness, while maintaining a sense of difference from the so-called natives or indigenous people of East Timor. What that means is that "East Timorese" identity has shifted to encompass a broad national identity, rather than the colonial category of the "native" East Timorese culture, although this is also increasingly being reevaluated and rediscovered to be incorporated into the wider East Timorese national identity.

Moreover, this national identity is, or has its roots, not in and from indigenous East Timorese culture. Those who created the idea of a single East Timorese nation and identity were mostly educated mestiços and assimilados from Dili. Many of these early political players had studied in Portugal and picked up political ideas from there, as well as from Mozambique via political exiles and East Timorese soldiers in the Portuguese military sent to fight against the African independence fighters. Moreover, those who arrived in Australia with the first groups of refugees in 1975 and 1976 were mostly from these elite ranks, many of whom formed the beginnings of the Australian arm of the independence struggle—and thus the political ideas and nationalist cultural imagery we have become familiar with. In a sense, this version of indigenous East Timoreseness has been abstracted from everyday lived practice into a reified anthropological schema of indigenous "culture"—dance, myth, food, ritual (see Baumann 1997; Kapferer 1988). More complex still is the fact that the "native" in East Timor is also what the Indonesian colonizer looks down upon as "uncivilized and barbarian." So inserting "European" is also an anti-Indonesian move.

Since living in Australia, class has become less of an issue. Rather, it remains an issue for the elites but has empowered their former "social inferiors," rendering old colonial categories obsolete, leveling the cultural playing field within the community, so to speak. As pointed out in Chapter 2, a number of elite families brought their servants with them when they came to Australia and are somewhat uncomfortable that their former subordinates now consider themselves their equals. For the formerly "inferior," this is of course a most positive turn of affairs and is seen as one of the most important benefits of living in Australia. But it is a deeply shameful and unhappy experience for the former elites, who feel that they have lost not only their homes and former positions of influence, but also lost the respect of other East Timorese, which they feel is their due. There are a number of anecdotal reports that former elites still feel they should be treated with the cordial respect they received in East Timor. I have heard many complaints (usually in the context of some playful character assassination) that those elites, especially former UDT members and leaders, expect other East Timorese to be at their beck and call. One young FRETILIN woman laughingly told me that the reason you never see UDT flags in photographs of protests in Sydney is that the UDT people always expect that someone else should sew their flags for them, as such tasks are beneath them. Because no one is willing to do such manual labor, UDT flags were often absent at the protests. I have also heard more than once that a number of UDT people refuse to speak Tetum with other East Timorese in public, instead replying in Portuguese, as they think Tetum is beneath them.

Despite the efforts of these older East Timorese elites, the old categories of "Portuguese," "mestiço," "assimilado," and so forth have virtually died out. Not once have I heard the term "mestiço" used by an East Timorese person in Australia, yet it had great currency as recently as 1991 when Thatcher's thesis was written. Nevertheless, the terms still do have an unconscious function for many in categorizing those they see around them, although a growing number, particularly those under forty see these cultural designations with a much more critical eye than their parents. There are a number of reasons these categories have ceased to have the same operative value as they did in East Timor and in the early years in Australia. First and foremost, they have no meaning in Australia, and enough time has passed that they are all but forgotten, while a whole generation of young East Timorese have lived in a system where they are not categorized thus. Second, the rise of East Timorese nationalism has meant that "East Timorese" has shifted from identifying the "barefoot natives," as they were known, to incorporating a broader national sense of East Timorese, which is not shameful for those "assimilados" to identify with. Moreover, it is readily apparent that living in Australia, many East Timorese find it simpler to identify as "East Timorese" because "Portuguese" is not available to them as an identity category in Australia.

The Relationship to Australia

Diasporic East Timoreseness must be considered in *relation* to local discourses. That is, we must understand how certain forms of identity are highlighted, or excluded, in the context of Australia. Ultimately, it is a question of belonging, and encompasses questions of racism, "cultural fit," and regimes of representation and recognition.

Many East Timorese, particularly those over thirty and especially those who have lived in Portugal, initially experienced Australia as a harsh, dull place without culture or tradition, and its people lacking animation. Many East Timorese feel uncomfortable at the lack of ritual and ritualized tradition in Australia, although the Catholic Church provides some respite from this perceived cultural blandness. This alienating landscape gives many a sense of not belonging. For some, this is no doubt exacerbated by experiences of racism. This may derive either from overt experiences or from a more subtle sense of never being "Australian" enough to fit in. One young man in Thatcher's research described this most movingly:

> I feel I am relegated to living in a no man's land. I am somewhere between being an alien and an accepted member of this society. No matter how expert I become with English, or at copying your ways, or how economically successful I am there comes a point where I cannot claim to belong to your world. Partly because your world will not allow me because I am Chinese, but also because part of me recognizes I am not of your world. I know what other worlds I do belong to. But I feel driven to seek the company of other Timorese people, because with them I don't have to pretend that all is well in this land of milk and honey. (young educated Timorese-Chinese man, quoted in Thatcher 1991, 214)

For many East Timorese such as this young man, this translates into a feeling that they are not part of the world here. They feel their difference will always deny them being part of Australia and being able to comfortably encompass "Australianness" as part of their own identity. Thatcher (206) notes that racism is more keenly felt by the former elite mestiços, who in East Timor, were not subject to discrimination. My own research indicates that older mestiços from the 1975 group are much more affected and angry about racism than are their East Timorese or Timorese-Chinese counterparts, who suffered racism in East Timor. Conversely, young East Timorese, those who have done most of their schooling in Australia and converse mostly in English, feel for the most part significant identification with Australia and Australianness along with their East Timoreseness. They are proud of their East Timorese identity but see themselves very much as young East Timorese-Australians. East Timoreseness then, may be felt sharply in relation to loss, in relation to the alienation brought about by unfamiliar landscapes and cultural and bodily practices. It may be felt in relation to the alienation brought about by racism. These are in turn patterned by previous class experiences.

Representations and Recognition

The politics of recognition (Taylor 1994) is an often underrecognized component to diasporic identities (Nederveen Pieterse 2001). By "recognition," I refer to the fact that recognition practices of the wider community make certain identities attractive, possible, or even unavailable.[4] We have seen this in the statements from those who no longer feel able to claim a Portugueseness in Australia. These politics of recognition have a range of impacts. There does, for example, seem to be a trend among younger East Timorese-Chinese (see also Thatcher 1991, 218) and other East Timorese youth toward being more disposed to identify publicly as East Timorese. Beyond the obvious reasons such as being moved by East Timor's situation, an element of attraction was added to East Timoreseness when East Timor became a rather "fashionable cause" among the wider Australian community. Moreover, as was pointed out in the previous chapter, unlike their perceptions of other refugee groups, the wider Australian public has looked kindly upon East Timor and East Timorese as true victims, as gentle Christian people, persecuted by the widely disliked Indonesian government. This played into a complex web of racism toward Indonesia, identification with Christianity, and images of "peaceful islanders" that permeate Australian representations of Pacific peoples. Moreover, as discussed in Chapter 3, there has also been a focus on drawing reference to the "debt" incurred by Australia during World War II when East Timorese people assisted Australian soldiers there against the Japanese. This links into powerful discourses of Australian mateship in war. Such discourses of representation and recognition provide a powerful framework within which "East Timoreseness" has been able to become a source of identity and pride for East Timorese in the diaspora. Moreover, the simple fact that East Timorese are recognized in Australia provides a source of satisfaction to many, preferable to the anonymity some have experienced in other parts of the world.

People look at you [in Australia] and go like, "oh you are Timorese." Instead of saying your name, they say—"oh you are from Timor, you are East Timorese." Whereas if you go to another place and people look at you and say—"who are you?". . . or you tell them you are from Timor—they will say like, "where the hell is that?" Where is East Timor? When I was in the States—some people asked me where I'm from. I said I'm from East Timor. And then they said—oh is that in Africa? Is that Jamaica? And it was like—it was really sad, people not knowing who you are. (Nuno, 33)

Similarly, the fact that Australia has a geographical and historical connection to East Timor, however troubled, makes it easier for many East Timorese to feel a sense of belonging and connection here, tempering the need to return to East Timor.

Thinking back to what Australia did in East Timor in the past—then it feels like I have another connection with both Australia and East Timor too. So in the future, maybe I will remain living here (in Australia) and not go back to Timor—because in a way, I still feel like I'm in Timor. Firstly, because it's closer and also the history between Australia and Timor. Also, because there are many Timorese in Australia. Let's say if I live in another country, like New Zealand, or let's say—another part of the world that has no connection at all to East Timor, then I wouldn't feel happy to stay there.

For Nuno, the sense that Australia has a history with East Timor means that there is not that feeling of absolute break from his homeland. It means that Australians have some sense of who he is, what his history is, where he comes from, and who East Timorese are. It also gives comfort to have a psychological sense of closeness to East Timor. East Timor is geographically close, there is a feeling that he could jump on a plane at any time and be back very quickly.

Nevertheless, as Fatima's story at the beginning of the chapter demonstrates, appearance also plays a strong role in people's ability to "place" you, making possible some but not other identifications. Fatima felt that in Portugal her appearance meant that people always knew that she was East Timorese (because there were few other cultural groups with similar appearance in Portugal), while in Australia she feels relegated to a generalized "Asianness." Somebody like Lihana, in contrast, has a rather different experience of this. From an indigenous East Timorese family, one of the hardest things for Lihana in Portugal was that "you look different from them." Over there, she says, "you are always thought to be from somewhere else." In Australia everyone is from somewhere else, and that is accepted. The *lived experience* of multiculturalism for many can be either a comfort or a source of alienation. For Lihana it provides a sense of being able to blend in, while for Fatima this blending in means a denial of the public recognition of her Portugueseness, which she felt was available in the more clear-cut ethnic landscape of Portugal.

Multicultural and Community Institutions

Definitions of ethnicity made by the federal government's Department of Immigration, Multicultural and Indigenous Affairs (DIMIA) frame the way that funding to community welfare groups is distributed. In the case of the East Timorese community, DIMIA makes no differentiation between East Timorese and Timorese-Chinese members of the community. It gives operating funds only to the Timorese-Australian Council whose charter it is to provide services and community activities to the East Timorese people in Sydney (Timorese-Australian Council 1994). However, the bulk of Timorese-Chinese have little if any contact with that organization, preferring instead to participate in the Timorese-Chinese Association, which is self-funded, receiving no government funds.

Such government definitions of ethnicity have an effect on community politics. However, attention must also be given to power relations within and between the different East Timorese community associations. As Thatcher (1991) has pointed out, having many strong leaders and political personalities among the first group of East Timorese to come to Australia has had a profound effect on the forms of and participation in East Timorese community organizations. From the beginning, the key organizations divided along party political and ethnic lines, creating splits and resentments within the community that remain today. Moreover, the "model" for ethnic community groups and the picture of what constitutes ethnicity and multiculturalism presented by the institutionalized version of multiculturalism in fact tend to push "East Timoreseness" into an ethnic box. The simplified, reified cultural aspects promoted by the East Timorese associations reinforce stereotypes of East Timorese ethnicity that revolve around dance, food, religion, music and so on. This institutionalizes a static form of indigenous Timorese ethnicity which is promoted as representative of East Timoreseness as a whole, while in fact, the East Timorese community are a highly diverse group, in terms of politics, ethnicity, age and influence from other places such as Indonesia, Portugal, Taiwan, and China.

The Complexities of Timorese-Chineseness in Australia

"Chineseness" among Timorese-Chinese is equally complex and situated. As I flagged at the beginning of the chapter, I wish to use "location" both metaphorically and to indicate a place within a physical geography. In this sense, there are three locations of importance to the Timorese-Chinese in western Sydney. The first are the relationships that existed in East Timor, between them and indigenous, mestiço and Portuguese Timorese. The second is the relationship to "China"—geographically, that has meant mostly Taiwan, and as a cultural category, to Chineseness. The third is the relationships in Australia, between other East Timorese, between Timorese-Chinese and other Chinese, and between Timorese-Chinese and Australia.

There has always been a small presence of Chinese in East Timor who played a role in the sandalwood trade from as early as the fifteenth century. However, the greatest influx came in the 1920s when Hakka-speaking Chinese came to East Timor. The Chinese formed approximately 2 percent of the population in post-World War II East Timor. Most were involved in trading occupations and dominated the commercial sector. According to Taylor (1999, 16), Chinese Timorese ran 397 of the 400 retail outlets. In the capital, Dili, the Chinese made up an estimated 50 percent of the population. They lived in the Chinese quarter, located in the neighborhood of Kulu-hun, often living at the back of their business premises (Morlanes 1991, 70). In the early days, many Chinese men, especially poorer Chinese in the villages, married East Timorese women. However, many elites preferred to bring a wife from China or marry a Chinese woman from East Timor. Despite this, Timorese-Chinese I have spoken to do not consider China as the motherland, identifying more readily with Portugal as homeland, or with *Portuguese* Timor. This does not indicate that Chineseness was relinquished by Timorese-Chinese; an estimated three-quarters of Timorese-Chinese identified as Buddhist and participated in ancestor worship (Thatcher 1991, 151). Prior to 1975, Taiwan's own nationalist aspirations played a significant role in the cultural politics of Chineseness in East Timor. Many Timorese-Chinese took up Taiwanese citizenship when offered, especially once Taiwan opened a consulate in Dili and sponsored a chamber of commerce. Importantly, China funded Chinese language primary and secondary schools, which the majority of Timorese-Chinese attended. These schools and the embassy proudly displayed Chinese cultural symbols such as flags on their buildings. The embassy became a very recognizable landmark in Dili, and China's national day was celebrated each year with a parade through the streets of Dili. However, a few Timorese-Chinese were sent to Portuguese schools for Portuguese, assimilados, and mestiços, which were run by the Catholic Church or colonial administration.

It's really up to the family what language school they send their children to. In Portuguese or Chinese. But I remember at that time—when I went to the Portuguese primary school—I was the only Chinese . . . student there. Because a lot of Chinese placed importance on being educated in Chinese. (Ana, late 30s)

Whether Timorese-Chinese attended a Chinese or a Portuguese school in East Timor appears to be one of the greatest factors influencing whether they mix easily across both groups, have a greater attachment to "East Timoreseness," or are more comfortable mixing and identifying with other Chinese or Timorese-Chinese. While the East Timorese elite sent their young to universities in Portugal, for wealthy Chinese families it was the norm to send their offspring to study in Taiwan or Macao.

Prior to 1974, there was never the option of Chinese identifying with or integrating themselves into an East Timorese national identity. In the early 1970s there were a small number of early nationalists derived from the educated Dili ranks of an embryonic FRETILIN. The vast majority of East Timorese understood themselves through colonial codes, such as mestiço, Chinese, Portuguese, or indigenous East Timorese via their language group such as Mumbai or Macasae. This meant that, prior to 1974, there was no room for Chinese to maintain a sense of their own culture while identifying with a broader East Timoreseness.

These are patterns common to the experience of many Chinese in Southeast Asia. There is a vast literature on the fate of "overseas" or diasporic Chinese in post-colonial nations such as Malaysia and Indonesia (see Wang 1992; Pan 1999; Ang 2001). This literature foregrounds two common threads—an increased ethnic consciousness in response to exclusionary anticolonial politics in the host nation and an increasingly deterritorialized collective identity.

In the Dutch East Indies, as in Portuguese Timor and British Malaya, colonial divide-and-rule tactics and Chinese dominance of the commercial sector played a significant part in establishing a sense of separate Chinese identity. There are many situational differences in each of those countries, but there are some common influences that scholars such as Wang (1992) have identified. After 1900 new policies were introduced in China to encourage the Chinese overseas to identify with and maintain strong links to China. These included "re-Sinification" policies to promote Chinese cultural values. Children were not encouraged to attend schools other than those teaching in Chinese and were expected to use textbooks produced in China (Wang 1992, 19). Chinese journalists, teachers and scholars went to these European colonies to promote greater awareness of Chinese culture (Wang 1992, 7, 275). As just discussed, China funded several Chinese-language schools in East Timor that existed right up until 1975. In the Indonesian case, Ang (2001, 27) points out that with the rise of anticolonial politics it was quite common for families to have a "foot in both camps" by sending one child to the Chinese school and one to the Dutch school (in the case of the Dutch East Indies). I have heard similar reports from East Timor.

At the same time, Chinese in each of these colonies were often seen as collaborators with the colonizers, profiting from their special position. The Chinese community did profit significantly from the colonial system in East Timor, where they dominated the commercial sector. In all these Southeast Asian colonies, this economic dominance caused resentment among local nationalists and anti-imperialists toward the Chinese populace (Wang 1992, 17). According to Daniel Chirot, "the rise of modern nationalism hardened attitudes toward those newly viewed as outsiders. Entrepreneurial minorities . . . now became, in the eyes of the new nationalists, something considerably more threatening" (Chirot, quoted in Ang 2001, 63). In East Timor as in Indonesia and Malaysia, Chineseness remained outside the bounds of the new post-colonial national identity. However, while there are common historical threads, the particularities of Chineseness nonetheless developed within the specific social and historical contexts of each community.

An estimated 90 percent of Timorese-Chinese have left East Timor, and more than two-thirds of those are living in Australia. Larger communities are in Darwin, Sydney, and Melbourne, with small numbers living in Brisbane and Perth. Of the Sydney Timorese-Chinese, none I have spoken to have any wish to return to an independent East Timor—most expressing the opinion that their lives and families are firmly established in Australia now. Nevertheless, there is still a distinct sense of being Timorese-Chinese rather than simply Chinese. However, for some, their "Chineseness" is foremost in their sense of self, while for others, their East Timoreseness has a greater significance.

Francisco's Story

Francisco is a Timorese-Chinese man then in his middle thirties. He is married to a woman also of Timorese-Chinese background, and both describe themselves as practicing Buddhists. Although they are both Buddhists, Francisco felt that he would have been equally happy to marry a Catholic, as long as she was Chinese. He came to Australia in 1984, after four years living in Portugal awaiting permission to emigrate. His family had relatives in Australia, and his father felt his children would have better educational and job opportunities there. His family in East Timor were relatively wealthy; his father had his own business and several properties. Fearing for their lives because of Indonesian persecution of Timorese-Chinese, they fled as a family by plane, via Jakarta. Francisco tells me that the hardest thing for his family was to leave behind their business and properties they had built up and all the family memories.

With some reservations, Francisco is very happy in Australia. When asked what it has been like to come to live in Australia, he does not express any of the sentiments of division or confusion that non-Chinese individuals such as Felismina or Fatima describe.

There are some things I don't like too much about Australia, but they are minor. I really love it here. I like every aspect of life here. If I have to pick something, I think Australians are too lenient on criminals and I don't like graffiti everywhere. I also worry about human rights abuses against Aborigines. Also it seems there is too much salary disparity between rich and poor, but because the welfare system is too easy, it creates a nation of laziness. I feel that I fit in, except for the drinking habits of many Anglo-Australians, I'm not too keen on. But you know, Australia is more than I could ever have expected. I really like Australians, we have cross-culture marriage within our relatives, and we appreciate Australian culture, especially the food, football, the sun and friendliness of people. I am lucky to have a lovely new house, a good job, and many Australian friends.

For Francisco, the challenges of migration have been experienced at a much more pragmatic level than for Felismina or Lihana, centered on negotiating everyday differences such as attitudes toward crime or the perceived propensity of Anglo-Australians to enjoy drinking. He also feels that being Timorese-Chinese makes it easier for him to fit in than other Chinese:

Because we are multilingual, most Timorese-Chinese, except the old, speak Portuguese. Because of this, most of us can speak English with little accent, which we are proud of. It makes it much easier to get on with Australians, we don't feel shy about mixing outside our culture like some Chinese. That is different to many ethnic Chinese, they stay more within their own group. Also, we have a blend of diets, Portuguese, Chinese, and Timorese, so most of Timorese-Chinese can tolerate sandwiches! It's not hard to live here.

For Timorese-Chinese like Francisco, the hybridity of Timorese-Chineseness operates as a kind of cultural passport, smoothing the transition between cultural spaces. It gives a sense of cosmopolitan cultural capital, which allows them to stand out against other more "Chinese" Chinese. This does not mean that Francisco rejects or devalues his Chinese background. As he takes pains to point out, his Chineseness and especially Hakka culture remain extremely important to him, and a source of great pride. I asked Francisco how important both China and East Timor are to his identity:

China is very important to my identity. All other nationalities including Chinese dwelling in places outside China have always been treated as secondary. A strong and respectable Chinese nation will uphold its people's dignity. East Timor is not as important as China because we still carry strong tradition from our ancestors. We do/die the Chinese way! So, in a way, both are my homeland. East Timor is my birthplace, but China is and will be my place for identity.

Francisco's Chineseness is mobile, having traveled with him from East Timor to Australia. While he may have good memories of East Timor as his home, he separates that from his cultural identity which is first and foremost Chinese. It is an important symbol of resistance in the face of historical discrimination against overseas Chinese everywhere. It perhaps gives him a sense of being linked to a wider "brotherhood of Chineseness"; it is a source of dignity linked to a mythical China. However in no way does this mean that he reduces his own identity to a universal Chineseness. In another conversation, Francisco was eager to point out that Timorese-Chinese are different from other Chinese. This is not simply because they are Hakka-speaking Chinese; he feels he is specifically Hakka-speaking *Timorese*-Chinese. In his view, Hakka-speaking Timorese-Chinese have a unique character unlike any other Chinese group.

My Hakka culture is important to me. It defines East Timorese-Chinese culture. Our Hakka has evolved and is different to mainland Chinese Hakka. Sometimes it's a problem, because it means we tend to mix more with only Timorese-Chinese. So we have marriages mostly with others in our community, sometimes with relatives, distant cousins which is hard, because most people know each other well. But we are different you know to *non-Timorese* Hakka-speaking Chinese. We are probably less challenging and ambitious and like I said, our diet is a combination of Chinese and Portuguese food, as well as some Indonesian and Goan, and also we have dual beliefs in Catholicism and Buddhism. But we are also different to Timorese. They follow voodooism[5] and follow different customs.

Francisco separates out his abstract "Chineseness," that sense of pride in belonging to a greater Chineseness, from the messy, more mundane lived sense of being Hakka Timorese-Chinese. These are not in conflict, the latter does not undermine the former in Francisco's experience. They coexist and are drawn upon as needed. The distinct sense of being specifically *Timorese*-Chinese does not however equate to an identification with non-Chinese Timorese. Since being in Australia, Francisco's patterns of social interaction with other (non-Chinese) East Timorese have changed. He now spends little time with non-Chinese Timorese, preferring the company of other groups.[6]

In East Timor, I mixed occasionally with Timorese, but still mostly with Chinese. But now in Australia I don't have much social contact with non-Chinese Timorese mainly because of language and cultural barriers. I mix more with other Timorese-Chinese and ethnic Chinese for social life, and we work and we marry with them. I also mix with Taiwanese Chinese communities. I have Australian friends from work. The only group I would find it hard to mix with here are Lebanese because they are very intolerant toward women. I like going to the Timorese-Chinese Association to make my community link and for social fun, and also to share home feeling among friends.

While the vast majority of Timorese-Chinese (such as Francisco) mix primarily within their own community, with other ethnic Chinese and more rarely with indigenous/mestiço East Timorese, a number of Timorese-Chinese mix happily across both groups or primarily with the non-Chinese Timorese. These individuals generally don't identify themselves as "Timorese-Chinese," preferring simply "Timorese." Most often they are from mixed families, or grew up in villages with no other Chinese around—such as children of village shop owners. Mostly they are Portuguese-speaking and Catholic, and quite comfortable speaking Tetum, even if they retain their Hakka language. The majority would have been schooled in the Portuguese system rather than in the Chinese schools.

Carlos's Story

Carlos, a gay man in his mid-fifties, lives in Liverpool with his partner. He describes his ethnicity thus:

I would say I'm Timorese. Because I'm happy to be with Timorese people and Timorese-Chinese people. But my family, my parents and grandparents all called themselves Chinese. They were very rich; my grandfather owned a coffee plantation where I grew up. Actually my father was Chinese, and his family were from China. My grandfather—my father's father—was Chinese. My grandmother—my father's mother was Chinese. But her father was Chinese and her mother, Timorese. On my mum's side: my mother's father, although he called himself Chinese, did have a Timorese mother. I still have Timorese relatives in East Timor today, on my mother's side.

As a child, Carlos lived with his family on the large coffee plantation belonging to his paternal grandparents in rural East Timor. He helped a lot on the farm growing up and attended the local Portuguese school. He was keen to escape his family and decided to move to Dili at the age of twenty-five, a move that allowed him the freedom to explore his sexuality. He made his living by designing and sewing clothes and earned extra income from making and decorating cakes and organizing parties and weddings. He also made a good income as an informal moneylender.

Carlos was thirty when he left East Timor on the M.V. *Macdili* in 1975. He came to Sydney with the first group of mostly Timorese-Chinese refugees and stayed in the Endeavour Migrant Hostel in the eastern Sydney suburb of Coogee. He was helped by members of the Portuguese community in Sydney to find work, and began working in a factory within a week of arriving, despite having virtually no English. He describes his life in Australia as extremely happy and has no wish to return to East Timor. He is very outgoing and flamboyant.

Now semiretired, Carlos continues with his cakemaking business, creating extravagantly decorated wedding and party cakes for East Timorese, Chinese, and Portuguese customers and for various multicultural friends he has met through an assortment of social groups he is involved in. He still enjoys designing and sewing clothes, and creating crafts as a hobby. He happily moves between the East Timorese and Timorese-Chinese communities, and is regularly involved in community activities on both sides. He also happily mixes with Anglo-Australians, many of whom he meets through his partner. He has been in a relationship for more than twenty years with the same man, a working-class Anglo-Australian whom he first met in East Timor before 1975. They own a small apartment together and openly socialize as a gay couple with a range of "everyday" people from different ethnic backgrounds in suburban western Sydney. Carlos enjoys attending "multicultural seniors" groups in the Liverpool-Fairfield area. One of his favorite pastimes is his line dancing group, which is a mixture of older Anglo-Australians and a range of other ethnic groups such as Filipinos, Vietnamese, and Portuguese. He feels a great sense of belonging and acceptance among many different groups.

I really enjoy my life because I have a lot of friends. I meet a lot of friends. They really love me. Sometimes I'm sick—"Oh, what happened, why are you not coming to dancing?" They will all see me and say "what happened, what happened?" They will ask you, they're friendly. I am very lucky and I have a lot of friends in Australia and I haven't heard anyone insult me or my neighbor everywhere I'm living. It doesn't matter, they're couple or single whatever they're all very friendly with me. This makes me so happy when I am dancing or something. Cause I'm dancing 5 days. Monday, Tuesday, Wednesday, Thursday, Friday with different groups.

Carlos doesn't express any sense of connection to China or his Chineseness. He feels that in East Timor the Chinese were very Westernized, and he is much more interested in his East Timorese roots—becoming an expert in East Timorese fabrics, dance, and food. I asked whether he follows both his East Timorese and his Chinese culture.

No, Chinese in Timor we have a culture but we didn't follow much in Chinese culture in my country anymore because we are all Catholic. My culture and country, we never follow like we don't have Buddha, here Buddha everywhere. We didn't have that. We followed just like European. We eat like European. We dress like European. We live like European just like how I live now. I remember, this one time. When we first came to Australia we went to Chinatown. We ask for a spoon and fork and knife—and they were looking at us. They didn't say it, but you can tell in their eyes they are thinking, "You're Chinese how come you can't use chopsticks?" But we never used chopsticks in my country. Very, very old people they used, but not many.

Carlos's version of East Timor is very much Portuguese Timor. His experience of Chineseness has only begun to confront him now in Australia. He seemed a little bit embarrassed about the "chopsticks" encounter, but overall he has little, if any, "identity anxiety," happily sailing between taking part in the Timorese-Chinese Association (he loves the dancing there) and learning more about indigenous East Timorese culture, learning about traditional cooking and practicing the traditional dances to teach to his multicultural line dancing group. That Carlos's sexuality has played an important part in shaping his comfortable hybridity is obvious. From breaking away from his rural coffee plantation to live in Dili as a young man, to challenging gender stereotypes with his clothing designs, cake decorating, and dancing from the early 1970s—all have paved the way for Carlos to feel comfortable challenging boundaries and slipping in and out of different identities. Clearly, Carlos's life trajectory is radically different from Francisco's. Carlos is a gay man living with an Anglo-Australian partner, was brought up in a proud Chinese family but schooled in Portuguese, and was from rural East Timor where his social contact was mostly with indigenous and mestiço Timorese. Francisco, son of a wealthy Dili businessman, is a Buddhist who attended the Chinese school in Dili, married to a Timorese-Chinese woman, and very involved with the Timorese-Chinese Association.

In Francisco's opinion, although influenced by Portuguese culture,

Timorese-Chinese always maintained their Chineseness in East Timor. They remained with Buddhism, attended Chinese schools, and celebrated Chinese National Day. In Carlos's opinion, Timorese-Chinese were virtually Western, ate with knives and forks, were Catholic, dressed and ate as Westerners, never had Chinese symbols around the house, and spoke both Hakka and Portuguese. As Carlos sees it, most Timorese-Chinese in Sydney have only started to *become Chinese* now that they are in Australia. What, then, are some of the processes by which Chineseness is, as Carlos would have it, being relearned? Or, as Francisco would have it, what processes play into a continuation of Chineseness and community? How is Timorese-Chineseness different in Australia, and why?

The Timorese-Chinese Community in Australia

In Australia, two factors play an important part in the cohesiveness of the Timorese-Chinese community. The core of the original community was drawn from the 672 Chinese who arrived in Darwin on the M.V. *Macdili*. Those allowed on the first ship out of Dili were the elites, mostly Portuguese, high level mestiços in the administration, and wealthy Chinese from Dili. Most were placed in the Endeavour Migrant Hostel in Coogee. Those on the second boat mostly ended up in the Cabramatta Migrant Hostel in western Sydney. Many lived in their hostel for up to a year, and the community ties and friendships they made there were formative in creating a Timorese-Chinese community that is very distinct from non-Chinese Timorese. Among those who arrived were also a number of community leaders who took a strong role in forming an association for the Timorese-Chinese. This association has played an enormously important role in creating a distinct Timorese-Chinese community, separate from non-Chinese Timorese.

Located in Greenfield Park (near Liverpool in Sydney's outer western suburbs), the current Timorese-Chinese Association, formed in 1991, plays an important part in reproducing Timorese-Chineseness in Australia. Among many activities at the association's meeting halls, they hold classes in Chinese dance, which they learned only after they arrived in Australia, and Portuguese folk dancing, which they were more accustomed to in East Timor. In recent years, the Taiwanese government has been funding classes in Mandarin at the association for Timorese-Chinese community members. They celebrate Chinese festivals, although this is a fairly recent phenomenon. They celebrate both the Western and the Chinese New Year, the latter only in recent years. The Western New Year is celebrated with Chinese food, dance, and other traditions normally practiced on Chinese New Year (see Inglis 1998, 285). On both occasions, they mix in Portuguese elements such as food and folk dancing.

Nevertheless, there is evidence of an increasing "re-Sinification" of the

Timorese-Chinese, especially those taking part in the Timorese-Chinese Association. For example, although Portuguese folk dancing was always the main form of dancing in East Timor, and it continues to be a staple part of all the dance activities in the association in Australia, there has been an increasing interest in traditional Chinese dance in the last few years. Interestingly, the two forms, although musically dissimilar, have much in common in terms of choreography. One fellow, an obviously rather camp gay Timorese-Chinese man like Carlos (although his sexuality is never commented on within the community), has taken a lead in developing traditional Chinese dance at the association. He bought videos of Chinese dance and studied them frame by frame over many days, noting the dance steps. He then started classes for the women at the association, teaching them set dance pieces picked up from the videos. He is also rather expert at sewing, producing exquisite copies of the traditional Chinese dresses he sees on the videos. However, he also produces interesting hybrid costumes, a fancy combination of the traditional Indonesian *kabaya* favored by Timorese-Chinese women in East Timor, with shiny Chinese fabrics. At the association meetings, older ladies teach the younger ones Chinese cooking, although the influence of Portuguese cooking is still readily apparent. Many Timorese-Chinese will go out of their way to mix with other Timorese-Chinese, rather than within the wider Chinese communities. A number of those—especially the elderly—who attend the Timorese-Chinese Association actually travel out to the Greenfield Park center from their homes in Maroubra Beach, in Sydney's beachside east, about an hour and half drive away.

The extraordinary lengths to which the Timorese-Chinese communities around Australia go to get together evidence both the sense of difference from other Chinese and East Timorese and identification with East Timorese-Chineseness. Each year, a community in Sydney, Melbourne, Brisbane, or Darwin hosts a celebratory get-together for all Timorese-Chinese from around the country. The annual bus trip to the get-together is the highlight of the Timorese-Chinese calendar. In 2000, the Sydney Timorese-Chinese played host. Some 1,500 members from the Melbourne and Brisbane Timorese-Chinese communities came to Sydney by bus (a ten- to fifteen-hour trip) to take part in several days of celebration. The Sydney community had been preparing for many months, practicing Chinese (learned from the video) and Portuguese dances, sewing costumes (shiny cheongsams and the Timorese version of kabayas and sarongs made from gold and maroon fabric), decorating the association hall, and cooking food from East Timor. The visit included dance performances and a special soccer match between the state teams, and culminated in a lavish dinner and dance at an enormous and richly decorated Chinese function center.

While they go to great lengths to mix with other Timorese-Chinese, there is relatively little interaction with other Chinese communities in Sydney. Celebration of Chinese festivals with other Chinese is a relatively new phenomenon for Sydney Timorese-Chinese. The Melbourne Timorese-Chinese in Thatcher's study (1991, 228) refused all invitations from other Hakka-speaking communities to have joint celebrations until 1992, when they came together to celebrate the August Moon festival; they have tentatively maintained this socializing since. In recent years in the Sydney community, there has been some joint socializing with Chinese from Cambodia, Vietnam, and Laos.

Primarily this contact has developed because of the geographical proximity of these other groups to the suburbs where most Timorese-Chinese live. Because it is close by, many Timorese-Chinese use the Laotian Buddhist temple in Bonnyrigg (a neighboring suburb to Liverpool), since they don't have their own. Friendships have blossomed through this contact, and socializing together has gradually increased. There are also "multicultural seniors" groups run by the local council, involving many Chinese from Laotian and Cambodian backgrounds, again providing an opportunity for Timorese-Chinese to get to know them. This is an important point. Often identities spring from pragmatic relationships. This is a very localized version of Timorese-Chineseness, centred on the micro-locality of Fairfield and Liverpool.

Most also read the Chinese papers, such as the daily *Chinese Independent*, the paper put out by the Kuomintang (KMT). Taiwan and increasingly China are ever-present in the community. As one interviewee pointed out, whenever the Timorese-Chinese Association holds a big event, they always make it a point to invite both Taiwanese and Chinese government representatives. Interestingly, the Portuguese community in Sydney also has links to the Timorese-Chinese. There have been a number of mixed marriages over the years. The Portuguese community made an effort to assist with housing and job hunting when the East Timorese first arrived. Many friendships have endured, particularly with those Chinese who attended Portuguese schools in East Timor.

All this makes it clear that there is a very distinct sense of *Timorese-Chineseness* within the community. Many made it a point to call my attention to the fact that their habits of dress, food, and dance are different those of other Chinese. Other Chinese perhaps also reinforce this sense of difference to some extent. There have been stories of discrimination from other Chinese toward Hakka-speaking Timorese-Chinese.

I heard a story about a Timorese-Chinese boy who was being teased at school by other Chinese kids—who were not Hakka speakers. And they were teasing him about his language. I think they were saying that Hakka is not a proper language and he ended up being beaten up. . . . I have heard such things. But I haven't really experienced it. But in Darwin I think it happens. I heard in Darwin—there is a sort of "Chinese aristocracy" in Darwin—who pick on the Timorese-Chinese because we are the poorest ones! (Tony, 36)

Comments like these must be placed in a wider context of class, urbanity, and Chineseness. Such discrimination would most likely emanate from urban mainland, Hong Kong, or Singapore Chinese, while a greater sense of affinity is felt with Chinese from places such as Cambodia, Vietnam and Laos because all derive from rural or "small scale" commercial backgrounds, are less educated, and commonly don't speak or write Mandarin or Cantonese. Many Timorese-Chinese (like their Cambodian and Laotian counterparts) work in manual labor. The Timorese-Chinese Association's premises were built entirely by voluntary labor from within the community. Proudly displayed on the walls are large color photographs of the various Timorese-Chinese laborers who helped—pictured tiling, painting, laying bricks, and cleaning. They perceive themselves to be simple, laid back, easy-going, yet hard-working and industrious. These characteristics are a great source of pride among Timorese-Chinese.

As Ang argues, it makes little sense to speak of a unitary Chinese community, or diaspora, as a whole (2001, 92). Indeed, for many Timorese-Chinese there is a clear sense of ambivalence about feeling a part of some greater "Chinese" community as most have a distinct sense that they are different because of their East Timorese background. One story I heard during my research illustrated this very well. The Sydney Olympic Organising Committee invited the Chinese of Sydney to have a contingent take part in the torch relay for the 2000 Olympic games as representatives of Australia's Chinese "community." A Timorese-Chinese woman was invited by the large Chinese organization in the city to take part. She was terribly confused and upset by the invitation, worried about such a public declaration of Chineseness. She finally went to visit a leading East Timorese (non-Chinese mestiço) community worker for advice on what to do. She felt that by participating in this important international event as part of the official Chinese "community" group, she would be saying that she was *Chinese*, and thus betraying her East Timorese background. In the end, she chose not to take part, feeling that the event would have forced her to publicly choose one community/identity over another. That is not to say that there is a rejection of belonging to a greater Chineseness; rather, it symbolizes the need for being able to be both Chinese in the wider sense and *Timorese-Chinese* at other times.

Since they have been in Australia, however, there has been a reduction in speaking Tetum and Portuguese and an increase in Hakka and Mandarin. This is partly a result of the little contact between the bulk of

Timorese-Chinese and other East Timorese, meaning that most of the Timorese-Chinese tend to speak Hakka to one another. It is also a result of the fact that most young Timorese-Chinese are sent to Mandarin classes, funded by the Taiwanese government and run at the association's premises. Most young people are no longer taught Tetum or Portuguese; they speak mostly Hakka at home, learn formal Mandarin, and communicate in English with friends at school. The only families who still speak Portuguese at home are those schooled under the Portuguese system or, in the case of Tetum, those in mixed marriages. Even so, many young Timorese-Chinese are more inclined to use the word "Timorese" hyphenated with "Australian" or "Chinese" than their parents, in part because the political identity this confers is rather fashionable, and in part to distinguish themselves from other Chinese. Which leads me back to the question of recognition and the politics that surround it.

Perceptions of Timorese-Chinese by Indigenous and Mestiço East Timorese

The sense of a distinct difference between the Timorese-Chinese and other East Timorese is as much imposed by non-Chinese as it is deliberately cultivated by Timorese-Chinese. The feeling among most East Timorese is that the Timorese-Chinese are just different and have always wanted to be their own community. Usually there is a slightly resentful indifference to this fact. However, with respect to fighting for East Timor's independence, and now finally rebuilding East Timor, there are definite boundaries drawn defining who can belong to the new East Timorese nation, and under what conditions. Among non-Chinese Timorese, the Taiwanese citizenship issue has become emblematic of the perceived lack of commitment by Timorese-Chinese to East Timor. When Taiwan opened its consulate in Dili, it offered Taiwanese citizenship to any Timorese-Chinese who would like to take it up. One particular story about citizenship claims is frequently told by non-Chinese Timorese to explain why the Timorese-Chinese are seen as not wanting to be East Timorese and not caring about East Timor or its people.

It's probably just rumors . . . but back home in East Timor during the Portuguese time, the Chinese wouldn't change their citizenship, even if they can be Portuguese citizens, they sign up to be Chinese. That's what I heard. They always say they are Chinese back home and they wouldn't change. But when the war started, they lied to get out—they say they are Timorese, for the first time wanted to claim they were Timorese and have Portuguese citizenship. Just to get out. And that meant that a lot of Timorese couldn't fit on the boats, because it was only for educated and wealthy Timorese who have Portuguese citizenship. (Lihana, 30)

This is how one young woman described what she had heard. She is referring to the fact that, although many Chinese in East Timor took Taiwanese citizenship, once the civil war started they claimed Portuguese citizenship. This was in order to escape on the boats taking evacuees, and later enter Portugal, so as finally to come to Australia. Very few Timorese-Chinese actually took the option to live in Taiwan. Another story often invoked relates to the Australian government's Special Family Reunion Program for East Timorese in the mid-1980s. The vast majority who were awarded places to come from Portugal were Timorese-Chinese. Apparently this is because the Australian government favored those who did not involve themselves in politics. My own research shows, and is supported by Thatcher (1991), that this outraged the wider East Timorese community, who felt that the Chinese deliberately avoided helping East Timor as a self-interested strategy to gain entry to Australia.

These two stories are told and retold to indicate that the Timorese-Chinese had no interest in belonging to East Timor. More recently, however, these sentiments have tempered somewhat, especially with East Timorese leaders such as José Ramos-Horta and Xanana Gusmão visiting to actively promote the return of Timorese-Chinese to help rebuild the commercial sector in East Timor.

We don't have any trouble about them having their own association. It is ok with us—as long as when you talk to them they are proud to say they are Timorese. Yes. They are proud to say—they are all Timorese. So as long as they don't say I'm from Mandarin, or from Chinese—they are proud to say that I'm a Timorese. When Xanana came here the first time, he looked at them and said—you are not Chinese, you are Timorese. And he told them, I went to China, and the Chinese say—how are the Chinese in Timor? And he looked at them and said, we don't have Chinese in Timor. And the government say—why you don't have Chinese. Xanana—says—I don't call them Chinese. I call them Timorese. (Nicolau, 33)

Here, Nicolau expresses a sentiment common in the diaspora, that while they accept Timorese-Chinese practicing their own culture they must not identify as Chinese and should have a first allegiance to East Timor. For others, there is an issue of maintaining a sense of East Timoreseness that is distinct and recognizable. For one young indigenous East Timorese woman, living in Sydney where more than half the East Timorese are in fact Timorese-Chinese, it creates a concern that others may not understand that she is East Timorese too:

The majority of Chinese left East Timor. They are the most here in Sydney. So everybody says—oh you are Timorese—you don't look like one. Timorese are supposed to be fairer—they are supposed to be like Asian. And you like NO! That's like—Timorese are supposed to be darker and curly hair like me. And its just um. . . . I would say an identity crisis again. And if they say like Timorese they speak Hakka. And I say . . . no, no . . . we don't speak Hakka, we speak Tetum! Yes. . . . So it's just a little clash there. (Lihana, 30)

For this young woman, the large number of Timorese-Chinese in Sydney threatens to dominate what it means to be East Timorese in the eyes of other Australians. This compounds for her the difficulty of maintaining a sense of stable identity living outside East Timor.

Chineseness, it is clear, is as much a process of inscription as it is ascription. It is by no means fixed, and frequently individuals shift comfortably between several senses of Chineseness, Timorese-Chineseness, and Hakkaness. As Ang has argued,

Chineseness is not a category with a fixed content—be it racial, cultural or geographical—but operates as an open and indeterminate signifier whose meanings are constantly renegotiated and rearticulated in different sections of the Chinese diaspora. . . . There are, in this paradigm, many different Chinese identities, not one. (1998, 225)

What does seem clear however, is that acceptance into the wider space of "East Timorese national identity" is provisional at best, and nonexistent at worst. Although the possibility of assimilation is offered, there is simply no option to be a hyphenated Timorese-Chinese and have full acceptance into the East Timor nation. In Australia at least, Timorese-Chineseness is still an option.

Analysis: Layers of Hybridity, Enmeshed and Anchored

The homeland is central to the conceptualization of diaspora. Many studies have explored the various ways in which homeland identities are played out in the diaspora. However the East Timorese case reminds us that there isn't necessarily a unilinear connection between the diaspora and the homeland. As with many other postcolonial contexts, it is far more complicated than that. These fragments from my interviews demonstrate that connection to *and* disconnection from the homeland are equally important. As Nederveen Pieterse warns, it is important to see hybridity as the product of *layers* of history, "each with distinct sets of hybridity, as a function of the boundaries that were prominent, and accordingly a different pathos of difference" (2001, 231). For East Timorese in the diaspora, this perspective is especially significant.

The most prominent aspect of the East Timorese case is the extent to which boundaries have changed and are shifting. Boundaries that were important in colonial Portuguese Timor are no longer so relevant, but they leave a sediment that still influences identity experiences today.

Those boundaries that existed in Portugal, where many East Timorese lived before coming to Australia, are no longer relevant in their new home. Those boundaries that frame East Timorese nationalism are different in East Timor from how they have been imagined in the diaspora. Colonization, invasion, exile in Portugal and then Australia, and finally East Timor's independence all imply different and changing sets of boundaries, which include or exclude particular identity possibilities, and which in turn frame the kinds of hybridities that arise within and between their layers. For example, the decline in the currency of Portugueseness has had a significant impact on Fatima, Felismina, and Nicolau. Fatima's case felt anchored in Portugal; although she was certainly hybrid, she found she could identify and be recognized as Portuguese. Her particular form of hybridity had currency in Portugal. In Australia, however, the boundaries of Portugueseness were different, locking her out of that identity space. She found that the discourses of "Asianness," and "East Timoreseness" were so powerful that in a way she was forced into them, which makes her quite uneasy.

As an indigenous East Timorese woman, Lihana experienced her time in Portugal very differently. For her, the boundaries of Portugueseness locked her out of belonging there at all. In Australia the system of multiculturalism provided a sense of belonging to East Timoreseness. However, she also felt some discomfort that Timorese-Chineseness was redefining the boundaries of East Timoreseness in Australia. She wanted to demarcate a more indigenous version of East Timoreseness, to which she feels she belongs. Ironically, it was only when faced with return that she discovered that East Timoreseness had shifted its meanings there.

For the first time, she recognized Australianness as part of her. This new sense of hybridity, overlaid with her former sense of Portuguese Timoreseness, meant that she felt a sense of only partial belonging, a sense of unhomeliness in the new East Timor. Portugueseness comes in again for both Fatima and Lihana when they express the importance of not wanting to be recognized as Asian, but feeling, for different reasons, that they are being forced into that category against their will. For members of the Timorese-Chinese community, though, despite their obvious hybridity, the category Chineseness has remained a stable constant. It seems that their experience of hybridity does not bring with it a feeling of loss in the way it does for, say, Fatima, or Felismina. Timorese-Chineseness provides a kind of anchor for them, an anchor around which they can float safely. However, as a gay man, perhaps the most "happily hybrid" of all my interviewees, for Carlos, escaping the rigid sexual boundaries of conservative East Timor has meant that he is able to be comfortable in all kinds of spaces.

What comes through forcefully in all these narratives is a sense of the power of boundaries and cognitive-affective maps to put in place certain identities and, in some cases, to force individuals to be recognized as something with which they don't identify and which is clearly an uncomfortable experience for them. To echo Ien Ang's reflections on Paul Gilroy's famous couplet, each of these individuals is dealing with the dilemma of "where you're from, and where you're at" in different ways. In this light, perhaps the most important question to arise from this chapter is, for whom is hybridity happy? For Ang, "so long as the question "where you're from" prevails over "where you're at" in dominant culture, the compulsion to explain, the inevitable positioning yourself as deviant *vis-à-vis* the normal, remains" (2001, 30). For whom is hybridity happy then?

This brings me to the importance of an anchor. By anchor, I mean some kind of identity or experience to which you feel you can at least partially belong, on the one hand, and on the other, one which has some currency, and to which you are *recognized* as belonging. So we can see that for Fatima, her hybridity gives her a sense of being rudderless, homeless almost, while most Timorese-Chinese, despite their hybridity, are much less tormented by it, because they have a kind of traveling "Chineseness" to which they can (and wish to) belong. An anchor does not necessarily have to be an ethnicity. It may be a high degree of cultural capital, it may be an empowered cosmopolitan identity (for example, the high flying East Timorese political cosmopolitans, or Carlos's more mundane version). By anchor, I don't mean that individuals embrace and are embraced by some all encompassing, essential, singular identity (Chineseness, Timoreseness, or whatever). Anchors, to continue the metaphor, allow a boat to float safely without drifting off to sea. Similarly, having a safe identity to fall back on, to speak from, but one which is open enough to drift away from when it suits, is the basis for a happy hybridity.

There is a second, related set of issues that arise from both the narratives in this chapter and the arguments in the previous one. These have to do with the very particular dilemma that has arisen now that East Timor is independent. To explain the processes behind this dilemma, it is useful to take a brief detour into some ideas put forward by Gerd Baumann (1997, 1996). Baumann has proposed two mutually constitutive forms of discursive praxis (Werbner 1997b, 18); the dominant and the demotic forms of ethnicity. The dominant discourse views "culture" as an essence, the reified possession of the "ethnic" group (Baumann 1997, 209). It is most often invoked in public forums for political ends. Demotic discourse, in contrast, involves a much more fluid concept of culture, and is actively negotiated and debated in the social process (215). The important aspect to recognize is that they coexist. They form dual discursive competencies. For ethnic activists, "reified cultural emblems are mobilising banners," which "draw on common-sense ideas to objectify culture, community, ethnos" as "self-evident homologues, while at the same time being aware of remaking, reshaping and re-forming these very terms in other contexts" (Werbner 1997b, 18).

Ethnic identity, then, can be seen to be an outcome of the negotiation of the dialectic between dominant and demotic discourses. Applying this conceptualization to the East Timorese case, however, throws up some important questions. As argued in Chapter 4, the independence struggle has been a powerful force in creating a map of "East Timoreseness" centered around symbols of indigeneity and the importance of exile. These processes are what Baumann is referring to by dominant discourse. However, East Timorese identities "on the ground" are far more complex. The important point is that, in a sense, it is easier to shift between the dominant and demotic discourses in a diaspora context. The big issue here is that, now that East Timor has its independence, those in Australia are for the first time confronted with having to carry through on the dominant discourse, which is centered on pure East Timoreseness and a commitment to return. Thus the two become intertwined in very painful ways.

Prior to independence, it had been possible for East Timorese to be tied into a community of suffering centered around the symbolic importance of exile, but *at the same time* also to feel ambivalence about how much they actually fit or could identify with the public identity put forward. However, now that the reality of return is available, these coexisting discourses, the dominant and the demotic, challenge and confront one another. Symptomatic of this is the immense guilt many feel at not wishing to return "home." In the next chapter, "From Exile to Diaspora?" I argue that increasingly East Timorese are attempting to negotiate the "where they're at," and "where they're from" through the creation of a new, hybrid translocale configured from, between, and across both East Timor and Australia.

Chapter 6
From Exile to Diaspora? On Identity, Belonging, and the (Im)Possibility of Return Home

> Perhaps the worst condemnation of all is to watch our country
> recede from our reach like a foreign, distant, indecipherable tide
> and to witness how indecisively our bodies begin to seek stability
> after many precarious years; our bodies, unconsenting and
> perhaps irremediably, grow accustomed to a country which they
> did not choose of their own free will.
>
> —exiled journalist

Darwin International Airport, March 2001. I am on a short stopover on
my way to East Timor. Darwin is Australia's stepping-off point to East
Timor—just a one-hour flight away—and the official transit point for
the United Nations UNTAET mission. Stepping off the plane and into
the airport lobby I am struck by the extent of East Timor's *presence* in
Darwin. The airport is a sea of blue-beret-wearing peacekeepers, clusters
of soldiers awaiting flights in or out of East Timor—faces ranging from
expectant to bored. In a taxi on the way to the city, the gruff, woolly-
bearded driver inevitably asks what I am doing in Darwin. On learning
that I'm on my way to East Timor, he proceeds to give me a rundown on
the intricacies of East Timorese politics, the peacekeeping forces, the
NGO and UN presence, and the ins and outs of the local Darwin East
Timorese community. For him, the comings and goings of East Timorese were simply part of the Darwin landscape. He told me that every day
he drives expectant local East Timorese to the airport—loaded with all
their worldly possessions to take back on their long awaited final return
to Timor. He also told me that he very frequently collects them again
some months later from the same airport—having changed their mind,

embittered and disappointed by their experience. Finding East Timor changed beyond recognition, saddened that they were not welcomed back with open arms as anticipated, and finding life in the "third world" is much harder than remembered, they have taken the heart-wrenching decision to give up and come back to Australia.

The driver also tells of how the local Darwin prostitutes are all investing in property—enjoying a booming trade servicing the peacekeepers taking their recreation leave in Darwin. In the city center I come across a cafe owned by Timorese-Chinese—and hear there are others—something unknown in Sydney. On the street I see many faces that could well be East Timorese, while in Sydney I would only very rarely encounter East Timorese anywhere by accident. I see peacekeepers wandering around in and out of uniform from every imaginable background—Portuguese, Brazilian, Kenyan, Jordanian, Australian. Back in the airport at the check-in counter for the flight to Dili, I line up behind a queue of East Timorese with piles of boxes, carrying all kinds of household paraphernalia, televisions, vacuum cleaners, stereos—all the luxuries of the West on delivery to family in East Timor. When someone in the queue finds the gifts exceed the baggage allowance, requests are passed down the queue to the (mostly white) aid workers and researchers like myself with little luggage, to allow the gift bearers to check their load in with our own to spread the weight. It appears a well-practiced ritual. In the waiting lounge all the aid workers and researchers exchange business cards and survival hints. Most seem to be NGO workers of varying kinds, and I unexpectedly meet several people I know from my Sydney East Timor networks—trauma counselors, aid workers, relatives of some East Timorese I know in Sydney. One friend, a trauma counselor, complains at having had to carry an entire dinner setting and a cappuccino machine up from Sydney (a four-hour flight north) on behalf of one of his East Timorese clients to deliver to her relatives.

Arriving in Dili, the first sight in the airport is an enormous troop-carrying plane emblazoned with "United Nations," surrounded by army trucks and soldiers milling about. I am struck by how familiar Dili seems—greeting passengers flying in is the famous statue of Jesus (reminiscent of its legendary Brazilian cousin) perched on the cliff top welcoming the plane. In the airport hall, I see people queuing at the check-in counter to return on the same plane to Darwin. The same faces, internationals and East Timorese, carrying reverse cultural baggage—having delivered their gifts from the West, they are returning with armloads of local cultural items, tais cloths, baskets, local crafts. Driving through the streets of Dili to the city center—it's almost as if I've been there before. In part, this is because for two years I've spent time with East Timorese in Sydney hearing every small detail of this place described to me. Also, the most uncanny part is that Dili is so much like Darwin—albeit with the sad addition of utter poverty apparent at every turn. There were the same troops, UN vehicles, aid workers, cafés, tropical heat, dust, and a certain style in the way people move about.

It struck me then that Darwin felt very much a kind of halfway point—a place of *both* East Timor and Australia, the tropics, but still the West, the landscape, the coming and going of people and goods. Now I understood why so many Sydney East Timorese say that, although they don't really want to move back to East Timor, they might just move to Darwin. Darwin represents that strange in-between state that mirrors who they have become. It is of both places, Australia and East Timor, and not quite belonging to either. However, beyond Darwin as a real place, I also began to contemplate these images of Darwin and Dili as a kind of metaphor for the hybrid, translocal space in which many East Timorese from other parts of Australia now live. This is a space created through constant coming and going, through relationships that intertwine at so many levels within, between, and across the two places, through the flows of cultural traffic, through the maintenance of kinship ties across space. This is a space I see many of Sydney's East Timorese creating in everyday interactions.

Questions of home, exile, and belonging became central for former East Timorese exiles following East Timor's independence. Now they had to decide whether to return to East Timor or remain in Australia. After the painful initial flight, possibly the greatest challenge for all exiles comes when it is finally safe to return to the homeland. For some, the final realization that they have grown accustomed to the new country is as painful as the initial exile, for these people can never *really* go home. There is, then, a fundamental ambivalence at the center of the post-exile experience. This increased engagement in processes of translocality reflects a fundamental shift, not from exile to home, but from exile to *diaspora*.

Theorizing Translocality

There is a range of processes apparent in the East Timorese community that represent strategies through which East Timorese returnees and "remainees" are able to create a kind of extended space of belonging. It is this space that I call *translocality* after Arjun Appadurai (1995).[1] Appadurai (1996, 178–99) has articulated a theory of the production of *locality*, wherein locality is an essentially relational and contextual knot of relationships, rather than something necessarily in space or place.

I prefer to use the term *translocal* rather than *transnational*. Earlier conceptualizations of the transnational, such as that put forward by Basch, Glick-Schiller and Szanton Blanc (1994, 7), characterize it as the building of multistranded social relations encompassing a disparate range of processes that include familial, economic, social, organizational, religious, and political relationships, giving shape to transmigrant identities connected to two or more nation-states. Appadurai's conceptualization of the translocal, in contrast, distinguishes those processes of actual everyday relations from those which can be referred to as transnational.

The transnational relates to elements that are not necessarily about relationships of locality. For example, a transnational community might be involved in a long distance nationalist project centered on the fantasy of homeland, but they are not necessarily involved with those in the homeland at the level of the everyday, the local, of "neighborhood." The transnational may be incorporated into the translocal imagination, but that is not to say they are one and the same thing. In other words, while the transnational functions at a more abstract level, at the level of ideas, political imagination, longing for homeland, and so forth, the translocal allows us to envisage the everydayness of material, family, social, symbolic networks and exchanges that connect East Timor and Australia. Locality encompasses the emotional and social character of neighborliness in a way the transnational doesn't. Locality, therefore, has an inherently phenomenological quality, constituted by a series of links between the sense of social immediacy, the technologies of interactivity, and the relativity of contexts, and expressed through particular modes of agency, sociality and reproducibility (Appadurai 1996, 178).

The important point in the East Timorese case is that the production of locality in Australia is translocal in character. This spatially discontinuous locality connects parts of Sydney and sites in East Timor into a single "neighborhood." The translocal does not neutralize space, it creates a new space that connects the two halves, East Timor and Australia. Indeed, given the very local nature of these processes, perhaps it is more correct to define this as a translocale between and across Dili and Fairfield. In other words, locality for East Timorese returnees and those who remain in Australia is produced in the imagination of a neighborhood by way of a set of social interactions that connect Australia and East Timor in very direct and practical ways.

The social immediacy to which Appadurai refers is manifest, for example, in phone calls, in the way information gathered about activities in Timor is shared in living rooms and on the streets of Fairfield. It manifests itself in extended family groups, those with one or more immediate family members working in East Timor. At the symbolic level, the exchange of cultural and everyday items between places has the effect of creating a kind of social contiguity. Beyond their material dimensions, these processes also function performatively, through cultural, political, and philanthropic performances, through material flows of goods and money, through gestures of giving or public service (Werbner 2002, 125), all of which intertwine to produce the translocale of Australian-Timoreseness. Where before independence East Timor represented a reified nostalgic version of "home" around which the desire for return centered, and which functioned as a kind of hinge for exilic identity, now home has entered the phenomenological realm of translocalized relationships and exchanges centered on the everyday.

For both remainees (in Australia) and returnees (to East Timor), charitable activities provide a focal point for demonstrating their participation in what can be characterized as the "moral community" of East Timor, as described in Chapter 4. Both groups are equally part of the translocal community spanning both places. Those in East Timor will have items sent over or delivered by visiting friends and relatives; there are the ever-present phone calls between Australia and East Timor; family ties are maintained in both places, as are homes, children, wives, husbands, and finances in Australia. Many are working on one-year contracts, having taken long-term leave to keep open the possibility of returning to their Australian jobs. Those in Australia travel for visits to East Timor, maintain close ties to family and friends there, help causes there, and constantly trade letters, cultural items, and news. A great many in the Sydney East Timorese community also have relatives at high levels in East Timor and are part of the "conversation" about the development of the new nation through these informal networks of family and friends. Through the choices they have made, both remainees and returnees are fostering a thriving translocale.

The *Reality* of Return Home

I visited East Timor in early 2001 to track down East Timorese from Australia who had made the "big move home" to East Timor to speak with them about their experiences and feelings toward this most significant event in their lives. Those who have decided to return for the most part share one important characteristic. They are almost all educated and were financially established in Australia, meaning they were able to afford housing in East Timor and had the ability to support themselves. This is an important point and should not be underestimated. Despite these similarities, not all returnees have had the same experience of resettlement. Of those I interviewed, I have chosen to relate Fernanda's and Osório's stories here because they represent different sections of the returnee group. Fernanda is a middle-aged mestiço woman who came to Australia in the early 1980s; Osório is a young man of twenty-six, schooled under the Indonesian system before fleeing East Timor in 1990. Their stories reflect their lives and perspectives in 2001.

Fernanda's Story

I met Fernanda in her modest newly built home in a suburb on the out-skirts of Dili. The house is at the end of a short dirt road and is sur-rounded by other small homes belonging to local East Timorese, all of which face onto a communal grassy area where the residents keep goats and chickens, and where the neighbors often congregate under the ubiquitous *hali hung* tree in the afternoon for coffee and a chat.[2] Fer-nanda had returned to East Timor from her home in suburban Sydney in the middle of 2000. She was seventeen when she fled East Timor with her family in 1975. After eleven months in Atambua in West Timor, she traveled to Portugal, where she lived for eight years before coming to Australia sponsored by a stepsister under the Special Family Reunion Pro-gram in 1983. She did not enjoy her time in Portugal at all, finding the economic inequalities and discrimination toward outsiders very difficult to cope with. She eventually married an East Timorese man in Australia and had three children: two girls, now teenagers, and a boy born a decade later. Until she left for East Timor, Fernanda and her family lived in the western Sydney suburb of Mt. Druitt, where a number of middle-class East Timorese families live. Their motivation for returning to East Timor was not necessarily because they were unhappy in Australia.

I have always had so much moral support from Australians . . . and even now I've left, even at the airport, when I'm trying to bring loads and loads of things in, they're always helping. Even in Timor now, you see an Australian person dealing with a Timorese child, and you see that it's completely different. They're more human than Portuguese! I think it's more, it's in the Australians' hearts. They're very kind people. . . . My father was born in Portugal and everything—but when I went to Portugal in '76, from Atambua, I found it a lot harder to get into the community. I found that the Portuguese people were not quite accepting us back. . . . But when I came in '83 to Australia, it was completely different. . . . I felt more accepted, for the first time since I left Timor, I felt at home. . . . So I am sad to leave in a way. I will always be part of Australia.

Fernanda's main motivation for moving back to East Timor was to find a simpler and less stressful life for herself and her family and to be able to bring her young boy up in East Timor. She had very fond memories of the East Timor of her youth and hoped to rediscover some of that life on her return. Fernanda's daughters chose to go back to Australia to finish school, and four of Fernanda's siblings remain in Australia with no wish to return, but her husband had no family in Australia and was always very lonely there without family support.

Even though I was settled in Australia, happy, I always missed the life I had before I had to leave East Timor. Very peaceful, nice. People from East Timor that I remember, from before '75, when I had to run away, were friendly people.

People that take you into their houses any time and you could walk in the bushes and you could do anything you liked and nobody would do anything wrong to you. I have very strong memories. . . . And my husband was a bit lonely in Sydney. The two of us were always talking that one day, if it's possible, we will return to East Timor. But that was something at the back of our minds, because while the Indonesians were here it was almost impossible. And then, when the referendum started to come up: OK! We started to come up with ideas. . . . It was difficult, because I had to leave my daughters there in Australia. They were still quite young, . . . they still need me. But, then again, I have to think about this one [her son], too. It was sort of like . . . "We have to sacrifice some things to get some things better."

Fernanda, then, was motivated by a combination of factors such as her husband's loneliness in Australia without family and the fact that they had always maintained a commitment to return. She had strong and fond memories of her life in East Timor, a fantasy life of warm weather, beaches, a comfortable and simple life, a safe place where she could be part of her culture and be part of a community, and, perhaps most important, her wish to raise her youngest child in East Timor. In part, this was to do with her need for her children to have a connection to Timorese culture, and in part it was motivated by the difficulties faced by low-income working parents in Australia.

I wanted my children, even though they are Australians, to know where their parents come from. I guess, what made me decide, it's sort of like, when I was in Australia I had everything I wanted to live comfortably. And I still have these things in Australia, because I still didn't get rid of anything! Even though I came back here, I wanted to keep my things in Australia. But family life I did not have in Australia. Because, like, I was waking up at 4 o'clock in the morning in Australia, leaving home at 4:30—leaving my children locked up in the house—because I lived in Mount Druitt and I worked at Bondi. And then arriving home at 5:30 in the afternoon. Dinner. Prepare uniforms for the next day. I had no life with my family at all. My daughters grew up without knowing me. . . . I didn't want to continue with my son. I could see him sometimes, sitting, playing in the backyard, even though he stayed with my father's aunty, they call her Grandma—which, we live back-to-back in Australia, different houses, but the backyards are back-to-back. So we open the gate and the back fence and the kids—[laughs] . . . Anyway, but my son—like, the old lady was old and she was always inside the house and he was playing outside, and sometimes people go, "Poor Ric! No mother, no father, nobody!" . . . This was the biggest part of my decision, and the other biggest part was trying to, in some way, help these people of East Timor.

Split families are common among East Timorese returnees from Australia—permanent returnees, and those testing the waters on twelve-month contracts. This situation forces many families with older children to make the difficult decision to leave one or more family members—children, husbands, wives, or siblings—in Australia. For Fernanda and those like her, her teenage children are Australian, born and raised there.

Many have no wish to "return" to East Timor—knowing nothing of the place, other than that it represents to them a place of danger and poverty. Whether to return if you have children is possibly one of the most difficult issues facing Timorese families in Australia. The situation is very difficult for Fernanda and for her two teenage girls, but one that she feels is sustainable because she has family support in Australia to help care for her daughters.

When we first came back, we brought our daughters with us, they stayed here with us for a while but then they went back to Australia in January to start school. They're with my husband's aunt. But they miss us. They ring us here every Sunday. Their [great aunt, they call her grandma] brought them up, so they're very close. So they are all right, because they grew up with their family. But they still miss us a lot. They do. But I hope they'll want to come back eventually. My oldest daughter already said, because she was here, she said—she's now in Year 11, so she's made a decision she would like to take courses she can use in Timor, so when she finish she will come, she would like to come to Timor.

Because her children had not been to East Timor before, it was somewhat of a culture shock for them. Nevertheless, Fernanda hopes that her daughters, particularly her younger one, will, with age, come to appreciate East Timor and choose to make a life there, or at least to pursue a strong connection to their mother's homeland. Her elder daughter has expressed a wish to work for a short time in East Timor when she is older, and this is very heartening for Fernanda. However this new situation has, not surprisingly, been difficult for her daughters.

For the first two weeks . . . it was very hard for them. . . . They were born in Australia, and in Australia you've got all facilities and hygiene, which—it's nothing in Timor. It was hard for them to learn to live with the family here. The younger one, . . . She still doesn't understand a lot. So for her, it was like, "Mum, I don't want to go back there! Yuk!" [laughs]. She doesn't think about the family, the people meeting us here to teach them all these things about our culture, she's too young to understand all this kind of thing. . . . I'm going to try to bring them over more often to visit. I would love to have them here permanently. We'll have to wait and see what they think once they've finished their studies. But of course, they're Australian-born, so they'll always go back to Australia anytime they want. Australia will always be a part of them. . . . The transition to come back it's not going to be quite as hard as for those from Portugal, because they know that Australia is so close and they know that anytime, they can go back.

The fact that individuals have often become very attached to their lives in Australia, or as in Fernanda's case have children who have either been born in or raised in Australia, presents perhaps the most fundamental difficulty for a great many individuals and families in Australia and East Timor. The most common strategy these people use to reconcile this difficult situation is to imagine, and indeed in many cases deliberately create structures for, leading *translocal lives* in order to have a connection to *both* East Timor *and* Australia. Common are strategies such as dual property ownership, working on short-term international contracts in East Timor, traveling back and forth, and having homes and family in both places. For Fernanda, this plays out in several ways.

We are back here permanently. But I won't sell. I won't sell my house. I'll rent it out. That is important for my daughters that we don't cut off from Australia. And for me too—I don't want to give up my things there. At the moment it's very important for my children, because they can see Timor, it's a country still not 100 percent. And, again, being Australians—they were born there, they were raised there, they are Australians! Yes, and even for myself, as Australians' mother— yes, I would very much like for Australia to still have an important part in East Timor. So I will be travelling there anytime I can to visit everyone.

In addition to the constant travel back and forth and the dual property ownership, there is, as stated earlier, a lot of phone contact and cultural traffic in the form of letters, cultural and practical goods, ideas and information. For those who remain in Australia, the "returnees" are an important link to East Timor. For those who have decided against returning, it is a wonderful link to their homeland to have family members or friends who have gone back, who can function as translocal mediators. They become a constant source of news from "home," go-betweens who can allow the nonreturnee into their lives. This gives those Timorese remaining in Australia both a sense of, and a real first-hand involvement in, East Timor, in the network of local social relations in East Timor.

There are always a lot of phone calls and letters and things a lot, a lot of backwards and forwards. They ring me up all the time. All my friends over there in Australia, my workmates. Yes, they do ring me up! [laughs]. They enjoy getting news from Timor, my brothers and sisters, my family over there, my friends, they all ring me up, they enjoy, and in one way they envy me being here in East Timor but again, they say, "We're not going to leave our lives, we're not going to leave everything here," they say, "You had enough courage to do it, but we're not." So in a way I can be like their link to East Timor, even if they don't want to come back here. It makes them happy.

Fernanda's translocal practice of everyday life comes out in several ways. As she says, she didn't want to give up her things in Australia. Her family have made the decision not to sell their Sydney home, despite having built a brand new home in Dili. This is as much, I think, to give a sense of security, an insurance policy if you like, to Fernanda, as it is to make her children feel safe and to demonstrate a continuing connection to Australia. Her elder daughter hopes one day to use her skills to work in East Timor. Fernanda plans to visit Australia whenever she can. She sees herself not simply as a Timorese very connected to East Timor, but as a "mother of Australians," her three children. She is aware that they are very much children of both places, and that this places her in a permanent relationship to both East Timor and Australia, a conundrum she reconciles by not severing all ties there. She is happy that her friends and family back in Australia are able to telephone often and that she can be their source in East Timor. Fernanda's story shows that translocality is embodied and material, not just imagined, as transnationalism can be.

Fernanda's return to East Timor has been a balance of positive and negative experiences. To finally "return home" was not quite as wonderful as she expected. But overall, she rates her return as successful. Perhaps the two biggest difficulties have been the shock at how much East Timor had changed, and her struggle to cope with the new culture of East Timor.

I can't believe it how much it's all changed. . . . , I still get lost in Dili, . . . I had a picture in my head before I came, about how it would be, and what our lives might be like. . . . But it has been very difficult for the family to accept what we find here . . . because the picture that we had, maybe was influenced by the way we live in Australia, it was a clean way, it's a healthy way, and these people over here, they live for twenty-five years under the Indonesians where they—the Indonesians are not clean, so that's how they grew up. And for them, the ones who left in '75, they still have that resentment towards us . . . so now, you're trying to teach them and they turn around and say, "You think that because you left, you went to live overseas, that you know better than us."

A former exile, South African Breyton Breytenbach, reflects on the difference between exiles, and those who stayed:

"Before" does not exist for "them," the "others," those who stayed behind. For "them" it was all continuity; for you it was a fugue of disruptions. The thread is lost. The telling has shaped the story. You make your own history at the cost of not sharing theirs. Their eyes, having seen too many different things, now see differently. (quoted in Gready 1994, 6)

The shock of change, and the sense of unhomeliness this can bring, are common to many former exiles. Among other things hinted in Fernanda's narrative is her deep concern with issues of hygiene and cleanliness. It represents everything that has changed for the worse in East Timor, and the lack of which seems to give her a profound sense of uneasiness. It represents the Indonesianization of Timor and the shift away from Portuguese, "Western" manners and practices, which she remembers from her youth in Dili and has become used to in Australia. This creates a kind of dislocation of home. The journalist in the opening quote to this chapter alludes to this in describing the ambivalence surrounding how bodies unconsentingly become accustomed to the country of exile (Kaminsky 1999, 1).

This "unhomely" feeling might be described as a lack of "attunement"

(Mar 2002, 295). Attunement references a kind of bodily "affective resonance" with a new place, person, or situation, which Mar describes as a visceral combination of physical sensation and emotional connection (or lack of connection) (295). In Fernanda's case, she feels unexpectedly ill attuned to her new home, demonstrated by her bodily discomfort at the "new" manners of East Timor, her feeling lost in the marketplace, and so on. The important element in the concept of attunement is its very bodily and affective character. Interestingly, however, Fernanda hopes that returnees might be able to play a role in subtly "educating" those who stayed into Western hygiene practices:

I know that a lot of skills that I have can help my country. Because I always worked in hospitals, . . . I can see that these people here can be helped, because diseases are spreading too quick here. . . . But it's not only in hygiene around the houses, but the person's acts as well. For example, they spit everywhere, there's no-one to go in and explain to them that they can't do that, that this is a method of spreading disease. . . . Not so much up the mountains, but in Dili . . . under the Portuguese, Dili was very clean, and the people . . . who lived around the Malae[3]—which is what they called the white people— they had to behave, they had to be clean.

This anxiety about cleanliness perhaps also represents an unconscious difficulty with living surrounded by poverty. She has become used to Western standards of health, and associates Westernness, Australianness, and *Portugueseness* with cleanliness. In a way, then, this anxiety and mild disgust about the "unhygienic Indonesian/mountain" ways of contemporary Dili underscores her new and rather unexpected foreignness. Despite the generally positive experience she has had of return, one of its most obviously painful aspects has been a feeling of rejection by the "locals," the "stayers," who see her as Western and foreign. This perception is caused primarily, she feels, by the many "show-off" overseas Timorese who have returned to East Timor and who "act superior," looking down on the local people. Despite her dislike of these high flyers, the "locals" do not differentiate them from her. She is targeted as an outsider along with them and the much-despised UN and international workers, a situation that is extraordinarily painful for her.

I feel that people are very unfriendly. I went to the markets a few times and a lot of people don't know that I'm Timorese because of my light skin, they think that I'm Portuguese or from another country, so they speak in Tetum between them but I understand because I can speak Tetum. And they all go . . . , "Run her over with your bike! Because she doesn't belong here, she belongs in her country." . . . Even though I want to cry—I just look at them with a smile on my face and I speak to them in Tetum and I say, "This is my country!" For them it's the whites . . . the malae are the targets. One problem is that lots of Timorese come back here just to show off. . . . So even though it is these show offs, and also UN workers that they hate most, it affects my life a lot. Because if the locals hate every malae who comes here, because of that then I'm a target too. . . . But then I just have to try not to let it get to me. It hurts because being a Timorese and wanting to do so much to your country, to contribute to your country, then you get here and you can't do it because you are taken as a foreigner. . . . I feel rejected in my own country. But this is still my home and I will be strong. I am a Timorese and no-one can say that I am not. I was born in Timor and no-one can say that I am not a Timorese.

Fernanda's mestiço background, her "pre-'75" identity, her western/Portuguese version of Timoreseness, all of these things have remained somewhat intact during her years in exile, while East Timor has, as it were, moved on. For Fernanda, the most important "other" that needs to be expelled from East Timor is Indonesianness. For many of the younger generation in East Timor, however, the influx of wealthy foreigners has in many ways become a more important focus of anger, creating a situation where Fernanda and those like her are marked as foreign because of their very Westernness and are thus a target of resentment.

Osório's Story

Fernanda's experience is by no means universal. For several reasons, returnees such as Osório seem to have had a far less ambivalent experience of return. The fact that he lived in East Timor until 1990 and was schooled under the Indonesian system is very important. He is fluent in Indonesian, Tetum, Portuguese and English. He comes from a very politically involved FRETILIN family, and was involved in protests and political activity throughout his time in Australia. He is young, of indigenous Timorese background, and still has a strong network of friends in East Timor from before, and with whom he has happily reestablished relationships.

Because Osório's father held a position with the FRETILIN party in the late 1970s, the family spent some time in the hills following the invasion but came down to Dili at the end of 1978. His father was arrested at the beginning of 1979 by the Indonesians, taken for questioning, and never heard from again. It was a fundamental trauma that in later years influenced Osório to become involved in the political struggle as a FRETILIN representative himself. Following his father's "disappearance," Osório's mother started trying in 1979 to get her family out of East Timor, succeeding only in 1990, when they fled to Portugal before coming to Australia in 1992.

When I was in Portugal, . . . I started to realize, bit by bit, about East Timor's history. . . . That's when I was involved in the struggle for East Timor politics. I joined demonstrations that were held in Portugal. . . . So by the time I got to Melbourne, even though I was still at high school, I had already had the awareness of the need to actually join the struggle, be an activist, and be active in the whole process. Also, you know my father—my whole family was FRETILIN. So when I went to Melbourne, it was automatic for me to be involved in politics. I had to be involved because well, I've always had faith in East Timor being independent one day. Having faith in independence is a big issue because lots of people, well, many people, have lost faith at some point in time about East Timor being independent. . . . But I've never lost faith. I just thought, if you have to struggle for 150 years I think that's—you know. We still can do it.

Osório's deep involvement from quite a young age in politics, the fact that he comes from a very political family and, perhaps most profoundly, the death of his father in the name of East Timor's independence at the hands of the Indonesian military created an enormously strong pull to return to East Timor. Another important factor is that Osório is from the Melbourne East Timorese community rather than Sydney. While Sydney East Timorese are geographically spread throughout three distant areas of Sydney and are cut through with a myriad old community arguments and resulting factions that refuse to meet or communicate, the Melbourne community is for the most part centered in an area near the inner city and is very linked geographically and socially with the non-Timorese students and intellectuals in the pre-independence solidarity support movement. The Melbourne community is generally seen to be much "tighter and more organized," and more localized, in terms of getting together and organizing community and political activities.

The community in Melbourne was very tight, so we kept our everyday lives, our interactions, much like we do here in East Timor. . . .when we first arrived in Melbourne, we felt isolation, . . . But as soon as we met all the other East Timorese, the feeling of community made it seem much closer to home than we ever thought possible. . . . Even though you were born outside, even though you had a foreign experience, . . . like Australia and Portuguese culture, I think if you keep in touch with the East Timorese community in a tight way then you get a sense of what it feels like to be in East Timor, you don't forget where you come from this way. This feeling of wanting to be back in Timor, this feeling of exile you ask about—I'd say I started to feel like that once I was in Melbourne. Once I started to mix with the Timorese, community and get that sense of East Timorese back again. I think that that is because we'd start to talk about how nice it would be to go back to our country, to go back to live. And then we also talked about how this place (Australia) don't belong to us, and we live here, we work here, we do our studies here, but it just doesn't feel right. . . . And when we mixed together, we felt closer to home, and it made you realize that it would be a lot better if you were in your own country.

The differences between the Sydney and Melbourne communities that Osório describes are similar to those raised in Malkki's (1995) important study of Hutu refugees in Burundi. In that study, Malkki compared those living a tight-knit refugee camp with Hutus who were living in and integrated into a nearby town. Her research showed that the camp refugees placed a great deal more emphasis on maintaining a kind of purity, a sense of exile, and a focus on returning home. For those in the camp, "refugeeness" formed a central part of their self-narratives (1997a, 67). Those in the town had a far less essentialist, bounded form of collective identity; they were more cosmopolitan, able to mesh with their town lives. For them, "exile" did not really have much operative or symbolic function at all. They did not define themselves solely in relation to the concept of return to homeland, the way the camp refugees did. There are both similarities to and differences from the Timorese case. The differences between the Timorese in Sydney and Melbourne mesh with Malkki's analysis in the sense that, anecdotally at least, Melbourne Timorese have been more likely to return than their Sydney counterparts. Their spatial togetherness and links with the solidarity groups have meant they are a much more cohesive group. Although the Sydney Timorese have been less likely to return, they nonetheless still have a sense of moral indebtedness to East Timor, and they are still subject to a great deal of guilt surrounding their decisions not to return.

As was flagged in Chapter 4, the forms of protest are an important element in the construction of exile. Osório reports that the regular protests, and in particular the creative aspects such as artistic exhibitions, music, and dance, had a great influence on his emotional attachment to East Timor and subsequently played a part in his need to return.

I remember in Melbourne, we always used to talk about the scenery in East Timor, the very beautiful scenery out there, about one day living somewhere in the interior, in the mountains. I remember seeing one of the exhibitions in Melbourne the solidarity and Timorese community used to promote our struggle. It was '98 or '99. About East Timorese artists, and most of the paintings were about scenery. East Timor art and photos, a lot of them have got scenery. I really think that these things worked in capturing people's hearts. What the scenery would be like, what beautiful beaches—you can actually go there and see for— it makes you can close your eyes and feel it. But it is funny—it was only in Melbourne that this started.

For various reasons, Osório's return has been much smoother than Fernanda's. The United Nations hired him as an interpreter, and although he lives modestly in Dili, his very healthy international salary made it easy for him to establish himself and to afford the airfare to visit friends and family in Melbourne. He did not find it a difficult decision to return to Timor. He expressed to me that he felt no culture shock and has had no trouble at all fitting in again, and he feels very much at home in East Timor.

It wasn't a hard decision at all to come back. . . . I felt that this struggle, I don't have a choice but I just have to be in it! . . . When I came back here, I felt like

I'd never left the place. Like, I'm used to the luxuries in Melbourne, but I'm also very well-adapted here. . . . I don't have any problems with anything at all. . . . most of my friends are still here, most of my relatives are still here, so when I came back I don't feel much like I left at all. No culture shock at all. The only difference that people are seeing between me and them was that I speak better English than anybody could. . . . But apart from that . . . people don't notice much difference in me at all. . . . I don't know how to put it, but the people who see me wouldn't even know . . . that I had been living in Australia . . . for ten years. . . . Also, you can tell if someone has been abroad for the past fifteen or twenty years by the way they're speaking Tetum. It would have mostly Portuguese words but no Indonesian words at all. So I can get away with it—no-one can tell—and I try not to tell people I've been abroad.

It is possible to see in Osório's story some characteristics specific to him and his situation that position him quite differently from Fernanda and have influenced profoundly his experience of return. First of all, Osório comes from a deeply political family. He has been involved in independence politics since his youth and has been emotionally driven by the loss of his father. He was involved in many of the kinds of activities discussed in Chapter 4, creating, I believe, a kind of embodied trajectory (see, for example, his musings on Timorese landscape) of exile and inevitable return. His experience in the tightly knit Melbourne community meant that he was much less linked into a life in Australia, which made return a simpler affair. He is relatively young and speaks fluent Indonesian and contemporary Tetum, mixed with Indonesian words, the same as that used by youth in East Timor today. This gives him an important ability to blend in, as does his darker skin and indigenous Timorese background.

Unlike Fernanda, whose skin color and Tetum mark her out as "foreign," Osório is able to pass as someone who has never left. He still has a strong network of friends in East Timor from his school days and has slipped happily back into friendships with them. He has a high paying job as a translator but keeps that quiet among his social network. All in all, the conditions for Osório's return were such that he was able simply to slip back into a very similar life in East Timor. He is working in a job where he is involved in the East Timor war crimes trials, heavily involved in the FRETILIN youth wing, is continuing his Australian studies from East Timor as an honors student (with plans to return to Australia to complete them), and is very much involved with the social and political life of East Timor, from the high flyers to the locals.

There are those like Fernanda whose decision to return is bound up with a range of issues, such as her husband's lack of family in Australia, her extremely strong-willed and determined nature, her desire for a quieter life for her young child, and her wish to escape the long hours she had to work because of her financial struggles in Sydney. And there are those like Osório who are compelled to return because they have not been gone as long and it is therefore not so much of a cultural shock. Osório has also lived in a much tighter knit community and has been very politically involved throughout his life. Unlike Fernanda, he never quite felt a sense of belonging to Australia, and the transition back has been much smoother than for Fernanda. Both, however, had a strong sense of exile identity and a strong desire and sense of responsibility to return.[4]

We have seen that return is no simple feat. The difference between those who stay and those who return is that the returnees are inevitably faced with the fact of their hybridity, that their Timoreseness will be put into question when faced with the reality of living in a new nation trying desperately to rediscover itself after so many years of colonization. Sadly, this rediscovery seems frequently to slip into essentialist notions of what it is to be Timorese. Arising from a range of processes, and regardless how progressive their intent, such proclamations have the effect of undermining the returnee's sense of return from exile to home. If I am no longer a true Timorese, how is it that I can return "home" to East Timor? Where is it then that I do belong? There are so many well-meaning forces working at present in East Timor to excavate some notion of Timoreseness from the rubble of Indonesian occupation. However, as Said so eloquently cautions:

No one today is purely one thing. Labels like Indian, or woman, or Muslim, or American are no more than starting points, which if followed into actual experience for only a moment are quickly left behind. . . . Yet just as human beings make their own history, they also make their cultures and ethnic identities. No one can deny the persisting continuities of long traditions, sustained habitations, national languages, and cultural geographies, but there seems no reason except fear and prejudice to keep insisting on their separation and distinctiveness, as if that was all that human life was all about. . . . [I]n Eliot's phrase, reality cannot be deprived of the "other echoes [that] inhabit the garden" (Said 1994, 407–8)

In many ways, the East Timorese returnees from Australia and Portugal represent the "other echoes" that inhabit the garden of contemporary East Timor. For numerous reasons, it does seem that the homecoming experience of many returnees reflects a trend in East Timor where those who left have a sense of only partial belonging on their return. The people of East Timor are going through a phase of rediscovering who they are. As with many anticolonial movements (understandably) this often turns into a process of trying, to use Hall's term (1990), to excavate traditional identities from under the cultural layers of colonial rule and occupation. These processes often slip into exclusionary practices of cultural boundary marking as a means to eject whichever otherness seems the biggest threat to a sense of "East Timorese Identity" (capitals intended). Ironically, in post-1999 East Timor, the cultural "other" many, especially the disempowered and the young, wish to evict is not so much Indonesianness as Westernness. Gradually since the United Nations intervention in 1999, there has been an increasing sense of disenfranchisement among local East Timorese, those who don't speak English or Portuguese and those who are poor or uneducated. They have been marginalized by many of the processes set in place by the United Nations and the international NGO community working in East Timor.

The international staff (and that includes East Timorese from the diaspora)—on international salaries, engaged in conspicuous consumption, and working in the best and best-paid jobs—have come to represent "the West" to Timorese locals. The imposition of Portuguese in the workplace and in schools compounds this resentment among the younger local generation, most of whom speak neither English or Portuguese.[5] They are disadvantaged in obtaining good employment because they must compete with East Timorese returned from Portugal and Australia, many of whom speak Portuguese, and those from Australia have the added advantage of English. There have been many angry clashes over this issue in particular.

Moreover, with the enormous influence of a very traditional Catholic church, gender codes have become important in East Timor as a central marker of ethnicity. During the period of my visit alone, there were several violent incidents surrounding the demarcation of "appropriate" codes of gender behavior for Timorese women. Some of these incidents demonstrated an unfortunate intersection of issues of masculinity, colonialism, poverty, and the marking out of ethnic boundaries. There were several reports of young local Timorese women being beaten by Timorese men simply for dancing with foreign soldiers from the Peacekeeping Force (PKF). The general opinion among young men at the time was that "these are our women and we don't want them corrupted and used by outsiders." In another incident, an Indian woman, who was a member of the UN civilian staff, was attacked on a Dili beach for swimming in a bikini, apparently having been mistaken for a local Timorese woman. In the Dili markets, three young Timorese women returnees were set upon by a group of men for wearing "revealing" Western dress. Such incidents as these and the incident in the marketplace reported by Fernanda earlier in the chapter highlight the fact that all returnees, whether high flyers or not, are in the precarious position of having come to represent that which threatens the *new* traditional East Timoreseness.

Gender and the comparative freedom of women in Australia compared with East Timor is one of the biggest issues surrounding return. One mid-thirties mother of two young boys said to me that she "feels like a stranger" in East Timor now because the men talk down to her and stare at her because of her Western dress. She particularly hates how conservative the Catholic Church has become in East Timor, especially the rules that she must wear a veil in church and that women must wear a skirt rather than pants. Another issue that arises over and over again is the sense that East Timor is different now, more "backward," more "Indonesianized." There are countless stories of how devastated many returnees felt when they discovered that those who stayed did not welcome them back with open arms as anticipated. Those who stayed often see the Australian Timorese as cowards who did not stay to fight like they did. They are seen as wealthy and privileged opportunists just coming back to steal jobs. Returnees are often shocked at how much has changed, and saddened by their inability to reconnect to family and friends who stayed. Paul Gready articulates similar difficulties of return after a long exile from South Africa:

More often than not there is no hero's welcome, no large cheering crowd to await the exile's arrival, no ritual slaughtering of the fattened calf. The returnee may, indeed, cower from such a reception. Could any welcome, anyway, compensate for all the years of farewells? People have grown up, grown old, and died; lives and relationships have changed, and those long absent have been forgotten. Absence strips away attachments and connections, makes the exile into a stranger who has no life left in that place called home. Even with close friends and family, returnees may still find themselves struggling "like tourists in a market place." (1994, 7)

Those who find it hardest are the East Timorese who left prior to the 1990s and are caught in the distinct cultural difference surrounding their Portugueseness as against the Indonesianized East Timor of today. People like Osório, on the other hand, are often those who were schooled under the Indonesians and left East Timor during the 1990s. They speak Indonesian, and their Tetum is inflected with Indonesian words that replace the Portuguese influences on the language used by the older generation. They find it easier because they have a valued space to slip back into in East Timor. They don't stand out as "foreign" as much as the 1970s and 1980s refugees do when they return. They are more likely to have networks of friends and family still in East Timor and find it easier to reconnect into their former social milieu. Moreover, they are less likely to be as connected to Australia as their 1970s and 1980s counterparts, and less likely to have significant assets, family, and other responsibilities there.

The importance of having a local "space" to slip back into in East Timor is paramount. By this I mean a social and family network, a good job that comes with significant social and cultural capital. Different strategies are employed to find such a space. While individuals such as Fernanda and Osório fit in by trying not to betray their foreignness, there is another group who live in quite a different world—the "high flyers," the educated cosmopolitan East Timorese with government, NGO, or UN jobs. These cosmopolitans usually live in Dili. In contrast to "everyday" individuals such as Fernanda, living and working in the local community, this group exists in a world that is rather abstracted from the everyday struggles of local life.

While Fernanda's world is very local and she negotiates her day-to-day existence within the same space as those East Timorese who stayed, this large group of very privileged individuals in Dili are the most visible of all returnees. You find them in the flashy City Café in central Dili, one block from UNTAET headquarters. This is the city's most fashionable café, with a contemporary Western menu (and prices to match), contemporary stainless steel décor, and English- and Portuguese-speaking waiters. They will be sharing a table with other cosmopolitan Timorese or international workers from the UN or international NGOs. There is a good chance that a high profile politician such as José Ramos-Horta, Xanana Gusmão, or some other government minister will be at a table nearby. Many of these returnees are on international rather than local salaries, allowing them to maintain a very high standard of living in East Timor, one not accessible to local Timorese. Such salaries also allow these individuals to maintain a more Western way of life, to travel back to Australia (or Portugal), and quite often to maintain a family and home back in Australia. You will find these individuals traveling the streets of Dili in a ubiquitous NGO or UN standard issue white four-wheel-drive vehicle. This is a world far removed from the local Timorese, the "stayers." The divide is visible in many ways. The City Café in Dili is situated on a street where more than half the buildings, at the time of my visit, were burned out and the remainder occupied by small businesses mostly set up to service the international trade—office services, other cafes, and so on. The hands of Timorese street urchins, who roam the streets of Dili, reach up through the railing of the raised deck where the café seating is located to beg for American dollars.

The average weekly wage of a worker on an international wage is in the vicinity of $1,000 Australian dollars per week while the average wage of local East Timorese is less than $40. There is a whole network of hotels, bars, restaurants, and cafes frequented by this cosmopolitan group, with prices linked to their international wages and therefore out of bounds to most locals. Indeed, there is a burgeoning industry of security guards posted outside such establishments to keep "undesirables" out. For this group of returnees, such conditions act as a strong inducement to stay, given that many of this group would, if in Sydney, be somewhat on the margins of Australian society, in average or below average occupations and salaries, living in the western suburbs, and always slightly "on the outside" as migrants from a non-English-speaking country. This group are able to achieve a significant climb in social status by returning. They instantly acquire a great deal of social and cultural capital, and as Tetum-, English-, and Portuguese-speakers, are in a position to take up the best jobs in East Timor. Once it was announced that the United Nations would go into East Timor, there was an intense movement of community leaders from Sydney back to East Timor, many seeking prime positions in the new government. This is not to imply that just because these returnees are doing well, they should somehow be the object of scorn and suddenly become unworthy of our sympathies. Mallki (1997b) identifies this trend among refugee workers who respond in such a way that only those who "look like proper victims" are worthy of attention. Rather, I want to emphasize the way in which this group of individuals live, to a large extent, in a different sociospatial milieu to "local" Timorese.

Between Worlds: On the Translocal Reconfiguring of Home

Despite some negative experiences, many have found that they are happy to have come back to East Timor, even if they have not quite found the original home they were looking for. However, it is increasingly apparent that the sense of only partial "homeliness" for both returnees and those remaining in Australia has led many to engage in various strategies to renegotiate a sense of home, post-exile. One key strategy to achieve a sense of belonging can be seen in Fernanda's and Osório's stories, whereby they deliberately minimize the aspects that mark them as "foreign" in public. What I would like to concentrate on here, however, is the fact that for quite a number of both returnees and remainees, processes outlined in previous chapters have resulted in a need to reconfigure home, which in turn has manifested itself in a kind of translocal outlook to link the neighborhoods of both East Timor and Australia.

At various points throughout the book we have seen some of the translocal aspects of the current situation with respect to Timorese in Australia and those who have returned home. In Chapter 4, I related the kinds of conversations one might hear in a Timorese living room or between Timorese meeting at the local shops in Fairfield. I gave the example of a young woman who regularly gets the latest updates at the supermarket or in the local shopping center on the ins and outs of what is happening at the highest levels in Timorese politics, by way of the elderly mother of a leading Timorese politician. There are a very large number of individuals in the community in Sydney with close family members who have returned to take up high-level positions in the East Timor government. There are also a large number of now translocal families, where one or both parents have returned to take up contract work in Timor, leaving a household in Sydney with little prospect of resolving the definition of "home base" in either place. Like Fernanda's translocal household, many maintain a home in both places. Quite a few are hoping that East Timor and Australia will have some kind of special structures put in place to allow them to work in both places (quite what those structures might be, I'm not sure). The idea of allowing dual citizenship between Australia and East Timor is also very popular.

In addition to the traffic in cultural goods referred to earlier, the telephone traffic between East Timor and Australia is phenomenal. Telstra (Australia's main telecommunications carrier) had the contract (at the time of writing) to provide the mobile telephone network in East Timor. Because of this arrangement, the cell phone system in East Timor was, beginning in 1999, operating on the same phone network as Australia, meaning that when one calls a mobile phone service in East Timor, it is not charged at an international rate but deemed a "national" call within Australia. This was both metaphorically and practically very interesting. It created a sense of "contracted space" between friends and relatives in the two countries.

Between 1999 and 2002, Telstra had a special deal in Australia whereby it was free to make a call from one Telstra mobile phone to another between 9 P.M. and 5 A.M. The local Timorese community have discovered this anomaly and every evening there is the 9 P.M. network overload, with a huge number of mobile phone calls between the two places. As can be imagined, this created a wonderful sense of connection for Timorese remaining in Australia, particularly given the fact that they were cut off from contact for many of the years of Indonesian occupation. As Fernanda pointed out, those remaining behind very much enjoyed these phone calls to relatives and returnees. They were able to get all the latest news and gossip from East Timor and have a sense of almost being there. Conversely, those in East Timor were able to put through their orders for goods from Australia and receive all the news from "home." There is also lots of cultural traffic of the everyday variety. One young Timorese woman in Sydney told me that when all the international workers were in East Timor, she received endless orders from her cousins in Timor for the latest fashions they saw on these international workers around Dili. Apparently cargo pants and strappy sandals were the latest must-have item among young Dili residents. Her cousin at one point telephoned to ask her to bring a whole box of these sandals (presumably to distribute to sisters and friends) when she next made a visit.

On a more symbolic level, the current debate surrounding Portuguese versus English as the working language is another interesting example. I noticed that there was a sense of competitiveness becoming apparent between returnees from Australia and from Portugal, manifest particularly around competition for jobs, and translating into support for one side or another in the language debate. Because many of the UN jobs required English, Portuguese, and Tetum, those English-speaking Timorese returnees from Australia were at a natural advantage in competing for these coveted positions, causing some resentment among returnees from Portugal. Similarly, the Australian returnees were much more likely to support having English rather than Portuguese as one of the official languages of East Timor; conversely, those from Portugal supported Portuguese against English. This probably has to do primarily with the competition for jobs just outlined, but based on conversations overheard in Australia and East Timor, it has also to do with returnees, and those in the diaspora, wanting to have a stronger connection between the two "homes." English represents the possibility to connect with and identify with Australia. For the first time, *Australianness* becomes part of their public identity.

While keeping in mind these examples of the production of translocality, I now want to turn attention to those who have decided to remain in Australia. They are, nonetheless, increasingly partaking in this translocal space from their side. This equally represents the possibility of renegotiating a kind of home that links both places. Osório's return is possibly one of the simpler cases. However, many Timorese who remain in Sydney have heard much more ambivalent stories from friends and relatives who've made the journey home—stories that no doubt have an impact on their own decisions to stay or go. It is to those who have yet to "make the big move" that I turn now.

On the *Possibility* of Return

One striking fact about the literature on refugees, exiles, and return is that for the most part it looks at only two aspects of the "post-exile experience": the decision to return and the experience of actual return. It is equally important to add to the analysis an understanding of the experience of those who decide not to go back. It is not correct to simply assume they are assimilated into the country of asylum and therefore have no wish to return or, conversely, have no sense of belonging to their country of origin. There are many factors surrounding the decision to stay, and assimilating to the new country or returning to the old does not necessarily achieve a sense of "home." Rather, simply wishing to return may be their "home."

Roger Zetter's (1994) study of Greek-Cypriot refugees and their perceptions of the possibility of return has shown that the protracted nature of their exile is an important and often overlooked aspect of their relationship to the possibility of return. This fact and the socioeconomic differentiation and processes of adaptation are central variables in what Zetter sees as the often contradictory and paradoxical attitudes to return he has identified in the individuals he interviewed. Like many refugee communities, those in Zetter's study, like the East Timorese, engaged in what we might call "strategies of not quite belonging," finding it difficult to develop new social relationships and patterns of belonging in the host country, difficulty in engaging in community development. However, the myth of return in Zetter's research is at variance with the actual reality where these people have in many ways broken with old social and cultural norms and practices. Moreover:

Those refugees who have experienced perhaps the greater psychosocial consequences of refugeehood and the associated dependency. . . have found the social fragmentation and the loss of autonomy the more difficult to overcome. But consistent with evidence of atrophy and dependency from elsewhere, rather than mobilized as a force of return, this has engendered a "loss of status. . . a surrendering of identity . . . for many this becomes a crucial factor in staying put." (Zetter 1994, 8)

Zetter's observations here are paralleled in my own research. It is by and large the more empowered individuals who are making the move back to East Timor. There is a group who are working through not wanting to return, mainly because their lives have become connected to and reasonably successful in Australia. But there is another significant group who fit Zetter's profile, the largely disempowered, highly traumatized group who are most likely to be welfare dependent, living in relative poverty, and, indeed, somewhat atrophied in the sense that they are caught up simply in the day-to-day struggle of getting by and don't have the skills, finances, or mental energy to contemplate a move either way. Approximately 1,200 of the "1600 group" (introduced in Chapter 2) have only temporary asylum and have been furiously fighting for years for the right to stay in Australia permanently. Because of their insecure financial and residential status, they have little hope of entering the cosmopolitan zone of the translocal, with no possibility for return visits, for coming and going, for taking up high level contracts. It does seem, then, that ability to come and go, to keep a stake in both places, as it were, has a large bearing on whether an individual feels comfortable returning to East Timor.

There are many reasons why a good percentage of the community are not able to or do not wish to return to East Timor. Despite this, the vast majority of non-Chinese Timorese still cling tightly to the notion of return; many say they will "one day" go home, or "if only I didn't have such and such responsibility," and so forth. The symbolic importance of the desire for return remains strong and poses one of the greatest challenges to East Timorese making the transition (by returning or not) from exile.

Josefa, a mother of mestiço background, Cristina, a woman of indigenous background, and Ana, a Timorese-Chinese woman, have very different feelings about the possibility of return to East Timor, with the clearest marker of difference between the two "Timorese" women and the "Timorese-Chinese" woman.

Josefa was thirty-six at the time of our interview in late 2000. She lives in a comfortable middle-class family home in one of the new housing developments surrounding Liverpool, which she and her husband are paying off. She works in the community sector and has two daughters, then six and ten. She speaks mainly Tetum with her husband and English with their children, something that she feels a bit uncomfortable about. Although Josefa is ambivalent about return, she places great emphasis on the fact that she was a forced migrant, a refugee, rather than someone who simply wanted to come here for a new life. She reminded me of this fact several times throughout the interview, which underscores her need to have a sense that she will go back, even if her present circumstances make this untenable for her.

I guess if you always believe—I mean not believe—if you always feel that you are a Timorese person in your heart then you have to have that desire of wanting to go back. I believe that that is among every Timorese that is outside. Simply because—the reason why we fled East Timor is different to any other migrant groups here, for example. That even though we are here, trying to assimilate, but at the same time, we know that our country is in chaos, going through a lot, and that we want to be a part of that. We have got a lot more settlement issues because of that. You know? Where do we fit in, how do we let go of East Timor, and then try to just settle and forget about East Timor?

She came to Australia in 1977 at the age of twelve after spending a year in West Timor and a year in Portugal. Her now elderly parents remained in Portugal until 1998, when they moved to Australia to be with her, meaning that the bulk of her family are now living in Sydney. For Josefa, the possibility of return is an enormously complex issue, bound up with feelings of guilt, obligation, identity, duty to family and children, the need to be financially stable, and the need to demonstrate a commitment to East Timor. These are in some ways not new feelings for her. She gives one the sense that there has always been a sense of guilt bound up in her relatively successful and settled life in Australia, that somehow by "settling" there—because of the importance of her refugee status—she was in some way betraying East Timor.

It's like you are trying to settle or survive in a new country—and of course you have commitments in a new country—you have responsibilities—you have to look after yourself—in terms of providing—whatever necessity—if you have children—you have to send your children to education, make sure they have shelter over their heads, so you have to work—so I guess even though we are all—caught up in this process of settling in here—but at the same time you know—there is the other side—the emotional side—that East Timor is still unresolved—that East Timor has to become independent. We all have to contribute towards the development of East Timor once it is independent. So it is you know—not "this is my new country and therefore forget about East Timor"—but it's always been, ok, we are settling in—but there is always the unfinished business back in East Timor—that also needs us.

Having young children that she is responsible for compounds this ambivalence about settlement in Australia. Josefa feels guilt for abandoning East Timor and an obligation to return and perhaps help the new nation. However, she feels an even greater obligation to make a good life for her children. These contradictory pressures place Josefa in a very difficult position, which is not easy to really resolve satisfactorily.

I think with any East Timorese person in Australia . . . it has always been our dream . . . to go back. But how and when—is the question. Because of other commitments that we have here. That's not to say that there is no responsibility back in East Timor as well. It is not an easy decision. . . . But yes—if it was easy— I guess to put it into umm—if I didn't have my children—if I didn't have to pay off a mortgage, for example—you know—why am I on a mortgage—because obviously I want, I want something for my children as well. If I didn't have all that—then yes—it would be easy for me to say—what would I be doing here? You know? I can go there and . . . help . . . anything that is required. . . . But I can't just be selfish—I'd like to also bring up my children—and to also feel the way I feel about East Timor too. But that doesn't necessarily mean that I have to be in East Timor to do that either.

This is a situation encountered by a great many Timorese I have spoken with in Sydney and is perhaps the most significant pattern apparent among the non-Chinese sections of the community. For Josefa, the only way to deal with this situation is to live in the moment, think practically, and focus on her children.

I think the way a lot of us cope is that we have to accept what is reality. . . . I am living here—I have made my own reality here as well—as well as what has happened back in Timor. . . . I guess because of my own limitations . . . at this particular moment . . . I try to focus on what I need to do at this stage, rather than looking ahead. Because if I do that, I'd be stuck. I cannot just—I'd be stuck. I can't. And I believe—its not easy to settle, and its not easy to—to be able to— what you are doing here also involves a lot of hard work, a lot of stress . . . and you are only a human being, and what you are going to do for East Timor too— is going to involve a . . . a lot of hard work—financially, emotionally, physically, and all that. So this is where you've got to draw the line. You just have to live in the moment and not think about all this.

Along with a deliberate bracketing of the "future" and the possibility of return, Josefa also uses a strategy of deferral, which is something I saw again and again in a large majority of those I interviewed in the non-Chinese Timorese community. I mean by deferral that many like Josefa seem to reconcile the guilt feelings—about not returning to East Timor after so much investment in the struggle, and with respect to the impor-tance of an identity bound up in refugeeness and exile—by way of a promissory strategy. They frequently declare an intention to one day go home and help rebuild East Timor, but return is always deferred to some future date "when the mortgage is paid, when my work commitments are fewer, when the children leave school, get married, when my hus-band retires," and so forth. I would argue that such deferrals are an unconscious way of ameliorating the guilt of not returning; a means of maintaining a commitment to the future of East Timor, while remaining an active participant in their Australian-based family lives.

I believe that eventually we'll all go back. Not in the immediate future—because—it's almost as if you need to sort out the bits and pieces. . . . But those who are already past that and gone past that already—these ones I can see them going back—if not already—then in the near future. . . . But also—I think because of the way East Timor is—you also need to build some base—you can't just let go here—and expect—I mean what would you do to East Timor if you go there empty handed with nothing? . . . But one day my biggest wish is to go back to Timor . . . but as far as what I can do at this stage—I want to contribute, I know that I don't have to be in East Timor to be able to do it. I just wish that there were proper structures put in place, where we, that are outside East Timor can also contribute. . . . but also, where do I fit in? This is also the question.

In addition to the strategy of pragmatism and deferral, Josefa also reconciles her position by knitting herself into East Timor's future from a distance. Again, this is a very common characteristic of the Sydney Timorese community. As she says, "you don't need to be in East Timor to help." Many Timorese ameliorate their guilt at not returning by actively participating in all manner of charitable assistance schemes set up to aid the people of East Timor. Many have their own "pet" aid projects in East Timor set up by themselves, friends, or family, often small-scale income-generating schemes. Such activities are means of intensification, ways of participating or performing membership in the moral community of East Timor.

Unlike Josefa, Cristina expresses no wish to return to East Timor. Nev-ertheless, like most other non-Chinese Timorese, she has a fervent need to help East Timor, even if from Australia. Cristina, thirty-two at the time

I interviewed her, is married to a Timorese man and lives in a small apartment in Fairfield. She works as a nurse and comes across as a very confident and independent young woman with strong opinions. Cristina visited East Timor in 1997, following the period of Indonesian *reformasi*, prior to the 1999 referendum. This visit had a profound impact on her view of return; it complicated her sense of home and belonging in such a way that she feels that return is not a tenable option now.

It's funny, when I'm here Timor means home. . . . But when I went there in 1997, I felt like I was a stranger there. I felt like I miss Australia—like oh—I could have gone shopping—and things like that. So after all these years—it was like an identity crisis. . . . But I guess because we have left for so long—things are different—people are different. You feel welcome, they treated you well and things like that—but all the things that you do, like you are adapting to a different lifestyle or environment. [and] . . . your friends have changed too. You are looking forward and really excited going there to see them—I don't know what happened—you can't have that conversation like you used to. Even your house is occupied by someone else. You go there like—even if you are told that that's your house—your parents say that you can stay there whenever you want . . . but you feel like you're somewhere else—even the garden is different—you know? It's like, everything is different. I feel like it belongs to someone else.

As Baldassar (2001) argues, the return visit in particular is an extremely important factor in the lives of migrants. In her study of Italian migrants, most did not decide whether to settle in Australia or to repatriate until they had made a return visit to San Fior (their home village in Italy). The majority chose not to repatriate, judging that life in Australia held better prospects for them. For many, this return visit allowed them to move beyond the yearning for "home," and to appreciate for the first time their Australian lifestyles (326). Those who decided not to return experienced a kind of "shift," or reversal, between their center, formerly San Fior in Italy, and their "periphery," Australia—which after the visit became home. San Fior became a place to visit for a kind of spiritual and cultural "renewal" (327), although such visits can also be disorienting and full of disillusionment.

Nevertheless, as Cristina's story shows, the return visit is an extremely important element in creating the translocal space, creating connections, establishing a translocal neighborhood with real elements of material and social connections that connect the two halves through visits, letters, gifts, and so forth. Cristina's insistence that her future children be taken to East Timor to learn about their culture also demonstrates that the return visit is a process through which cultural renewal can take place.

Like many Timorese, Cristina had grown up in Australia hearing stories from her parents about "home." Many families fled their family homes in East Timor believing that they would one day be able to return to them.

These family homes have existed in people's minds as a kind of fantasy place envisaged exactly as they were when they were left behind. After twenty-five years of absence, the reality is of course much different. In most cases extended family back in East Timor have taken over the homes, and in many cases where no family is left, homes were simply taken over by squatters or by senior figures in the Indonesian military or sold to locals.

One can only imagine the shock, sadness, and confusion returnees encounter when they find their longed-for home occupied by someone else and changed beyond recognition. There are many cases presently before the courts in East Timor where former owners are trying to claim homes or land that they left all those years ago—claims being fought vigorously by present-day tenants who claim their own rights over the property on the grounds of long-term residence and abandonment by the original owners. For Cristina, this situation, along with her discovery that both she and East Timor had changed, undermined her sense of home and belonging in a way that she is yet to resolve. Although she feels determined now not to return to East Timor, she is resolute that she will maintain a link to East Timor.

Is it possible that you have two homes? Because you are settling in here and like of course I want this to be my second home. But you still have your past and you like to go back and visit or whatever. . . . But just because I have roots in Australia now—I'm not cutting any relationship to Timor!! I would like to take my kids there—when I have kids—you know to learn the culture and things like that—but I just don't want to go through it again—whatever happens. I would say only if I'm not married and I have no one to care for. Because it is too painful if you lose someone. Or you know that—you have to go through it again.

As with many Timorese in the diaspora, Cristina's perspective on return is further compounded by a fear of the insecure environment in East Timor. Having suffered trauma and lost loved ones, many Timorese are understandably reluctant to return to the scene of that trauma, where all the memories are relived and where there is still a less than secure environment in which many still feel endangered. For Cristina, as for others, the concern for loved ones and family overrides any personal need to return. This concern for loved ones may also be invoked as a way to ameliorate the guilt of not wanting to return. One of Cristina's strategies for resolving her situation is through imagining how she might raise her future children—and create a cultural link between them and East Timor while living in Australia.

But um it would be good when I have children in the future, for them to know—to learn about the culture—you know the—about the tais, the lulik—I'd like them to experience it. Not to teach them—to tell them stories or whatever. And I would also like them to see how—wonderful living here in Australia is—you know comparing the situation and taking advantage of it. Like going to school, not to drop out—you know. Things like other stuff that they can learn from here.

And, like other East Timorese, Cristina is able to have a sense of belonging to the East Timor nation, despite living in Australia, through participating in the rebuilding from afar.

I think we are looking more at . . . building East Timor. Like some people are going into business, or some people they like to go back—I've known a couple of them—they'd like to go and live there. But I don't know—it's such a hard thing. . . . Because they still have people there—it's not like everybody came out. There is going to be a clash between—like—we are the ones that are going to be the outsiders this time. Isn't it?—like "oh you left East Timor now you coming back?" So, I can't really talk for other people. . . . But initially I was thinking that—I'm a nurse—I would like to go there and help. But . . . I'd like them to take over back home, and anyway, I don't think we are really wanted there. If I go there, I feel like I'm not helping either. . . . The only thing we can do is to send them money to rebuild. Because I still have a sister there. That's my priority at the moment.

For those like Cristina there is an immense guilt at not wanting to return. On the one hand, Cristina feels that East Timor is home and that she is East Timorese. On the other, she is aware that after so many of her formative years spent in Australia, she is also inextricably linked there. She ameliorates her guilt feelings through imagining a future linked to East Timor, via her future children, and by participating in national rebuilding through assisting in charitable activities and sending money to family remaining in East Timor. This is not a simple process. There is still a sense of confusion and guilt surrounding her identity and belonging, compounded for her since the reality of return has become a possibility.

It is important, as I noted earlier, to give equal emphasis to the experience of nonreturnees, the stayers, those who have chosen not to return. Many of those still in Australia are ambivalent about going back. Particularly hesitant are those from poorer families, who are elderly, or who do not have legal status to reside in Australia permanently. Some are simply unable to countenance the possibility of return for financial reasons. Indeed, many cannot even afford airfare to take the all-important "testing the waters" visit home. Others, like Cristina, feel afraid to go back until they are sure it is politically stable. They are afraid of civil war, and full of fear at the possibility of having to relive war trauma and risk losing loved ones again. Those like her also experience home as a kind of shifting center, but have increasingly become more connected to their lives in Australia; many have established careers, have relationships, own their own homes, and have children born in Australia. The majority of the younger generation are not interested in "returning" (indeed, many have never been there, or left when they were very small), although a few, especially children of political leaders, are training in occupations such as nursing in hope of working for a period in East Timor to "try to help our nation rebuild." Others, such as the majority of the Timorese-Chinese community, are well and truly established in Australia and do not have the burning desire or guilt surrounding the issue of return that other Timorese have, although most still express a wish to participate in the moral community of East Timor through charitable activities.

Stuart Tannock (1995) defines nostalgia as a structure of feeling that invokes a "positively evaluated past world in response to a deficient present world." He argues that "the nostalgic subject turns to the past to find/construct sources of identity, agency, or community that are felt to be lacking, blocked, subverted, or threatened in the present" (454). A powerful mix of guilt, nostalgia, and desire characterizes the attitude toward return among the vast majority of non-Chinese Timorese with whom I have spoken. Deciding not to return to East Timor does not mean that this nostalgia and guilt have disappeared from their lives. As with Josefa, many have a kind of deferred intention to return home: "I will go back when . . . the kids are older, the mortgage paid off, the economy is better in Timor, and I don't want to take the jobs from those who stayed there." At the beginning of my research, every East Timorese said they would go back. Three years after the 1999 referendum, about half said they would eventually return, while others made deferral statements such as those in Josefa's story. For quite a few, return has been gradually translating into a less sure intention. Many now look at ways to help East Timor from Australia instead. Nonetheless, for a great many Timorese who either outwardly admit to not wanting to return or engage in deferral strategies, there is very frequently a feeling of immense guilt about not wanting to go back to their homeland. This guilt derives from the important role that exile and refugee status has played in Timorese diasporic identities until now. As Malkki has shown (1992, 35), the status of "refugeeness" is sometimes valued among refugee communities as the ultimate sign of the temporariness of exile.

In the Timorese case, as I argued in Chapter 4, the ritual and dramatic forms of protest that many in the community in Sydney were involved in or exposed to throughout the years of the independence struggle, combined with the highly traumatized nature of the community, created a kind of embodied moral identity structured around the condition of exile and the symbolic power of the desire for return. This has very specific implications for the way that the members of the post-independence community were able to imagine themselves in place in Australia, juxtaposed with the reality of return which never quite matches up to the exile's fantasy of return.

The importance of exile induces an enormous guilt now that the possibility of return is here. For some this has translated into an actual return to East Timor, for those who decide to stay, this manifests in some of the "guilt ameliorating" strategies sketched above. However, as we have seen the situation is not as simple as those "Timorese" in their identity fitting neatly back into the place where they can achieve full belonging.

In Chapter 3, I put forward the concept of "two East Timors," which, because of the imaginative resources available in the diaspora, transnational discourses, and interconnections with the solidarity movement, implies that their imagined Timor is something different from that imagined by those who remained at home. After 1999, many Timorese have been taking part in translocal practices that try to fuse the two East Timors into one, through lived experience, material practice, and the imagination. Similarly, in Chapter 5 I explored the ways East Timoreseness is situated within cross-cutting, hybridizing identity processes which are often at odds with the traditionalist discourses influenced by the independence struggle, and indeed, at odds with the kinds of Timoreseness at work in contemporary East Timor itself. The implications with respect to return are many, and indeed, influence the experience of both returnees and those who remain in Australia.

On Timorese-Chineseness and the Irrelevance of Return

One of the most striking findings to emerge from my research was the sharp difference between the Timorese-Chinese and Timorese communities on the question of return. While most East Timorese rationalize family as an impediment to returning home, the Timorese-Chinese overwhelmingly see family *as* home. While more than half of all East Timorese I have spoken to express a wish to return home, whether now or some time in the future, I have not met a single person who identifies as Timorese-Chinese who has expressed a need to return "home" to East Timor. It does not seem to matter if a person is of mestiço Timorese-Chinese background and educated in Portuguese, or if the person's family and background is mainly Chinese. The most determining factor is the identification with Chineseness, with Timorese-Chinese community and Chinese cultural practices, however hybrid.

Geographical location seems also to be a determining factor. While few if any Sydney Timorese-Chinese wish to return, there are a small number of Darwin Timorese-Chinese who have explored that option, primarily, I understand, to investigate business opportunities. Of those I interviewed, most cited family roots in Australia, business or financial roots there, and, with respect to East Timor, a fear of violence and loss of property. According to Carlos, the Timorese leadership have made attempts to encourage Timorese-Chinese to return, but there is little evidence that any feel confident to take up the offer:

A lot of the leaders now, they say that they want the Chinese to come back, with all their business skills. Some have gone back. You know, but they all come back and say—and they don't think that it is safe to go and live there. No. People don't want to go back. There have been people coming back from visits, and say they won't go to live. There are a lot of reasons. There is no money there, it is poverty. Umm . . . people don't have money—and looting still happens. They want survival. As soon as they know, "oh you've come from overseas, oh, you have money—let's go and target them." It happens. So why would we want to go back to that place? Life is good here now.

As is often the case with Chinese in Indonesia and Malaysia (see Wang 1992), the focus of the country's leaders is on the commercial importance of the Chinese, rather than on promoting a sense in which they are part of the East Timorese nation. This clearly demarcates who it is that can belong, in all senses of the word, to the new East Timor. Their commercial skills are appreciated, but this does not translate to embracing them within the broader notion of Timorese national identity. Indeed, such demarcating practices are emerging in East Timor at the highest levels. Some MPs in East Timor have called for fluency in Tetum and Portuguese as prerequisites for Timorese citizenship—a move clearly aimed at Indonesian transmigrants, but one that has ramifications for the mainly Hakka-speaking Chinese.

Ana is a typical representative of the Timorese-Chinese community. Her story illustrates how many Timorese-Chinese have a much more mobile sense of Timoreseness, which is not predicated on any notion of exile or return. Thirty-seven at the time of our interview, she is married to a Timorese-Chinese man with whom she has two children. A Buddhist, she was educated in both the Portuguese and Chinese school systems in Timor. In Australia, she identifies as Timorese-Chinese and is very involved with the Timorese-Chinese community center. Although Ana expresses some nostalgia for East Timor, this nostalgia centers on the prosperous lifestyle her family had there. Unlike non-Chinese Timorese, this does not translate into a desire for actual return.

When I left I was quite young, I was ten, but I still have a lot of memories of East Timor. If you want a glass of water—you just call the maid . . . I always asked my parents; why couldn't we have that here? . . . And that's how I always picture that time. . . . I guess we were lucky because I mean like, my parents had a business, they were very wealthy there. We lived very comfortably. We had a huge double storey house, I think we had about seven people working for us, like the house maid, and each of us had our own nanny . . . they were there just to look after us and play with us. I thought it was fantastic. In the afternoon, they would take us to the beach . . . and whatever we want, we got. So I mean like, it was really. . . fond memories, compared to now . . . we have to go to work and come home late and when the parents get home, there is nobody to help them, and they still have to feed the family.

There does not seem to be the sense of guilt tied up with not wanting to return, which is so apparent in the non-Chinese section of the community. For Ana and her family, their feelings about return center on the fear of violence and loss of property. Because the Timorese-Chinese dominated the commercial sector in East Timor, which translated into personal wealth, the loss of substantial homes and business is perhaps felt more keenly by them and forms a central part in their perceptions of the dangers of return home.

A lot of the people that had business back in East Timor, if you talk to them, it's just like, you know, we don't want to go back. We were hurt very badly, we lost everything. . . . They've got nothing to go back to anymore and a lot of them are old now. . . . Also, a lot of the next generation, . . . they have already got their home here they have already got good jobs, and they've all got kids. Why would they want to go back to Timor? For what? . . . why would they want to start all over? . . . And there is no security. . . . It could happen worse if things got bad again. . . . It's too uncertain. . . . At one stage, I talked to my father and my sister. And I said, you know, why not? Maybe we should all go back and live, you know, just for the family name, and they said why? You want to risk it? We lost everything once. . . . In my family, no, we don't want to go back. We consider ourselves very lucky that we are together, we are very happy, each of us are. . . well educated now, we've got very secure jobs, we are very happy, by all means we would go back as a holiday. We will never forget our homeland. . . . But I think Australia is our homeland now. We consider it our home.

It is interesting that Ana considers East Timor her homeland, but obviously "homeland" is a shifting thing for her. A key theme running through Ana's narrative is the importance of family and how family becomes the litmus test of return. The fact that her son considers Australia home is the measure of her own sense of home. For Ana, home is future-oriented and is bound up with family. Where the family is, home is. Ana's family, like most Timorese-Chinese I have spoken with, are well and truly settled in Australia: most have good jobs, are paying off mortgages, and feel that their lives are secure and successful. Family is similarly important for her father.

I said to them—do you want to go back? And my dad said no, what guarantee have I got? He said I could go back, and in a year or two years, I could lose the whole thing again. He said all the children are now married, they have got their own family. He said—we can only hope that we, the children, would do well, and carry the name on. You know, that's how it is. It's the family now. I mean that's all that mum and dad says. All they're concerned with now is the family. If the family is together then they will do well.

Although most Timorese-Chinese express little interest in returning to East Timor and do not seem to have the same guilt feelings around this choice that non-Chinese Timorese do, they nonetheless express a continuing connection to East Timor, which many demonstrate through involvement in charitable activities.

> I don't feel that I'm obliged to go back. . . . But we are doing a lot of stuff here, in Australia, in Sydney—for the Timorese people back home. . . . At the beginning of the year—we made a huge collection. And we did a charity function. . . . And we did quite well. . . . We find the Chinese people, they know that they can't go back. But . . . there is always a little bit of space in their heart . . . so they have to do something. Because they haven't forgotten their homeland. They haven't forgotten those that have lost—you know innocent lives for nothing. . . . Because they know, just because we are all settled in now, we've got family, we've got good homes, we have income coming in, that we can not forget about the people there. . . . Like my sister and myself, we, on our weekends, we go around and collect food, clothing, we collect everything. And we ship it home. We ship it to Timor. We can't go home to do it, so that is our contribution.

The important point here is the difference between the two groups. Ana's narrative demonstrates a common sentiment among many Timorese-Chinese. On the one hand, they have no wish to return; they feel no guilt or sense of responsibility to go back and rebuild. On the other hand, they have a desire to participate in the moral community, to assist what they still see as their homeland. I believe this signals the kinds of processes outlined in Chapter 4 to do with how mestiço and indigenous Timorese have been bodily and affectively tied into the moral community of East Timor through the years of participation in the struggle for independence. For Timorese-Chinese, there has been available a history of only very partial belonging to East Timor and the category "East Timoreseness."

Because of these two processes, Timorese-Chinese have not really been constructed as belonging to the moral community of East Timoreseness. Their image was never invoked in the emotional protest years. This is underscored by the fact that prominent Timorese leaders such as José Ramos-Horta and Xanana Gusmão have made visits to the Timorese-Chinese Association to request that its members return to help build the East Timorese economy. As I pointed out, Timorese largely perceive the Timorese-Chinese contribution to the nation of East Timor as a commercial one. However, it is important to note that the Timorese-Chinese community in Sydney provide the largest and most organized fundraising for East Timor-related causes. This indicates their need to demonstrate a moral relationship to East Timor, but it also shows that their identities, unlike those of other Timorese, are not predicated on the desire for return. For them, there is no "trans" remaining in their sense of locality. In the same way that their Chineseness is mobile, not necessarily attached to the physical place that is China, this community also experience their Timoreseness as something that travels with them. This is a characteristic of many Chinese from Southeast Asia. For example, the Chinese from Vietnam have reportedly had fewer settlement difficulties, and less sense of needing to return to Vietnam, than their Vietnamese counterparts.[6]

Remaining, Returning, and Negotiating Partial Belongings

Who is it that is most predisposed toward returning to East Timor? As seen earlier, those who are very politically involved have been most likely to return. In particular, a good number of very cosmopolitan political activists have returned to take up high level positions in the government.[7] Also, those who are financially established are far more likely than the economically and socially disadvantaged to return. Those who have little family in Australia but have family remaining in Timor are similarly more likely to go. Conversely, those who identify as Timorese-Chinese are the least likely to return, as are those with lives well established in Australia, especially those with satisfying careers, families, and children. There is also anecdotal evidence that those from Melbourne are more likely than their Sydney counterparts to return.

However, simply returning or conversely deciding not to return does not guarantee a sense of homely belonging. Because of the role of guilt and the symbolic power of exile, I believe there is, and will be, a gradual shift among (non-Chinese) Timorese, from the condition of exile to what I have termed a translocal *diasporic* community formation. A central challenge to this shift is how those remaining in Australia will deal with the question of how to translate the symbolic function of exile now that the possibility of return is available. This parallels the dilemma faced by many diasporic Jewish people following the creation of Israel. David Palumbo-Liu asks:

Who was the "real" Jew? . . . Did leaving the diaspora mean that one was belying the fictionality of the compensation, that bargain with history, that had kept the Jewish people intact for centuries? But more vexingly, what did it mean to *remain* in the diaspora when the state was there now, available and viable, and one's political identity realizable in an actual political state. (Palumbo-Liu, quoted in Carruthers 2001, 274)

The symbolic importance of return and refugeeness in many ways masks the reality of contemporary East Timorese experience. The desire for return has been an important way of imagining and demonstrating

"we-ness." Faced with the reality of return, Timorese have had to negotiate the very painful contradictions that can undermine the sense of
self and identity inherent in the performance of loyalty to homeland,
which the desire for return embodies. As we have seen, many find they
do not wish or are not able to return. Furthermore, those that do frequently find that return does not fulfill the fantasy of home. However,
the notion of return still holds an important place in Timorese identity.

This gradual process of shift from exile to diaspora manifests, for
example, in participation in long-distance charitable activities, which we
might, following the argument put forward in Chapter 4, call "strategies
of intensification" (Hage 2002). Similarly, many of those remaining in
Australia, like Josefa, engage in deferral strategies so as to maintain a
sense of belonging while not undermining this symbolic importance of
the desire for return. In other words, the moral imperative inherent in
the symbolic importance of return may be transferred to other strategies to engage in the moral community of East Timor. By participating
in these philanthropic activities and by maintaining, to some extent, the
myth of returning one day, coupled with an involvement in translocal
practices, the guilt surrounding return can be ameliorated without sac-
rificing the possibility of homely belonging.

This implies that for returnees there may well be a process not so
much of homecoming as of negotiation between homecoming and a connection to the diaspora. The move to a dual or diasporic translocal relationship to East Timor and Australia may become one strategy by which
returnees deal with the in-between state of returned exile. And for those
who have decided not to return, becoming translocally diasporic is one
way in which they are able to dissipate the sense of guilt and longing at
not returning. It provides a way of participating in the moral community
of East Timor without actually taking the big leap to repatriation.

From Exile to Home

Exile, diaspora, translocalism; all these terms are ghosted by some notion
of home or the pursuit of it. The notion of "home" remains central to
the experience of both exile and return, and it is no surprise that returning exiles do not necessarily find the "home" they left behind. We must
therefore ask: what is home, and is it possible to return to one from
exile? If not, does that render the exile permanently homeless? Or is
home for post-exiles able to be refashioned, renegotiated? If so, what are
the power relationships involved?

In his moving ethnography, *At Home in the World*, Michael Jackson
expresses a deep ambivalence toward attempts to too closely describe
and categorize the notion of home as some kind of essence that can be

defined. Home has multifarious meanings that differ across time and cultures. He prefers to see it as a lived relationship; the movement he hints at is captured in his phrase "being-at-home-in-the-world," which he describes as a balance between being acted upon and acting. In typically elegant fashion, he describes this as a state of "grace," which for me, beautifully captures the idea that home has a hopeful, fluid dimension. It is not where you've come from, where you were born, where you've been since, or where you are going. It's the comfortable combination of all those things, that place in the world "where you can come into your own" (1995, 125). Jackson describes how for the Walpiri, "home is where one hails from . . . , but it also suggests the places one has camped, sojourned, and lived during the course of one's own lifetime" (122).

Such approaches to home displace the universal connection between humanity and hearth and disentangle the link between culture and place. It follows that there are many intersecting kinds of symbolic, bodily, psychological, material, or national (to name just a few) spaces that order, interpret, transform, and resonate as "homely belongings." Still, the experience of homely belonging in the contemporary world is a highly differentiated one, drawn to a large extent along lines of empowerment and disempowerment. Differently available symbolic and material resources influence the way people "make themselves at home" under global conditions (Massey 1997). Home, then, implies a complex temporal juxtaposition, and flexible dialectic of objective conditions and subjective appropriation of a symbolic, bodily, and material milieu. The idea of "mobility" is placed within, not in contradistinction to, the understanding of "home."

Home framed around a past-oriented, culturally over determined homeland politics is a pathological one in this sense, denying the lived messiness, hopefulness, and fluidity of home. Yet, as Jackson points out, denial of land rights (in his case referring to aboriginal Australians, but we can equally apply it to occupied East Timor) disrupts the homely balance between being acted upon and acting, "acquiescing in the given and choosing one's own fate" (123). Importantly, Jackson is not saying home is all about fluidity and movement: the "where you come from" is just as important, and if that is denied through traumatic forms of displacement, a pathological disequilibrium prevails. For the East Timorese, then, returning home from exile is not simply the winning of the homeland, but its return is certainly a core element in the move to "grace."

For most East Timorese, the return from exile is not necessarily a return *home* to the East Timor that was left many years ago. Such a return is impossible. But it is possible, as we have seen, to think of home as *translocal*, operating across an extended, yet distinctly local milieu, and that home can be found at the intersection of a range of symbolic and material spaces. In the East Timorese case, these perhaps represent possibilities for moving not from exile to return, but from exile to diaspora. The difference between exile and diaspora is that, whereas exile derives from political necessity, the new diaspora has an element of voluntariness, what Jackson might call grace. What I see in the community is a shift to diaspora, and translocality represents one *mechanism* by which this is occurring.

For some Timorese, then, the simple fact of being able to return allows them to shift from exile to a feeling of being at home with oneself, perhaps a "being at home in the world" again, without having to follow through with an actual return.

As a refugee . . . it's like, you don't have any plans for the future. We were forced out. It's not like I'm going to another country and going to start over. It's not like you have a plan where you want to go. But for Timorese people, I think they felt, or for myself, I felt like I was floundering—you know? Like I didn't have a plan. You know . . . because I was always waiting to go back. That feeling of, I've got a country, one day I'm going back. But since Timor became independent, suddenly I felt like, this [Sydney] is my home, you know what I mean? Like that burden has just lifted off. Suddenly I feel like I can be anywhere. You know? I can call any country my country. Um . . . that, that . . . feeling. That's how I experience it. But prior to that, you try so hard to belong, you know? To belong. And . . . I never overcame that, until Timor was freed. (Paulo, age 36)

For some East Timorese, post-exile represents a freedom to look to the future, to finally be at home with themselves. For others, the affective power of refugeeness and exile, which was cultivated so strongly during the years of Indonesian occupation, means that the need to come to terms with post-independence East Timor, find an identity beyond exile, and achieve a new sense of home, is that much greater. For members of the Timorese community, although there may never be truly a *return* home, home is nonetheless something they will move toward in new ways.

Chapter 7
Conclusion: Independence Day: Looking to the Future

Epilogue—Monday, 20 May 2002

Today is East Timor's Independence Day. Just imagine: five centuries of Portuguese colonization, twenty-four years of Indonesian occupation, two years of United Nations administration, and finally East Timor's long-awaited independence day is here. I am in the town hall of an inner Sydney suburb at a party for East Timorese and solidarity supporters to celebrate Independence Day. At midnight last night, watched by an audience of international dignitaries and thousands of East Timorese, the United Nations flag was lowered in Dili and the new flag of an independent East Timor was raised for the first time. I experienced an extraordinary rush of emotion and found myself crying tears of sadness and joy as I watched these remarkable scenes on television. I felt privileged to have been involved with the Timorese community for the years leading up to this historic moment. I felt so very sad thinking back to all the stories I'd heard over the years, yet so happy that finally this tiny nation could, against all the odds, find itself free at last. I felt a kind of release, perhaps on behalf of those I'd worked with, that finally, here is the day that marks the beginning of their future. And I felt sad, because today is the last day of my research, the end point of an extraordinary journey.

Just months before, the first parliamentary elections had been held in East Timor. These elections were an important symbolic turning point in the lives of the East Timorese diaspora. While they could vote in the 1999 referendum that ensured East Timor's independence from Indonesia, they weren't permitted to vote in these elections. This official signal of noncitizenship marked the fact that, in legal-political terms at least, they were no longer part of the national space of East Timor. A few of the more committed traveled to East Timor to vote, but most couldn't justify the expense. Many more made the journey to East Timor for Independence Day; they weren't going to miss this big moment.

The Timorese community in Sydney had been partying hard all weekend. It began with the "Timorese active seniors" party in Cabramatta in the western suburbs on Saturday night, a local event in which all the funds raised from going door to door went to their community group. On Sunday night, Independence eve, a celebration soccer match was held between the local East Timorese youth team and a team of returned Australian peacekeepers. Another party at the Portuguese club followed this, where lots of drinking, dancing, and fun was to be had. Tonight, Monday night, in the town hall marks the end of those celebrations. There are speeches from two local mayors (whose councils have partnership/sister city projects in East Timor). There are presentations, awards for contributions to the struggle and to East Timorese culture. There are performances by Australian bands and choirs. The audience are predominantly middle-class Anglo-Australian, with perhaps a quarter Timorese.

Quite a few Timorese leave early, exhausted by the earnestness of the performers, especially when a well-known Australian musician replayed his multimedia visual performance featuring images from the years of occupation. There is little sense of fun and celebration from the solidarity people, and I think the East Timorese here are a bit disappointed. They just want to party and to celebrate this momentous occasion with all the joy it deserves.

Close to midnight, a raffle drawing takes place. The prize is a pair of plane tickets to Dili, donated by Qantas. What a wonderful surprise it is when the name drawn from the barrel is that of one of the main organizers of the event, an East Timorese woman who has been a tireless activist and organizer over the years but who has decided to remain living in Australia and hasn't been back to visit East Timor. When her name is announced, there is resounding applause and genuine joy that she, more than perhaps anyone else in the room, really deserves those tickets. She comes to the stage, shaking, and cries, "oh my God . . . I can't believe I'm going home!!!" . . . although, to be sure, they *are* round trip tickets.

Implications: For Theoretical Debates on Ethnicity, Diaspora, and Identity

At the level of intercultural interaction and understanding, it is undeniable that the study of transnational mobility is of paramount importance in today's world. Since September 11, ideas such as those in Samuel Huntington's *Clash of Civilizations* (1996) have gained increased currency. Against such all-encompassing visions of irreconcilable differences between the "West" and the "rest," my book has shown that cultural identities are in fact much more fractal and multidimensional than the simplistic dichotomies implied in discourses such as Huntington's. They shift and are cut through with multiple alliances and identifications that move us beyond the "East-West/West-Rest" divide. Rather than speaking simply in negative terms of disjunctures, displacements, and clashes, my research demonstrates the relevance of thinking equally about issues of multiple cultural affinities and belongings.

I also hope I have been able to show how certain affective cultural affinities arise and perpetuate themselves, yet are at the same time marked by ambivalence, contradiction, and change. In this way, although the book has focused on just one example, the East Timorese in Australia, the processes I have illustrated have much broader relevance.

The Timorese case demonstrates the strength of arguments put forward by scholars such as Werbner (1997a, 239), that communities are sites of struggle. The right to name, to describe and inscribe the community, to say who belongs to it and who is included within it, is cut through with relations of power and complex sets of moral relationships. Supporting Werbner's assertion that it is often the groups who are oppressed that strive to make their voices heard from the widest public platforms, the Timorese case demonstrates the soundness of her caution that it is in these contexts "that national images and public agendas are formulated which affect the destiny of these groups" (246). In this instance, the import lies in the kinds of discourses invoked in the independence struggle and the bodily modes through which the struggle was fought and performed, because they promote an identity firmly fixed on exile and return.

Despite the fact that a great many of the diasporic peoples today are made up of those officially classified as refugees—forcefully displaced by war or persecution—little has been said about the specificities of their experience as refugees, in reference to their experience of diasporic identity. The Timorese case throws important light on issues surrounding long distance nationalisms, especially in terms of what happens to those who invest much of their identity in such nationalist projects when, as it were, the project succeeds and there is indeed a new nation to which to return. Their case also contributes to debates on refugee studies and policies of repatriation. An important aim of the book has been to give refugees "some culture." That is, following Malkki's (1997b) groundbreaking work, my book shows that refugees are not cultureless, "speechless emissaries" without identities, agency, or lives beyond their refugeeness. I believe my use of theoretical material more usually applied to diasporas offers a more nuanced reading than the "refugee studies" perspective could offer.

Perhaps most important, I hope that I have been able to show the importance of giving bodies and emotions to those we study, as I believe this is one of the most vital avenues of research today. Like the East Timorese, long distance nationalist projects such as the Tamil Eelam movement, the Sikh diaspora, and many others invoke bodies and emotions to create an affective identification with their cause. In the case of the Middle East, Palestinians parade the bodies of dead martyrs amid huge crowds of emotionally and politically connected people. Lest we think such politico-affective crowd behavior is confined to "others," think of America post-September 11 and the mass outpouring of grief centered on the endless stories and images of those who died in the World Trade Center, and how this has translated into unprecedented patriotic fervor in that country. The important thread connecting each of these examples is the way in which bodies, politics, trauma, affect, and crowd behavior converge.

Implications: For the Timorese Case and Beyond

Beyond the theoretical implications, my research also has specific implications for the East Timorese case. Contrary to some material in refugee studies that promotes repatriation as the ideal resolution for the "displaced," my research shows that it is not possible to universalize such recommendations, and that each situation must be taken on a case-by-case basis. In this instance, the "ideal solution" might, for example, be a situation where state policies and structures, such as dual citizenship, in both East Timor and Australia, would allow them to continue and build on their translocal activities.

State actors in East Timor are fully cognizant of the potential of a "remittance culture." Timorese leaders in East Timor with whom I have spoken often reference the Philippines as a good example of how the diaspora can be incorporated into the nation in a way that is economically beneficial to those at home. Indeed, leaders such as José Ramos-Horta and Xanana Gusmão visited Australia more than once in the year prior to Independence Day, to speak to Timorese and Timorese-Chinese community gatherings in Sydney and encourage them to participate in East Timor "from a distance" through participation in aid projects, fundraising, and remittances to family. Australian aid programs and international NGOs are equally interested in the "potential" of East Timorese in Australia. I have been approached by several organizations to help them "access" the East Timorese community, who they feel could give them insights on how to approach their projects in East Timor. Some have come to me with specific requests for information on how they might go about enlisting the East Timorese in Australia to participate actively in their programs in areas such as fundraising, language training, assistance in cultural awareness, and, most interestingly, to act as mediators providing contacts to returnees now working in the East Timorese government.

It is wonderful for the East Timorese community in Australia to be able to take a role in East Timor. Many seem genuinely to appreciate the opportunity to assist East Timor. However, some elements within NGO and solidarity groups have regularly made comments to the effect that they feel it is the *responsibility* of East Timorese in Australia to help East Timor, preferably by returning or otherwise by actively assisting from Australia. Here solidarity turns into moralistic interference. I was at a seminar on East Timor where a member of the audience commented that he thought it was important that East Timorese from Australia return. He felt that with their "Western education and sophistication" they could help "modernize" East Timor and bring it economic success.

Such sentiments also translate onto the street. I heard a story where an Anglo-Australian woman confronted an East Timorese woman (one of the "1600 Group" threatened with involuntary return) who wishes to stay in Australia. The Australian woman apparently said something like, "You can't stay here and bludge on welfare, you should be back in East Timor helping to rebuild your country." This was distressing for the woman involved, who has no family left in East Timor and little prospect of employment or housing if forced to return, yet is made to feel guilty for wishing to have a better life for herself in Australia. As I have shown on many levels, there is no possibility for a seamless, untraumatic return. My research fundamentally undermines the arguments of those who believe it is a simple matter of repatriating those who belong "naturally" back in East Timor now that it has its independence.

I hope I have been able to show how important it is to see East Timorese people, and refugee communities like them, not as helpless victims but as complex and active human beings, constrained by circumstance but actively working with their situation in meaningful ways to negotiate a new space for themselves. In this light, I'd like to close with the telling words of a young East Timorese friend in Sydney:

Maybe I'm a gypsy. Like the way I see it . . . I'm moving from place to place. I don't have a general identity of who I am. I can't be Australian, I can't be Portuguese, I can't be East Timorese in the eyes of the people, and so I will just be a gypsy. But the concept of gypsy just scares people. So I don't know what I'm going to be. I don't know what title I want to have.

Afterword: January 2005

Almost two years have passed since East Timor's Independence Day, and five since the 1999 referendum. Much has changed in East Timor in that time, but the lives of many former exiles remain in limbo.

Alexandre—a gentle and intelligent young man of twenty-seven—is one of the "1600 Group" who came after 1991 and were denied asylum status in Australia. As one of those who escaped the Dili Massacre, physically and mentally scarred by the experience, he fled to Australia when he was seventeen and since then has lived with the traumatic uncertainty of potential deportation to East Timor. On a temporary bridging visa that denied him (and those like him) some of the most basic human rights expected of a Western democracy—access to higher education and to the welfare system—Alexandre's formative years as a young man were severely curtailed. Unable to access the education system, he was forced to work in low-paid casual work; what little funds he had to spare were sent to support his mother and siblings who live in the poorest of circumstances in East Timor. It is not hard to imagine how damaging these years have been for him and their impact on his ability to fulfill his potential and build a life for himself.

Knowing of his wish to work in the computer field, a group of us undertook to gain a scholarship for him at a local educational institution. Many phone calls and letters later, we were lucky enough to stumble upon a director of one of the private colleges who had worked in East Timor before 1975 and felt grateful for the opportunity to assist a young East Timorese by waiving his course fees. Alexandre completed the course while working nights to support himself and his family back home. A year after completion, however, he has felt unable to seek permanent work in the field because of his still uncertain residency status; employers have felt hesitant to take him on for similar reasons. He tells me that it is much too hard to think about a career when he doesn't even know if he'll be able to remain in Australia. Instead, he takes casual shifts as a waiter and works the night shift at a mail sorting center.

We speak every couple of months and he seems increasingly depressed and frustrated over his situation. When we last spoke two weeks ago, he told me he just feels like throwing it all in and going back to East Timor. He wants to stay so badly but has simply had enough of the uncertainty, poverty, and exclusion from the sorts of everyday opportunities the rest of us take for granted. For the last year he has had to report once a week to the Immigration Department office so that they can "keep tabs on him." The inconvenience, stress, and indignity of this is almost unimaginable. Remember, this young man is not a criminal. He was a refugee at seventeen years old and simply came to Australia to be safe and have some kind of future. We chatted some more and eventually he said, "but don't worry, I won't throw it in. I've waited this long and sacrificed so much. Besides, my mum needs me to be here, they rely on the money I send to survive. I'll just have to wait."

Alexandre is one of about 200 of the 1600 Group who remain in limbo. In the last two years the government has granted permanent residency to about 1,000 of them and sent about 200 home; another 200 simply had had enough and went back of their own accord. World affairs in the last few years—September 11 and the wars in Afghanistan and Iraq—have had an impact on the seemingly unconnected lives of remaining 1600 Group Timorese. September 11, which occurred during an election campaign, created a moral panic around Middle-Eastern asylum seekers arriving in Australia by boat from Indonesia. Most of these Iraqi and Afghani asylum seekers ended up on temporary three-year visas, or in detention.

Despite an increased sympathy among some sections of the Australian government toward the East Timorese 1600 Group, they were in the politically awkward situation where, if concession of permanent residency was made for them on compassionate if not legal grounds, it could set a precedent for the Afghani and Iraqi asylum seekers whose three-year visas are coming up for renewal. With the wars in Iraq and Afghanistan came calls for their visas not to be renewed on the grounds that their claims to asylum no longer held with the overthrow of the Afghan and Iraqi regimes. While there is much positive sentiment toward East Timorese in the Australian electorate, the latter two groups are not so lucky.

The government, so the rumor goes, has in response taken a "softly, softly" approach to the issue, awarding Timorese visas on a case by case basis very quietly and very slowly in order to avoid any media attention. There are good indications that the majority will be allowed to stay, but it may well take some time for the government to work its way down the list. The elderly and those with relationships or close family ties in Australia have been allowed to stay, but a number of young men have been sent back. Those like Alexandre still awaiting news remain in limbo, still waiting, still uncertain as to the land of their future.

For the rest of the East Timorese community, the pattern of shuttling back and forth, of split families and short-term contracts remains. Quite a few more of the politically active elites have returned, but very few of the rest of the community. The promises that "one day I'll go back" seem to be as frequent as before. Conversely, some of those I interviewed in East Timor have come back to Australia. Osório, the young politically active man from Melbourne introduced in Chapter 6, is one. His work translating for the war crimes unit has finished and he has returned to university studies in Melbourne. It is unclear whether this is a temporary or permanent "return" to Australia.

The community in Sydney is, I gather, gradually finding its post-independence feet. A couple of new leaders are beginning to emerge, and more locally oriented activities are happening. A soccer team has been established, and a yearly event to mark the anniversary of formal independence is held each May. The East Timor Cultural Centre closed down at the end of 2002, but the Timorese Australian Council remains active, as do the Catholic sisters of the Mary MacKillop Institute of East Timorese Studies, who continue to provide emotional and practical support to Australian East Timorese.

Meanwhile, East Timor itself has moved to a new phase in its nascent nationhood. There is much more cynicism among East Timorese in Australia and in Timor about the new government. From the idealistic heroes of independence, the FRETILIN government has been subject to accusations of nepotism, censorship, and corruption. They are fighting a new kind of independence struggle now. The homeland has entered a power struggle for autonomous rule in the face of powerful Western interests. Australia has been behaving like a bully on the Timor Gap oil issue, refusing to accept international sea boundary standards and holding East Timor's budding oil industry for ransom. Despite the fact that East Timor is now a democracy, most major decisions on reconstruction are made by international donor organizations and countries. A program of tariff reduction and privatization of state utilities has been effectively forced upon East Timor by the IMF; strict donor conditions determine much of the reconstruction paradigm; the civil service has been restricted to 17,000 from approximately 33,000 under the Indonesians. The East Timorese government is increasingly defensive and wary of "foreign politics," in part directed at left-wing radical solidarity supporters who have organized protests and campaigns against some of the less popular government policies, and in part in response to the perceived political interference of "democracy-promoting" U.S. organizations such as the International Republican Institute (IRI), the foreign policy wing of ultra-right wing of the U.S. Republican Party, an organization seen by U.S. conservatives as a key tool in directing the political agenda in countries like East Timor. This organization sees itself as supporting democratic opposition in East Timor, but FRETILIN see it as interfering. The government has responded to these perceived threats to East Timor's independence by enacting a restrictive immigration law banning foreigners from "engaging in political activities" (Moxham 2005).

Yet East Timor and its new government are doing their best to carve out a space for their nation in the region and mend relations with important neighbors such as Indonesia. Despite the terrible atrocities committed by the Indonesian military, East Timor sees Indonesia as a friend and most Timorese bear little grudge toward its people. Their justice and forgiveness approach to foreign policy is admirable. A wonderful example of this emerged following the Asian tsunami on 26 December 2004. Within days of the disaster, East Timor pledged $50,000 in aid to tsunami victims in Indonesia. A small amount in dollar terms, this was a most poignant gesture of goodwill, and a most significant gift given East Timor's status as Asia's poorest nation.

And then there is Xaviér, the young man introduced in Chapter 4, "Embodying Exile," who went into post-traumatic shock at the sound of fire engines during our interview. Unable to bear the isolation and pain of life in Australia any longer, unable to escape the terrible memories that had possessed his body for so long, he recently moved back to East Timor in the hope that finding a normal life back there would help his mind heal. He hoped returning would help him move past that point where he was trapped, by his recurring memories, in a time bubble of Indonesian-occupied East Timor. He wants and needs time for his body to absorb positive memories of the new East Timor. After that, who knows? His younger brother and older sister have decided to remain in Australia permanently. Ermelina, his elderly mother, passed away just six months ago, without fulfilling her dream to return to her village in East Timor to die. She is buried near Fairfield, but perhaps her spirit is now free to settle where it needs.

Notes

Introduction

1. The crocodile is the most important symbol in the Timorese creation myth. The island of Timor is said to be shaped like a crocodile. According to this creation story, a young boy came across a sick crocodile that was burning in the sun. The boy took pity on the crocodile and carried it to the sea so that it wouldn't die. To repay the boy's kindness, the crocodile took the boy, as was his wish, on many long journeys across the sea, carrying the boy on his back. Despite being tempted to eat the boy, the crocodile kept his promise and let the boy ride safely. They journeyed until the crocodile became old. When he realized he was dying, the crocodile said to the boy, "I will change into a land where you and your descendants will live from my fruits, as payment for your kindness." According to Timorese tradition, that crocodile became the island of Timor, and the Timorese are the descendants of that boy. The title of the exhibition and of Chapter 2, "Leaving the Crocodile," refers to the pain of Timorese leaving their homeland.

2. FRETILIN (Frente Revolucionara do Timor Leste Independente / Revolutionary Front for an Independent East Timor), East Timor's ruling party, was formed in 1974 and won East Timor's first election in 1975, before being deposed in a coup. See Chapter 1 for more details.

3. I realize that "community" is itself a contested term. Later in the book I explore the internal heterogeneity of the "Timorese Community." Nonetheless, I find I have to use the term as there is, as yet, no less controversial alternative to describe a group of people.

4. Although East Timor did not officially receive its independence until 20 May 2002, the referendum held in August 1999 to ask if they wished to remain a part of Indonesia is widely talked about within the Timorese community as the date East Timor became independent. This date has significance because it was following that vote that the Indonesian administration and military left. Therefore, when I refer to the time period "following East Timor's independence" I mean the time frame after September 1999. I detail the background to the referendum and subsequent independence in Chapter 1.

5. See Rosemary Preston's article "Researching Repatriation and Reconstruction" (1999) for a brief review and chronology of the literature on refugee return.

Chapter 1. East Timor: A History of the Present

Epigraph: Homi Bhabha, cited in Gupta and Ferguson (1997, 34)

1. In the Foucauldian sense.

2. This section on East Timorese history is compiled from a number of sources that I'd like to specifically acknowledge, including in particular Taylor (1999), Thatcher (1991), Morlanes (1991), and Dunn (1996).

3. For a more in-depth account of the early history of Timor, see "The Portuguese in the Moluccas and in the Lesser Sunda Islands" www.geocities.com/Athens/styx/6497/ternate.html. See also Gunn (1999).

4. These were mainly local slaves taken to serve on Dutch plantations in Java (Macedo, Braz, and Monteiro 2000), or sent to the South African Cape.

5. See two early important works on the development of East Timor's anti-colonial movement: Nicol (1978) and Jolliffe (1978).

6. Interviewed by the author April 2001, translated by Manuel Branco.

7. By mid-2002, all but an estimated 30,000 of these had returned to East Timor, by way of a concerted campaign by the East Timorese authorities to repatriate and reintegrate them.

8. There is still much argument on the Timor Gap oil issue. For an overview, see Dez Wildwood's "Backdoor" site http://www.pcug.org.au/~wildwood.

Chapter 2. Leaving the Crocodile: The East Timorese Community in Sydney

1. These were not forced marriages as such. Timorese in Portugal who were not able to gain Australian permanent residency "voluntarily" married Timorese in Australia because there was no other way to get here to join extended family and friends.

2. These two theses are useful accounts of pre-1990s Timorese communities in other parts of Australia. Thatcher's work (1991) focuses on Melbourne and looks at settlement issues and the differences between the Timorese and Timorese-Chinese communities. That of Morlanes (1991) is based on the Darwin Timorese community and looks at processes of ethnonational identity formation. To my knowledge, these are the only two works on the Timorese in Australia, although there are one or two Ph.D. projects in process as I write.

3. There are a number of excellent resources on the background to the Timor Gap oil issue. Particularly recommended is the *La'o Hamutuk Bulletin*, which can be downloaded at http://ww.etan.org/lh/bulletins/bulletinv4n34.html (Hamutuk 2003).

4. Exact numbers are difficult to come by, mainly because, between 1976 and 1996, the Australian Census counted East Timorese as Indonesians. The estimates have been arrived at by a complex process of cross-matching refugee arrivals from Indonesia who list their first language as Tetum or Hakka and multiplying by the anticipated birth rate. For an explanation of the anomalies in the data, and the process by which these estimates were arrived, see Thatcher (1991).

5. I wish to thank Nancy de Almeida from the East Timor Cultural Centre for her valuable assistance in compiling the information for the following sections.

6. James Jupp's article "Australia's Refugee and Humanitarian Policies" (2002) gives a good overview of the changing nature of Australia's stance and policies toward asylum seekers and refugees.

7. See the 1970 Census of Portuguese Timor, compared to the 1990 Census undertaken by Indonesia, listed in the appendices of Thatcher (1991).

8. For a breakdown of figures relating to employment, language, and housing, and comparing the East Timorese to the Timorese-Chinese sections of the community during 1994, see the excellent reports commissioned by the Timorese Australian Council: Rawsthorne (1994) and Chung (1994).

9. Centrelink is the Australian government social security agency.

10. Timorese use the word "party" to refer to any collective gathering—dance, dinner, barbeque, or open community gathering in a public hall where food and drink are available. The most common community event is a "party" in a local community hall, where anyone can purchase a ticket, usually for $10. Women cook Timorese and Portuguese food and bring it to the hall, and are reimbursed from the funds raised through ticket sales. Alcohol is usually on sale, and there is always dancing and a Timorese band. The dancing is usually the Timorese version of traditional Portuguese folk dancing or a kind of waltz shuffle. The music is either "Timorese reggae" or Portuguese folk songs. Usually parties were held to raise funds to assist East Timor, and there is nearly always a speaker from one of the political organizations.

Chapter 3. Nation, Transnation, Diaspora: Locating East Timorese Long Distance Nationalism

1. Indonesia's period of "political reform" was officially known as "reformasi."

2. Most of these organizations have ceased to exist, changed their focus, or radically downsized their activities since the successful referendum vote in 1999. Most of their key leaders have returned to East Timor. ETRA has been virtually dormant since the beginning of 2000, with its most active members returning to East Timor to take positions in the new government. CNRT no longer exists, and the UDT is virtually nonexistent as a political entity. FRETILIN in NSW still has representatives and is engaged in charitable activities. The Timorese Australian Council still exists; its charter is to provide services to the community in Sydney. This has left an enormous vacuum in the community, as virtually all community activities were centered on these kinds of political activities prior to 1999.

3. Despite this coalition, many (particularly those over thirty-five) still identify themselves and each other as "I'm UDT" or "he's FRETILIN." The two parties remain strong reference points when community members speak about one another, and political affiliations are the source of ongoing animosities. UDT people won't go to events where there is outward FRETILIN symbolism, and vice versa.

4. As one of my anonymous referees pointed out, photos of torture were often bought by the independence movement from the military who took them. This was a highly controversial tactic, particularly when in the late 1990s pictures of women being tortured were put on display by a range of "solidarity" groups. This was condemned, by ETRA women especially, as a violation and as fostering the image of Timorese as passive victims. For a discussion of the circulation of torture photographs in the Croatian and Bosnian diasporas, see Kolar-Panov (1996).

5. Only one station exists now, Radio Timor Oan (Timor people), formerly Radio FRETILIN.

6. I deal with these protest rallies in more detail in Chapter 4.

7. The Josephites are a fairly liberal Catholic religious order, known particularly in Australia for their progressive, outspoken activist stance on contemporary

social issues. A Josephite herself, Mary MacKillop is the first and only Australian to be beatified. Among other charitable activities, she ran schools for the poor in the nineteenth century.

8. I do not want to imply irony by the use of "scare quotes" here. Their use is to emphasize the discursive dimensions to these values.

9. After East Timor's independence, the University of New South Wales formalized the Diplomacy Training School, with the support of Ramos-Horta, and it now trains other third world students and NGOs (especially from the Asia-Pacific region) in advancing their causes for democracy and human rights internationally.

10. See Malkki (1994) and Wilson (1997) for their respective critiques of internationalist human rights discourses. Wilson argues that human rights reporting codifies human rights violations according to a universal template, which, among other things, has the effect of silencing all the messy contextuality of the situation and stripping them of their subjective meaning (134).

11. The flag eventually chosen was a version of the 1975 independence flag, based on FRETILIN colors of red, black, and yellow.

12. Although nationalism is frequently deemed "reactionary" by Western commentators, it is important to recognize the liberatory nature of the East Timorese case. Descriptions of the "imagined homeland" and "nationalism" in this case should not be read as shorthand for "reactionary" and "false." East Timorese anticolonial nationalism from afar has held enormous affective meaning for the population, and its success has been important in securing an independent future free of the severe human rights abuses committed by the Indonesian military. This is, of course, not to suggest that some of the rhetoric of East Timorese nationalism is beyond critique; rather, I want to recognize its positive dimensions as well. As Hall argues (1990, 224) "We should not for a moment underestimate or neglect the importance of the act of imaginative rediscovery. . . . Such images offer a way of imposing an imaginary coherence on the experience of dispersal and fragmentation."

Chapter 4. Embodying Exile: Embodied Memory and the Role of Trauma, Affect, Politics, and Religion in the Formation of Identities in Exile

1. Post-traumatic stress disorder (PTSD) has been criticized by counseling professionals for overuse for categorizing diverse experiences of trauma survivors into a prescriptive chart of symptoms. Nevertheless, it is still seen as a useful diagnostic tool and remains the main diagnosis for trauma survivors. There are also issues to do with the extent to which it is a useful tool when dealing with less individuated non-Western psyches.

2. My work follows an important ethnographic tradition developed in earlier Australian studies of settlement issues among refugee and migrant groups. See, e.g., Martin (1972), Viviani (1996), Bottomley (1979), and Thomas (1999).

3. Despite the fact that, as I argue in Chapter 6, few are carrying through with return now that East Timor has independence.

4. Indeed, many argue that, at least in the early years of the Indonesian occupation, the Indonesians were more likely to target the Timorese-Chinese.

5. The Dili Massacre, as it has become known, took place on 12 November 1991 in the Santa Cruz Cemetery in the East Timorese capital of Dili. Indonesian

military shot dead between three and four hundred peaceful protesters attending a memorial service. The massacre was secretly filmed by British journalist Max Stahl and was shown on news services around the world. That video is credited with raising international awareness of and sympathy for the East Timorese cause for the first time.

6. For a related discussion, see also Noble (2002). Noble, working in the Australian context, explores how everyday cultural objects such as Australian landscape paintings and other household decorations articulate in a homely way with national identity. In his view, "The extent to which we furnish our house and make it our home, our own, entails in part weaving into everyday experience objects of personal and familial significance which also carry, in often submerged ways, a national experience—as ornaments, memories of childhood, photos, touristic memorabilia, aesthetic artefacts, and so on. This constructs the nation not so much as a project of active affiliation and identification but as the furniture of everyday life, or what we might see as a "very banal nationalism'" (55).

7. See also Canetti (1973) on crowds and power.

8. See song words reproduced in Chapter 3.

9. In East Timor, the lulik house is the centerpiece of each village. It is a tall thatched hut with an elongated roof stretching into the air. The spirit ancestors of the village group are said to reside in the house. It is the most spiritually significant site in each village. In recent times, the distinctive looking lulik house has achieved icon status and is now a widely recognized symbol of East Timor and East Timorese culture.

10. The Dili Massacre is known in East Timor as the Santa Cruz Massacre after the cemetery where it took place. It is occasionally referred to as this in Australia too.

11. See also Csikszentmihalyi and Rochberg-Halton (1981) for a discussion on the dialogic aspect of objects, persons, and meaning.

Chapter 5. Locating Timoreseness in Australia: Layers of Hybridity, Anchored and Enmeshed

1. See Noble, Poynting, and Tabar (1999) for an interesting discussion of the shifting and contextual identifications among Arabic-speaking schoolboys in southwestern Sydney. They relate the story of a Syrian boy who, because there were no other boys of his ethnic background in his school, mixed with a group of mainly Lebanese boys. Although proudly Syrian, he identifies as Lebanese at school. As he says, "around here, it's more like you have to be Lebanese . . . Lebanese is sort of like slang for Arab" (40).

2. There is a difference in East Timor between the under-thirty generation, schooled under Indonesia, and the older generation (especially former exiles), who identify with Portuguese culture. The younger generation wish to invoke a more traditional, indigenous version of Timorese identity, while the older generation of politicians draw heavily on the Portuguese elements in Timorese culture.

3. Although he has expressed his preference to stay in Australia, rather than live in Portugal or East Timor—mainly because it is close to Timor.

4. I use Nederveen Pieterse's (2001) formulation of "the politics of recognition," although it is Taylor's famous work (1994) that coined the term. Taylor refers more to state practices, whereas I am focusing more on civil society.

5. Many Timorese and Timorese-Chinese use the term "voodooism" in English. They are really referring to the traditional animist religious beliefs and practices of East Timor.

6. The term "Timorese-Chinese," in that word order, is how this community prefer to be identified. In other parts of this chapter and others, I sometimes use the term "non-Chinese Timorese" to refer to East Timorese of indigenous or mestiço descent. I do this when comparing the two groups, rather than using the more general "East Timorese" label I have used elsewhere to describe these groups. Although it is a little clumsy, I use the term "non-Chinese Timorese" because I do not want to play into the racial exclusion of Chineseness from Timoreseness.

Chapter Six. From Exile to Diaspora? On Identity, Belonging, and the (Im)Possibility of Return Home

Epigraph: Exiled journalist, cited in Kaminsky (1999, 1).

1. I'd like to thank Deirdre McKay for helping me develop Appadurai's concept.

2. A kind of fig tree similar to the Indian banyan tree. It is said that they carry ancestral spirits, and that every village is built around one. In Dili, despite being urbanized, groups of houses are still built in a circular fashion around a shared yard area, at the center of which more often than not is the *hali hung* tree and, at its base, a wooden bench, plastic chairs, or milk crates for seating—where residents will often come to relax and to escape the afternoon sun.

3. *Malae* translates as "stranger" in Tetum. It is the term commonly used to refer to foreigners and was used in particular to reference white foreigners—especially Portuguese. It is still used today, especially in a derogatory way to refer to the international workers that have descended on East Timor since 1999.

4. Those who have returned have also left a mark on the community in Sydney. Moreover, there is an enduring sense that there is a vacuum in the community because many of its most active leaders have returned to East Timor. Since these important figures have left, there have been few community events. Prior to the referendum, most events were part of the independence campaign. There is for many a feeling of loss. Even now, the majority of community activities are centered on fundraising for East Timor, rather than being community building activities per se.

5. The government in East Timor is dominated by returned exiles and East Timorese of the pre-1975 generation. All identify strongly with Portugal and Portuguese language and culture. The decision was made early in the administration that Portuguese and Tetum would be the national languages, but that Portuguese would be the language of education, law, and government. This has had a profound effect, given that most East Timorese under thirty-five who remained under the Indonesian occupation speak little or no Portuguese. This created a huge generational split whereby older Timorese and those who lived in exile have been favored for the best positions in the government. It is one of the main areas of political tension in East Timor at present. Interestingly, a second layer of tension has arisen, with some returnees from Australia advocating English as a second national language with Tetum, in contrast to returnees from Portugal pushing for Portuguese.

6. From conversations with Mandy Thomas, author of *Dreams in the Shadows: Vietnamese-Australian lives in transition* (1999). For more debates on these Chinese

diaspora issues, see also Ang (2001), Ong (1999), Pan (1999), Mar (1998), Wang (1992). This of course also relates to the history of colonial relations discussed earlier in this chapter.

7. Off the top of my head, I can think of several individuals from the Sydney community who have connections and family still here. Of course, Nobel Laureate José Ramos Horta is the most famous former Fairfield resident to return, taking up the position of foreign minister. Estanislau da Silva, whose wife and children remain in Sydney, has taken the post of minister for agriculture. A Sydney woman now heads the Save the Children East Timor operation, and another resident is East Timor's ambassador in Canberra. Ines de Almeida, also of Fairfield, is now the media adviser to East Timor's president, Xanana Gusmão. The Timorese priest who conducted services for the community in Tetum through the years in Sydney's western suburbs, Father Alves, has returned and runs the Motael church, one of the main churches in Dili. Then there is João Carrascalão, member of parliament, head of UDT, and member of one of East Timor's leading families (his brother was governor of East Timor under Indonesia and is now leader of another of East Timor's opposition parties). Carrascalão was a prominent community leader in Sydney. This is a short list of names that spring to mind. There are many more, in Sydney and in equal numbers from Melbourne. It gives a sense of the extent to which the local communities in Australia are connected at the highest levels in East Timor.

Glossary

AETA	Australia East Timor Association. The main Australian solidarity organization for East Timor.
APODETI	Associão Popular Democratica (first called the Association for the Integration of Timor into Indonesia). 1974/75 party with only minor support.
ASIET	Australians in Solidarity with Indonesia and East Timor. A left-wing Australian solidarity organization aligned with the Australian Socialist Workers Party, now known as Action in Solidarity with Asia and the Pacific (ASAP)
Assimilado	Portuguese term for Timorese officially deemed "assimilated." Usually of mestiço or Chinese background.
Atambua	West Timorese border town where many East Timorese fled the civil war and during the 1999 post-referendum violence.
Baucau	East Timor's second largest city.
Blacktown	Northwestern working-class suburb of Sydney where a number of East Timorese live. It is neighbored by Mt. Druitt and Penrith, also suburbs with concentrations of East Timorese. The Mary MacKillop Institute of East Timorese Studies is located in St. Marys, next to Penrith.
Baino	Timorese term to describe a "civilized" indigene.
Cabramatta	Suburb neighboring Fairfield, where most East Timorese lived. A large number of Southeast Asian refugees made this suburb their home because of its proximity to the former migrant hostel where they lived on first arrival to Australia during the 1970s.
Bupati	Indonesian term for head of a district.
Caetano	Marcello Caetano, Portugal's dictator, ruling between 1968 and 1974. His regime was overturned in what became known as the "Carnation Revolution."
Calade	Derogatory term for the unassimilated indigenous, meaning stupid or ignorant.
Civilizado	Portuguese term for "civilized Timorese."
CNRM	Conselho Naçional da Resistençia Maubere; National Council of Maubere Resistance. The predecessor of the CNRT.

CNRT

Conselho Naçional da Resistençia Timorenses; National Council of Timorese Resistance. The main independence coalition group made up of FRETILIN and UDT supporters and others. Disbanded following the referendum.

Coogee

In Sydney's beachside eastern suburbs, close to Bondi. Location of one of the migrant hostels that mostly Timorese-Chinese were sent to in 1975.

Concelho

East Timorese administrative division.

Darwin

Capital of Australia's Northern Territory, a small city of around 105,000 people. The northernmost capital city and seen as Australia's "gateway to Asia," it is closer to Jakarta than to Sydney, and only about 600 km from East Timor. Unlike the southern states of Sydney and Melbourne, Darwin is in the tropics, has a laid-back semi-"outback" feel, is home to large numbers of aboriginal people, and has a long history of migration from Asia, particularly Japan, Malaysia, and Indonesia, reflected in its cosmopolitan food and street culture. Because of its location it was also the transit base for the UN mission to East Timor. A large population of East Timorese people live there because of its proximity to East Timor.

Cnua

Indigenous settlement within a suco.

Dato

Indigenous nobility.

Dato fakun

Indigenous nobility, or "important people."

Deportado

Portuguese exiled under Salazar to East Timor.

Dili

East Timor's capital city, the primary center of Portuguese life before 1975.

Ema

"The people" or "free men."

Fairfield

Working-class western suburb of Sydney, about forty minutes west (inland) of the harbor and central business district, home to many migrants. In the 1970s Fairfield and neighboring Cabramatta housed migrant hostels where many migrants and refugees were sent on first arrival in Australia. A large number of migrant services were set up in this area and migrants continue to settle there for this reason. Many Southeast Asian refugee communities are in this area, particularly Vietnamese, East Timorese, Cambodian, and Laotian.

ETRA

East Timor Relief Association. East Timorese organization based in Australia, main front for aid relief and information gathering before 1999. Now focused on rebuilding activities.

FALINTIL

Armed Forces for the National Liberation of East Timor.

FRETILIN

Frente Revolucionaria do Timor Leste Independente; Revolutionary Front for an Independent East Timor.

Gentio

Portuguese term for non-Christian or non-baptized people.

INTERFET

International Force for East Timor. The initial Australian-led international force that entered East Timor in September 1999 to restore and enforce peace following the post-ballot violence.

Liverpool

Neighboring suburb to Fairfield and Cabramatta. Liverpool is a slightly more middle-class suburb, generally less disadvantaged, with new housing estates and apartments and a large shopping mall. Many migrants from Fairfield and Cabramatta move to Liverpool when they are more established. A large number of middle-class East Timorese families live in the area.

Kupang	Capital of West Timor.
Liurai	Timorese royalty, ruler of a Timorese kingdom or rai.
Lulik	Adjective or noun for a sacred item or something pertaining to the indigenous spiritual belief system of East Timor. For example, a lulik house is a sacred house found in each village, containing ancestral spirits.
Maubere	Son of Timor, dweller in the mountains. Originally "my brother." Took on political meaning under FRETILIN.
Mary MacKillop	First and only Australian to be beatified in the Catholic Church.
Mestiço	Person of mixed Portuguese and Timorese race.
O nativo dos pés descalços	Portuguese term meaning "barefoot natives"; refers to "unassimilated" indigenous Timorese.
Pensão; plural pensões	Very basic hostel accommodation in Lisbon where many poor Timorese lived.
PKF	Peacekeeping Force
Posto	Portuguese territorial administrative unit within a concelho.
Rai	The major indigenous territorial political unit.
Rai-ten	Tax collected by dato in exchange for granting gathering, planting, and hunting rights to their land.
Reformasi	Period of Indonesian political reform leading up to 1998.
Salazar	António de Oliveira Salazar, Portugal's dictator between 1926 and 1968.
Suco	Small administrative area, collectively make up a posto.
Tais	Traditional woven cloth produced in East Timor, woven in coarse thread, similar in size to a sarong. It has become the best-known national cultural symbol.
Tetum/Tetun	Lingua franca of East Timor; spelled both ways.
Timor Leste	Official name of the new nation of East Timor. This Portuguese spelling was favored by the new government over the Tetum "Timor Loro'sae," which translates as "Timor where the sun rises."
Timor	Used to describe "unassimilated" natives, meaning son of Timor, ignorant.
Topasses	Early Catholicized mestiço population from around 1566. Known as "black Portuguese," they formed a distinct and powerful ethnic group in early Portuguese Timor.
Tumukum	Chief of a cnua or village.
UDT	União Democratica Timorense; Timorese Democratic Union. The conservative pro-Portugal political party that lost the 1975 election and fought a bitter civil war with FRETILIN.
UNAMET	UN Mission to East Timor; supervised the referendum ballot.
UNTAET	UN Transitional Administration in East Timor; administered East Timor between September 1999 following the referendum and Independence Day, 25 May 2002.
Villawood	Suburb neighboring Fairfield and Cabramatta, site of one of the three original migrant hostels where East Timorese arriving in 1975 were sent.

Bibliography

Al-Ali, Nadje, Richard Black, and Khalid Koser. 2001. The Limits to "Transnationalism": Bosnian and Eritrean Refugees in Europe as Emerging Transnational Communities. *Ethnic and Racial Studies* 24 (4): 578–600.

Allen, Tim, and Hubert Morsink, eds. 1994. *When Refugees Go Home: African Experiences*. Geneva: United Nations Research Institute for Social Development.

Anderson, Benedict. 1991. *Imagined Communities: Reflections on the Origin and Spread of Nationalism*. London: Verso.

———. 1998. *The Specter of Comparisons: Nationalism, Southeast Asia, and the World*. New York: Verso.

———. 2001. Imagining East Timor. *Lusotopie* 2001: 233–39.

Ang, Ien. 1998. Can One Say No to Chineseness? Pushing the Limits of the Diasporic Paradigm. *Boundary 2* 25 (3): 223–42.

———. 2001. *On Not Speaking Chinese: Living Between Asia and the West*. London: Routledge.

Antze, Paul and Michael Lambek. 1996. Introduction: Forecasting Memory. In *Tense Past: Cultural Essays in Trauma and Memory*, ed. Paul Antze and Michael Lambek. New York: Routledge.

Appadurai, Arjun. 1995. The Production of Locality. In *Counterworks: Managing the Diversity of Knowledge*, ed. Richard Fardon. London: Routledge.

———. 1996. *Modernity at Large: Cultural Dimensions of Globalization*. Minneapolis: University of Minnesota Press.

Aubrey, Jim, ed. 1998. *Free East Timor: Australia's Culpability in East Timor's Genocide*. Sydney: Vintage.

Axel, Brian Keith. 2001. *The Nation's Tortured Body: Violence, Representation, and the Formation of a Sikh "Diaspora"*. Durham, N.C.: Duke University Press.

Baldassar, Loretta. 1999. National and Cultural Identities: Introduction. *Australian Journal of Social Issues* 34 (4): 291–99.

———. 2001. *Visits Home: Migration Experiences Between Italy and Australia*. Melbourne: Melbourne University Press.

Bariangaber, Assefaw. 2001. The Refugee Experience: Understanding the Dynamics of Refugee Repatriation in Eritrea. *Journal of Third World Studies* 18 (2): 47–70.

Basch, Linda, Nina Glick-Schiller, and Cristina Szanton Blanc. 1994. *Nations Unbound: Transnational Projects, Postcolonial Predicaments, and Deterritorialized Nation-States*. Langhorne, Pa.: Gordon and Breach.

Baumann, Gerd. 1996. *Contesting Culture: Discourses of Identity in Multi-Ethnic London.* Cambridge Studies in Social and Cultural Anthropology 100. New York: Cambridge University Press.

———. 1997. Dominant and Demotic Discourses of Culture: Their relevance to multi-ethnic alliances. In *Debating Cultural Hybridity: Multi-Cultural Identities and the Politics of Anti-Racism,* ed. Pnina Werbner and Tariq Modood. Postcolonial Encounters. London: Zed Books.

Black, Richard and Khalid Koser, eds. 1999. *The End of the Refugee Cycle: Refugee Repatriation and Reconstruction.* New York: Berghahn Books.

Bloul, Rachel. 1999. Beyond Ethnic Identity: Resisting Exclusionary Identification. *Social Identities* 5 (1): 7–30.

Bottomley, Gillian. 1979. *After the Odyssey: A Study of Greek Australians.* St. Lucia: University of Queensland Press.

Bottomley, Gillian, Marie de Lepervanche, and Jean Martin, eds. 1991. *InterSexions: Gender/Class/Culture/Ethnicity.* Sydney: Allen and Unwin.

Bourdieu, Pierre. 1994. *Distinction: A Social Critique of the Judgement of Taste.* Trans. Richard Nice. London: Routledge.

Bracken, Patrick J. 1998. Hidden Agendas: Deconstructing Post-Traumatic Stress Disorder. In *Rethinking the Trauma of War,* ed. Patrick J. Bracken and Celia Petty. New York: Free Association Books.

Brah, Avtar. 1996. *Cartographies of Diaspora: Contesting Identities.* London: Routledge.

Button, James. 1997. Birth of an Underground. *The Age,* 3 May, 24.

Canetti, Elias. 1973. *Crowds and Power.* Trans. Carol Stewart. Rev. ed. Harmondsworth: Penguin.

Cardoso, Luís. 2000. *The Crossing: A Story of East Timor.* Trans. Margaret Jull Costa. London: Granta.

Carruthers, Ashley. 2001. Exile and Return: Deterritorialising National Imaginaries in Vietnam and the Diaspora. Ph.D. Thesis, Department of Anthropology, University of Sydney.

Caruth, Cathy. 1995a. Recapturing the Past: Introduction. In *Trauma: Explorations in Memory,* ed. Cathy Caruth. Baltimore: Johns Hopkins University Press.

———, ed. 1995b. *Trauma: Explorations in Memory.* Baltimore: Johns Hopkins University Press.

CDPM (Commission for the Rights of the Maubere People). 1997. São Paulo Manifesto. *Timor Leste* (Monthly Bulletin, original language Portuguese), November.

Chung, Mantchu. 1994. *Timorese-Chinese in South West Sydney.* Sydney: Timorese-Australian Council.

Clifford, James. 1994. Diasporas. *Cultural Anthropology* 9 (3): 302–38.

———. 1997. *Routes: Travel and Translation in the Late Twentieth Century.* Cambridge, Mass.: Harvard University Press.

Cohen, Robin. 1997. *Global Diasporas: An Introduction.* London: University College London Press.

Csikszentmihalyi, Mihal and Eugene Rochberg-Halton. 1981. *The Meaning of Things: Domestic Symbols and the Self.* Cambridge: Cambridge University Press.

Culbertson, Robert. 1995. Embodied Memory, Transcendence, and Telling: Recounting Trauma, Re-Establishing the Self. *New Literary History* 26 (1): 169–96.

dos Reis-Piedade, Maria Immaculada. 2001. Me & My Tradition. In *Leaving the Crocodile: The Story of the East Timorese Community in Sydney,* ed. Amanda Wise. Sydney: Liverpool Regional Museum.

Dunn, James. 1996. *Timor: A People Betrayed.* Sydney: ABC Books.

ETRA. 2000. *East Timor Relief Association* (Website) (cited 30 November 2000). Available from http://www.etra.zip.com.au/

FETWA. 1995. East Timor: The Inside Story. *Newsletter of Friends of East Timor (W.A.)*, 10–11.

Fortier, Anne-Marie. 1999. Re-Membering Places and the Performance of Belongings. *Theory, Culture, Society* 16 (2): 41–64.

———. 2000. *Migrant Belongings: Memory, Space, Identity*. Oxford: Berg.

Foucault, Michel. 1974. *The Archaeology of Knowledge*. Trans. A. M. Sheridan-Smith. London: Tavistock.

Fuglerud, Oivind. 1999. *Life on the Outside: The Tamil Diaspora and Long Distance Nationalism*. London: Pluto Press.

Gilroy, Paul. 2000. The Sugar You Stir . . . In *Without Guarantees: In Honour of Stuart Hall*, ed. Paul Gilroy, Lawrence Grossberg, and Angela McRobbie. London: Verso.

Goertz, Karein. 1998. Transgenerational Representations of the Holocaust: From the Memory to "Post-Memory." *World Literature Today* 72 (1): 33–38.

Goodman, James. 2000. Marginalisation and Empowerment: East Timorese Diaspora Politics in Australia. *Communal/Plural: Journal of Transnational and Crosscultural Studies* 8 (1): 25–46.

Gready, Paul. 1994. The South African Experience of Home and Homecoming. *World Literature Today* 68 (3): 509.

Grossberg, Lawrence. 1998. *Rock Resistance and the Resistance to Rock* (Website) (cited 3 September 2002). Available from http://www.gu.edu.au/centre/cmp/Grossberg.

Guarnizo, Luis Eduardo and Michael Peter Smith. 1998. The Locations of Transnationalism. In *Transnationalism from Below*, ed. Luis Eduardo Guarnizo and Michael Peter Smith. New Brunswick, N.J.: Transaction Publishers.

Gunn, Geoffrey C. 1999. *Timor loro sae: 500 Years*. Macao: Livros do Oriente.

Gupta, Akhil and James Ferguson. 1997. Beyond "Culture": Space, Identity, and the Politics of Difference. In *Culture, Power, Place: Explorations in Critical Anthropology*, ed. Akhil Gupta and James Ferguson. Durham, N.C.: Duke University Press.

Gusmão, Xanana. 1994. Congratulatory Letter from Xanana to Mandela, 1 September 1994.

———. 1996. Action Is Worth More Than a Million Letters. Pamphlet, June 1996.

———. 1998. Letter from Xanana Gusmao to the Timorese National Convention, Lisbon, 23–27 April. http://www.geocities.com/CapitolHill/Senate/7112/essay_xanana_01.htm (accessed 17 February 2005).

———. 2000. *To Resist Is to Win! The Autobiography of Xanana Gusmão*. Melbourne: Aurora.

Hage, Ghassan. 2002. The Differential Intensities of Social Reality: migration, participation and guilt. In *Arab Australians Today: Citizenship and Belonging*, ed. Ghassan Hage. Melbourne: Melbourne University Press.

Hall, Stuart. 1990. Cultural Identity and Diaspora. In *Identity: Community, Culture, Difference*, ed. Jonathan Rutherford. London: Lawrence and Wishart.

Hamutuk, La'o. 2003. Timor Gap Oil and Brazilian Aid to East Timor. *La'o Hamutuk Bulletin* 4 (3–4) (August).

Havely, Joe. 2002. *Xanana Gusmao: East Timor's Reluctant Leader*. CNN Hong Kong 2002 (cited 12 August 2004). Available from http://www.cnn.com/2002/WORLD/asiapcf/southeast/04/16/pres.gusmao.profile/.

Hirsch, Marianne. 1992. Family Pictures: Maus, Mourning and Post-Memory. *Discourse* 15 (2): 3–29.

Hobsbawm, Eric and Terence Ranger. 1983. *The Invention of Tradition.* 1st paper-back ed. Cambridge: Cambridge University Press.

Human Rights Solidarity. 1999. Free Xanana Gusmao Now. *Human Rights Solidarity* 9 (4 April).

Humphrey, Michael. 2000. From Terror to Trauma: Commissioning Truth for National Reconciliation. *Social Identities* 6 (1): 7–27.

Huntington, Samuel. 1996. *The Clash of Civilizations and the Remaking of World Order.* New York: Simon and Schuster.

Ileto, Reynaldo Clemeña. 1979. *Payson and Revolution: Popular Movements in the Philippines, 1840–1910.* Manila: Ateneo de Manila University Press.

Inglis, Christine. 1998. Australia. In *The Encyclopedia of the Chinese Overseas*, ed. Lynn Pan. Singapore: Archipelago Press.

Inui, Miki. 1998. Assimilation and Repatriation Conflicts of the Hmong Refugees in a Wisconsin Community: A Qualitative Study of Five Local Groups. *Migration World Magazine* 26 (4): 26–28.

Jackson, Michael. 1995. *At Home in the World.* Durham, N.C.: Duke University Press.

Jolliffe, Jill. 1978. *East Timor: Nationalism and Colonialism.* Brisbane: University of Queensland Press.

Jupp, James. 2002. Australia's Refugee and Humanitarian Policies. In *Refugees and the Myth of the Borderless World*, ed. William Maley, Alan Dupont, Jean-Pierre Fonteyne, Greg Fry, James Jupp, and Thuy Do. Canberra: Department of International Relations, RSPAS, Australian National University.

Kaminsky, Amy K. 1999. *After Exile: Writing the Latin American Diaspora.* Minneapolis: University of Minnesota Press.

Kapferer, Bruce. 1988. *Legends of People, Myths of State: Violence, Intolerance, and Political Culture in Sri Lanka and Australia.* Washington, D.C.: Smithsonian Institution Press.

Kenneally, Paddy. 2001. Personal communication, August.

Kolar-Panov, Dona. 1996. *Video, War and the Diasporic Imagination.* London: Routledge.

Lague, David. 1995. Canberra "Calming Jakarta" on Exodus. *Sydney Morning Herald*, 16 October, 2.

Lo, Jacqueline. 2000. Beyond Happy Hybridity: Performing Asian-Australian Identities. In *Alter/Asians: Asian-Australian Identities in Art, Media and Popular Culture*, ed. Ien Ang, Sharon Chalmers, Lisa Law, and Mandy Thomas. Sydney: Pluto Press.

Macedo, Jorge Braga de, José Braz, and Rui Sousa Monteiro. 2000. *National Development and Economic Transition Under International Governance: The Case of East Timor* (cited 5 August 2002). Available from www.fe.unl.pt/~jbmacedo/papers/timor.html.

Mahler, Sarah. 1998. Theoretical and Empirical Contributions Toward a Research Agenda for Transnationalism. In *Transnationalism from Below*, ed. Michael Peter Smith and Luis Eduardo Guarnizo. New Brunswick, N.J.: Transaction Publishers.

Malkki, Liisa. 1992. National Geographic: The Rooting of Peoples and the Territorialization of National Identity Among Scholars and Refugees. *Cultural Anthropology* 7 (1): 24–44.

———. 1994. Citizens of Humanity: Internationalism and the Imagined Community of Nations. *Diaspora* 3 (1): 41–68.

———. 1995. *Purity and Exile: Violence, Memory, and National Cosmology Among Hutu Refugees in Tanzania.* Chicago: University of Chicago Press.

————. 1997a. National Geographic: The Rooting of Peoples and the Territori-alization of National Identity Among Scholars and Refugees. In *Culture, Power, Place: Explorations in Critical Anthropology*, ed. Akhil Gupta and James Fergu-son. Durham, N.C.: Duke University Press.

————. 1997b. Speechless Emissaries: Refugees, Humanitarianism, and Dehis-toricization. In *Siting Culture: The Shifting Anthropological Object*, ed. Karen Fog Olwig. London: Routledge.

Mar, Phillip. 1998. Just the Place Is Different: Comparisons of Place and Settle-ment Practices of Some Hong Kong Migrants in Sydney. *Australian Journal of Anthropology* 9 (1): 58–73.

————. 2002. Accommodating Places: A Migrant Ethnography of Two Cities (Hong Kong and Sydney). Ph.D. dissertation, Department of Anthropology, University of Sydney.

Martin, Angela K. and Sandra Kryst. 1998. Encountering Mary: Ritualization and Place Contagion in Postmodernity. In *Places Through the Body*, ed. Heide J. Nast and Steve Pile. London: Routledge.

Martin, Jean. 1972. *Community and Identity: Refugee Groups in Adelaide*. Canberra: Australian National University Press.

Massey, Doreen. 1997. A Global Sense of Place. In *Studying Culture: An Introduc-tory Reader*, ed. Ann Gray and Jim McGuigan. London: Arnold.

McDowell, Christopher and Marita Eastmond. 2002. Transitions, State-Building and the "Residual" Refugee Problem: The East Timor and Cambodia Repa-triation Experience. *Australian Journal of Human Rights* 8 (1): 7–29.

Mellor, Philip A. and Chris Shilling. 1997. *Re-Forming the Body: Religion, Commu-nity and Modernity*. Theory, Culture, and Society. London: Sage.

Melo, Carmen. 2001. FALINTIL and the Diaspora. Personal communication, 20 January 2001.

MMIETS. 2000. Pamphlet, Mary MacKillop Institute of East Timorese Studies, Sydney.

Morlanes, Teresa. 1991. East Timorese Ethno-Nationalism: A Search for an Iden-tity—Cultural and Political Self-Determination. Ph.D. dissertation, Department of Anthropology and Sociology, University of Queensland, Brisbane.

Moxham, Ben. 2005. US AID in East Timor. *Z Mag* 18 (1).

Naficy, Hamid. 1991. The Poetics and Practice of Iranian Nostalgia in Exile. *Diaspora* 1 (3): 285–302.

Nederveen Pieterse, Jan. 2001. Hybridity, So What? The Anti-Hybridity Backlash and the Riddles of Recognition. *Theory, Culture, Society* 18 (2–3) (January): 219–45.

Nicol, Bill. 1978. *Timor: The Stillborn Nation*. Melbourne: Visa.

Niessen, Sandra A. 1993. *Batak Cloth and Clothing: A Dynamic Indonesian Tradition*. Kuala Lumpur: Oxford University Press.

Noble, Greg. 2002. Comfortable and Relaxed: Furnishing the Home and Nation. *Continuum: Journal of Media and Cultural Studies* 16 (1): 53–66.

Noble, Greg, Scott Poynting, and Paul Tabar. 1999. Youth, Ethnicity and the Mapping of Identities: Strategic Essentialism and Strategic Hybridity Among Male Arabic-speaking Youth in South-Western Sydney. *Communal/Plural: Jour-nal of Transnational and Crosscultural Studies* 7 (1): 29–44.

O'Connor, Kath, Sister. 1999. Sanctuary Network. *Sanctuary Network Newsletter*.

Ong, Aihwa. 1999. *Flexible Citizenship: The Cultural Logics of Transnationality*. Dur-ham, N.C.: Duke University Press.

Pan, Lynn, ed. 1999. *The Encyclopedia of the Chinese Overseas*. London: Curzon.

Parkin, David. 1999. Mementoes as Transitional Objects in Human Displacement. *Journal of Material Culture* 4 (3): 303–20.

Preston, Rosemary. 1999. Researching Repatriation and Reconstruction: Who Is Researching What and Why? In *The End of the Refugee Cycle: Refugee Repatriation and Reconstruction*, ed. Khalid Koser and Richard Black. New York: Berghahn Books.

Rafael, Vicente. 2000. "Your Grief Is Our Gossip": Overseas Filipinos and Other Spectral Precences. In *White Love and Other Events in Filipino History*, ed. Vicente L. Rafael. Durham, N.C.: Duke University Press.

———. 2002. Imagination and Imagery: Filipino Nationalism in the 19th Century. *Inscriptions* 5: 1–11.

Ram, Kalpana. 2000. Dancing the Past into Life: The Rasa, Nrtta and Raga of Immigrant Existence. *Australian Journal of Anthropology* 11 (3): 261–73.

Ramos-Horta, José. 1987. *Funu*. New York: Red Sea Press.

Rank, S. R. 1977. Recent Rural-Urban Migration to Dili, Portuguese Timor. Master's thesis, Department of Geography, Macquarie University, Sydney.

Rawsthorne, Margot. 1994. *Settlement of the East Timorese Community in New South Wales*. Sydney: Ettinger House on Behalf of the Timorese Australian Council.

Renan, Ernest. 1996. What Is a Nation? (1822). In *Nation and Narration*, ed. Homi K. Bhabha. London: Routledge. 8–22.

Safran, William. 1991. Diasporas in Modern Societies: Myths of Homeland and Return. *Diaspora* 1 (1): 83–99.

Said, Edward. 1994. *Culture and Imperialism*. London: Vintage.

Schech, Susan and Jane Haggis. 2001. Migrancy, Multiculturalism and Whiteness: Re-Charting Core Identities in Australia. *Communal/Plural* 9 (2): 143–59.

Seremetakis, C. Nadia. 1996. The Memory of the Senses. Part I: Marks of the Transitory. In *The Senses Still: Perception and Memory as Material Culture in Modernity*, ed. C. Nadia Seremetakis. Chicago: University of Chicago Press.

Smith, Anthony D. 1991. *National Identity*. London: Penguin.

Smith, Michael Peter and Luis Eduardo Guarnizo, eds. 1999. *Transnationalism from Below*. New Brunswick, N.J.: Transaction Publishers.

Steen-Preis, Ann-Belinda. 1997. Seeking Place: Capsized Identities and Contracted Belonging Among Sri Lankan Tamil refugees. In *Siting Culture: The Shifting Anthropological Object*, ed. Karen Fog Olwig and Kirsten Hastrup. London: Routledge.

Stein, Barry. 1994. Ad Hoc Assistance to Return Movements & Long Term Development Programs. In *When Refugees Go Home: African Experiences*, ed. Tim Allen and Hubert Morsink. Geneva: United Nations Research Institute for Social Development.

Sturken, Marita. 1999. Narratives of Recovery: Repressed Memory as Cultural Memory. In *Acts of Memory: Cultural Recall in the Present*, ed. Mieke Bal, Jonathan V. Crewe, and Leo Spitzer. Hanover, N.H.: Dartmouth College, University Press of New England.

Summerfield, Derek. 2001. The Invention of Post-Traumatic Stress Disorder and the Social Usefulness of a Psychiatric Category. *British Medical Journal* 322: 95–98.

Tang, Kristina. 1999. East Timor Care Centre: Establishing a Drop-In Centre for the East Timorese Community of NSW (Executive Proposal). Sydney: Service for the Treatment and Rehabilitation of Torture and Trauma Survivors NSW & Psychiatry Research and Teaching Unit.

Tannock, Stuart. 1995. Nostalgia Critique. *Cultural Studies* 9 (3): 453–64.

Taudevin, Lansell. 1999. *East Timor: Too Little Too Late.* Sydney: Duffy and Snellgrove.

Taylor, Charles. 1994. The Politics of Recognition. In *Multiculturalism: Examining the Politics of Recognition*, ed. Amy Gutmann. Princeton, N.J.: Princeton University Press.

Taylor, John G. 1999. *East Timor: The Price of Freedom.* Sydney: Pluto Press.

Thatcher, Patsy. 1991. The Timor-Born in Exile in Australia. Master's thesis, Department of Anthropology and Sociology, Monash University, Melbourne.

Thomas, Mandy. 1999. *Dreams in the Shadows: Vietnamese-Australian Lives in Transition.* Sydney: Allen and Unwin.

Timorese Australia Council. 1994. Timorese Australia Council Brochure. Sydney.

Tölölyan, Kachig. 1991. The Nation-State and Its Others: In Lieu of a Preface. *Diaspora* 1 (1): 3–7.

Turner, Michelle. 1992. *Telling: East Timor, Personal Testimonies 1942–1992.* Sydney: New South Wales University Press.

United Nations. 2002. UNTAET Background (Website). http://un.org/peace/etimor/untaetb.htm.

Van Alphen, Ernst. 1999. Symptoms of Discursivity: Experience, Memory and Trauma. In *Acts of Memory: Cultural Recall in the Present*, ed. Mieka Bal, Jonathan V. Crewe, and Leo Spitzer. Hanover, N.H.: University Press of New England.

Viviani, Nancy. 1996. *The Indochinese in Australia, 1975–1995: From Burnt Boats to Barbecues.* Melbourne: Oxford University Press.

Wahlbeck, Osten. 1998. Transnationalism and Diasporas: The Kurdish Example. Paper read at International Sociological Association Fourteenth World Congress of Sociology, Montreal.

Wang, Gungwu. 1992. *China and the Chinese Overseas.* Singapore: Times Academic Press.

Werbner, Pnina. 1997a. Essentialising Essentialism, Essentialising Silence: Ambivalence and Multiplicity in the Constructions of Racism and Ethnicity. In *Debating Cultural Hybridity: Multi-Cultural Identities and the Politics of Anti-Racism*, ed. Pnina Werbner and Tariq Modood. Postcolonial Encounters. London: Zed Books.

———. 1997b. Introduction: The Dialectics of Cultural Hybridity. In *Debating Cultural Hybridity: Multi-Cultural Identities and the Politics of Anti-Racism*, ed. Pnina Werbner and Tariq Modood. Postcolonial Encounters. London: Zed Books.

———. 1998. Diasporic Political Imaginaries: A Sphere of Freedom or a Sphere of Illusions? *Communal/Plural* 6 (1): 11–31.

———. 2002. The Place Which Is Diaspora: Citizenship, Religion and Gender in the Making of Chaordic Transnationalism. *Journal of Ethnic and Migration Studies* 28 (1): 119–33.

Werbner, Pnina, and Tariq Modood, eds. 1997. *Debating Cultural Hybridity: Multi-Cultural Identities and the Politics of Anti-Racism.* Postcolonial Encounters. London: Zed Books.

Wilson, Richard A. 1997. Representing Human Rights Violations: Social Contexts and Subjectivities. In *Human Rights, Culture and Context: Anthropological Perspectives*, ed. Richard A. Wilson. London: Pluto Press.

Winters, Rebecca, ed. 1999. *Buibere: Voice of East Timorese Women.* Darwin: East Timor International Support Centre.

Wise, Amanda, ed. 2001. *Leaving the Crocodile: The Story of the East Timorese Community in Sydney*. Sydney: Liverpool Regional Museum.

Zetter, Roger. 1994. The Greek-Cypriot Refugees: Perceptions of Return Under Conditions of Protracted Exile. *International Migration Review* 28 (2): 307–22.

Zournazi, Mary. 1998. *Foreign Dialogues: Memories, Translations, Conversations*. Sydney: Pluto Press.

Index

Page numbers in italics indicate illustrations.

Acknowledgments

Many friends and colleagues provided moral and intellectual support while I waswriting this book. I am especially grateful to Mandy Thomas, Ien Ang, and Greg Noble. Ien's insights into the diasporic condition have been an inspiration for many years, and I am sure the traces are present in this book. Through Mandy I learned how to do sensitive and creative ethnography, and Greg's keen theoretical eye helped me pull it all together. For their comments, criticism, and advice, I am particularly indebted to Pnina Werbner, Loretta Baldassar, and Deirdre McKay. I am especially grateful to Paul Stoller for his guidance, friendship, and support and for creating a space in his series for detailed narrative centered ethnography. I'm also sure his Songhay incantations smoothed things along the way for me. I would also like to express my thanks to Peter Agree at the University of Pennsylvania Press for being such a terrific, efficient, and supportive editor, and the editorial board at Penn Press for their comments on this work.

Thanks are due to my former colleagues at the Centre for Cultural Research at the University of Western Sydney, where most of the writing for this book was done. Thanks to Elaine Lally, Aneela Babar, Francis Maravillas, Barbara Bloch, David Kelly, and Cristina Rocha for their support, enjoyable company, and Friday night dinners. Thanks especially to Tanja Dreher for her friendship and help in developing my ideas and to Ricardo Peach for introducing me to the therapeutic delights of Rooibos tea and chocolate.

Invaluable financial and institutional support made my work possible. I thank in particular the Centre for Cultural Research at the University of Western Sydney for financial support, for funding my field trip to East Timor, local and overseas conferences, and a period in residence at the Australian National University. I also thank the German Academic Exchange (DAAD) for funding my time at the International Women's

University in Germany during 2000, and the Research School in Pacific and Asian Studies at the Australian National University for funding a visiting fellowship there. I'm grateful to the Centre for Cross-Cultural Research at the ANU for funding a postdoctoral fellowship during 2003 and 2004. I have fond memories of the collegial environment there, and I particularly thank the Centre for Research on Social Inclusion at Macquarie University where I am currently a research fellow. Their support during the revision phase of this book has been invaluable.

There are also publishers to thank. An earlier version of Chapter 3, "Nation, Transnation, Diaspora: Locating East Timorese Long Distance Nationalism" appeared in *SOJOURN: Journal of Social Issues in Southeast Asia* 19 (2) (October 2004): 151–80, reproduced here by permission of the Institute of Southeast Asian Studies, Singapore. An earlier version of Chapter 4, "Embodying Exile," appeared in *Social Analysis* 48 (3) (Fall 2004): 24–40, reproduced by permission of Berghahn Books.

Last, but not certainly not least, I am deeply and eternally grateful to all those in the East Timorese community who have assisted this research project. I thank particularly my generous and brave interviewees whose names I cannot mention for reasons of anonymity. Of those I can, I thank especially Mrs. Nancy Ezequiel-de Almeida for the hours she spent filling me in on things East Timorese, Noni dos Reis Piedade for her invaluable assistance in introducing me to many of my early interviewees, and also to Nedia Mendonça, Manuel Branco, Brigida de Andrade, Nairana de Almeida, and all the others who assisted in the Leaving the Crocodile" exhibition. I am grateful to all at the Mary MacKillop Institute of East Timorese Studies, especially Sisters Josephine Mitchell, Susan Connelly, and Therese Dagg. They generously allowed me access to their extraordinary collection of photographs, many of which appear in this book. They were also so helpful in assisting me to understand many of the issues facing East Timorese people in Australia and East Timor. Thanks also to Australians in Solidarity with Indonesia and East Timor (ASIET) and East Timor Relief Association (ETRA) for allowing me access to their archives and to reproduce the material here, and to the Australia-East Timor Association (AETA), the Timorese Australian Council, and the Timorese-Chinese Association for their assistance with my research. I am also deeply indebted to those East Timorese who extended their hospitality to me on my field trip to East Timor, whose names I am unable to mention here as they were all interviewed for this book and wish to remain anonymous. To the Sydney East Timorese community as a whole, I thank you for allowing me to write about your lives. I wish you well and hope that you all find a sense of home soon, wherever in the world you choose to be.

Viva Timor Leste!